THE COMPLETE
KALORIK MAXX
AIR FRYER
OVEN COOKBOOK
FOR BEGINNERS

600 Quick and Easy Air Fryer Recipes to Help You
Master Your Kalorik Maxx Air Fryer Oven

SHARON HERNDON

D1716347

Table of Content

Chapter 4 Fish and Seafood 44

Chapter 5 Poultry 70

Chapter 6 Rotisserie Recipes 94

Chapter 7 Meats 100

Chapter 8 Wraps and Sandwiches 123

Chapter 9 Appetizers and Snacks 129

Chapter 10 Desserts   145

Introduction

Kalorik was founded in Belgium in 1930 and has been manufacturing kitchen appliances for over nine decades. The name Kalorik is synonymous with superior technology and innovative products. The MAXX is the culmination of our mission to make cooking easier for everyone.

Discover the new generation of fryer ovens! The Kalorik Maxx 26 Quart Digital Fryer combines 10 appliances in one.

Works as a fryer, roaster, roasting pan, rotisserie, dehydrator, oven, toaster, pizza oven and slow cooker.

The Kalorik digital Maxx air fryer oven uses special Turbo Maxx technology to prepare food faster than ever. Upper and lower heating elements ensure even heat distribution for perfectly cooked results. An optimized airflow system and high performance turbojet engine ensure maximum blood circulation and deliver the same crispy texture and rich taste of fried foods - with little to no oil. This cuts down on fat and calories for healthier meals.

The unique rotisserie setup rotates the included rotisserie accessories during cooking, allowing the meat to roast evenly in its own juices and develop maximum flavour.

The Kalorik Maxx digital deep fryer reaches temperatures up to 500 ° F and is perfect for browning meat or vegetables to caramelized perfection.

The oven can hold a large chicken, a 12-inch pizza or up to 9 slices of toast in its cavity. The modern and multifunctional Kalorik Digital Maxx air fryer has glass doors that can be opened with one hand to prevent drips or burns.

A built-in safety function for automatic shutdown automatically stops operation when the doors are opened. A user-friendly digital LED display contains 21 presets for easy cooking.

Accessory elements include an air frying basket, baking pan, air rack, crumb tray, bacon tray, meat tray, roasting pan, grill handle and grill handle.

Features

- The air fryer multi-functional oven can fry, bake, toast, roast, grill, braise, dehydrate and broil

- Optimized air circulation system and powerful turbojet cook food up to 30% faster

- Bakes foods to crisp and golden perfection with little to no oil and reduces fat by up to 75%

- Easy to use digital LED display with 21 presets

- Seals up to 500 ° F for perfectly caramelized meat and vegetables

- One-pull glass French doors prevent drips and protect against burns

This powerful 1700W Turbo MAXX technology with accelerated airflow cook's food 25-30% faster. This fryer oven reaches up to 500F for perfectly caramelized protein, vegetables and more.

Pros

- 9 great accessories

- Indulgent meals

- Less Fat

- Modern French door system

Chapter 1 The Basics of Kalorik Maxx Air Fryer Oven

Air Fry: This function is used to air fry meals as a healthy alternative to deep-frying in oil.

- For best results, use the provided air fryer basket.

- Flip or shake food halfway through the cooking process to cook food evenly.

- Air Frying does not require oil. A tablespoon of oil may be added to enhance flavour.

Bacon: Cook bacon to perfection with the bacon tray.

- The wave design keeps bacon up and away

- from draining grease.

- Accommodates multiple slices at once.

- Use the bacon air fry function when cooking

- bacon.

Fast Air Fry: Cook food even faster by placing the basket on the top rack.

- Reduce your cooking time and shake your food halfway to ensure even results.

- Air Frying does not require oil. A tablespoon of oil may be added to enhance flavour

Steak Tray: Use the steak tray to sear and caramelize your foods to perfection.

- Slotted design allows excess fat to drain into the drip pan.

- Place steak tray on the top slot to obtain perfect searing.

- Use the steak air fry function when cooking steaks, chops, chicken, seafood and veggies.

Rotisserie: Use the rotisserie spit and its handle to cook whole chickens and roast all types of food.

- Press the "Rotate" button to allow the rotisserie spit to rotate during cooking, allowing meat to roast evenly in its own juices and develop maximum flavour.

- Rotisserie automatically turns on under the Chicken preset, for all other presets button must be pressed.

- This setting can be turned on and used during the air fry, bake, and roast cooking functions.

Dehydrates : all types of food with a dehydration function. Select the defrost function and set the temperature to 130 ° F and the time to 1 hour. Add time as needed.

- Use the 2-in-1 dehydrator and steak bowl. Turn the bowl of meat over and slide it into the slot in the dehydrator (above). Put your food in the air

- Slide the frying basket into the slot for quick frying. Press the on / off button to start.

- The built-in fan and low heat generation are used to create a hot air flow which reduces the air

- Water content of fresh foods.

- Arrange foods in a single layer without overlapping.

- Lemon juice can be used to pre-treat fruits and vegetables to prevent browning.

- Use it to dehydrate or order fruits and vegetables

- Dry beef and more.

Baking rack: The baking rack can be used for both air frying and the oven functions.

- This accessory can be used for a variety of foods including pizza or used when cooking with cake pans to place on top.

The Specification

Out Dimensions: 15.75 x 12.5 x 14

Inside Dimensions : 12.5" x 11" x 7.5

Capacity : 26QT

Weight: 17.2lbs

Materials: Stainless steel

Temperature Ranges: 500 ° F

Voltage: 1,700 Watts

Accessory: Comes with everything needed to prepare delicious meals right out of the box. Includes an air frying basket, air rack, bacon tray, baking pan, crumb tray, rack handle, rotisserie handle, rotisserie spit, and steak tray. Also includes a cookbook with inspirational recipes to help you get started.

The Control Panel

Knobs: - knob / Select button. During hot air frying, hot steam is released through the air outlet ... Kalorik Smart Fryer Oven uses advanced technology that gives you.

Button: Rotate: Use when cooking with the rotisserie spit. Press the Rotate button to turn on the rotisserie mode and make the accessory rotate to achieve an evenly crispy outcome. Press again to turn off the rotisserie function.

1. **Light:** Press the Light button to turn the oven light on or off. The light can be turned on at any time to help monitor your food while cooking. The light turns off automatically after one minute.

2. **Air Fry:** Press the Air Fry button to select the air frying function. 14 presets are available for use with this mode. Use the selector dial to select your desired preset.

3. **Oven:** Press the Oven button to use the unit as a conventional oven. 7 cooking modes are available when using the Oven function. Use the selector dial to select your desired cooking mode.

4. **Selector dial:** Use the dial to select your desired preset. Press the dial to adjust cooking time and temperature.

5. **Start/Stop:** Press Start/Stop to turn the unit on, begin, or end the cooking cycle. Long press 3 seconds to switch off the machine directly.

Display Screens: LED Screen

The LED screen displays the Countdown Timer and Temperature (4),

Rotisserie signal symbol (2), Air fry signal symbol (3), and Presents (1).

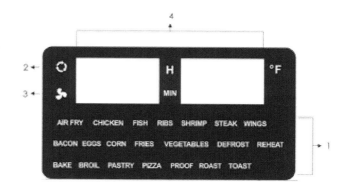

Cooking Timetable:

AIR FRYER

Air frying can be used as a healthy alternative style of cooking, requiring little to no oil and using rapid hot air to cook meals faster.

Food	Default Temperature (°F)	Default Time(min)	Adjustable Temperature (°F)	Adjustable Time (min)
Chicken	435°F	40 mins	140-450°F	1-90
Fish	375°F	10 mins	140-450°F	1-90
Ribs	400°F	25 mins	140-450°F	1-90
Shrimp	375°F	10 mins	140-450°F	1-90
Steak	500°F	13 mins	140-450°F	1-90
Wings	450°F	15 mins	140-450°F	1-90
Bacon	425°F	6 mins	140-450°F	1-90
Eggs	400°F	5 mins	140-450°F	1-90
Corn	440°F	15 mins	140-450°F	1-90
Fries	450°F	15 mins	140-450°F	1-90
Vegetables	400°F	10 mins	140-450°F	1-90
Defrost	80°F	40 mins	80-140°F	1-90
reheat	280°F	6 mins	140-450°F	1-90

OVEN

This mode is for use of the bake, broil, pastry, pizza, proof, roast, and toast functions. Place the baking tray or rack with food inside the oven. Use the selector dial to scroll through the presets, when desired preset is flashing, press the Start/Stop button to confirm the preset and start cooking.

Food	Default Temperature (°F)	Default Time (min)	Adjustable Temperature (°F)	Adjustable Time (min)
Bake	375°F	25	140-450°F	1-90
Broil	450°F	15	140-450°F	1-90
Pastry	400°F	30	140-450°F	1-90
Pizza	400°F	20	140-450°F	1-90
Proof	100°F	60	140-450°F	1-90
Roast	425°F	35	80-140°F	1-90
Toast	400°F	7	140-450°F	1-90

Different Advantages from Other Air Fryer Oven

1. Healthier Meals:

You don't need to use a lot (or none at all) of oil in these devices to make your food crispy and golden! Most users simply spray oil on the product and then continue with the cooking cycle. The hot air takes advantage of the little oil and the excess oil simply drains from the food. This makes these devices ideal for making fresh and frozen fries, onion rings, mozzarella sticks, chicken wings and nuggets.

Unlike a conventional fryer oven, the Kalorik Maxx air fryer oven cooks faster and excess oil does not get into the food.

2. Accessories Included:

It has everything you need to start preparing delicious meals right away. Contains a roasting basket, grid, bacon, baking dish, crumb dish, grill handle, pan handler, drip pan and steak pan.

3. Extreme Performance:

Highly efficient Turbo MAXX air circulation system generates air temperatures of up to 500 ° F to cook food 30% faster than other air fryer ovens and 50% faster than conventional ovens standard. This provides the same crispy texture and rich taste of foods fried with little to no oil, which cuts down on fat and calories for healthier meals.

4. Modern And Multifunctional:

The Kalorik MAXX air fryer oven combines the functionality of 10 different appliances in one unit. The MAXX's user-friendly LED digital display contains 21 presets for easy cooking, whatever the occasion.

5. Good for Large Families:

You will see some fryers advertised for "large families" but what does that actually mean? Most air fryers are best suited to making food for 1-4 people (depending on the capacity). There are very few that can handle making food for more than 4, and they often still require cooking in batches. For large families, a true convection air frying oven would probably be a better choice.

The MAXX's extra-large 26-quart cavity can roast a whole chicken, bake a 12" pizza, or toast 9 slices of bread with room to spare—perfect for preparing dinner for the whole family.

Tips and Tricks to Cook with This Air Fryer Oven

1. Always use oven mitts or oven mitts while in use when touching an exterior or interior surface of the oven or when handling accessories.

2. To reduce the risk of fire, keep the interior of the oven clean and free from food, oil, grease, and other combustible materials.

3. Do not use metal utensils such as knives to remove food particles from the heating elements, as this may damage the appliance and cause electric shock.

4. Do not store materials in the oven when not in use.

5. Unpack the device and accessories, wash and dry everything. Clean the inside of the oven with a damp cloth or sponge. Pat dry with a paper towel. Make sure the oven is dry before using the appliance.

6. Place the oven on a flat, heat-resistant surface so that it is also at least 10 cm from surrounding objects.

7. Unwind the power cord and plug it into the electrical outlet. Place the sliding crumb tray in the bottom of the appliance under the lower heating elements. Make sure the appliance is clean and everything has been removed from the oven.

8. It is normal for smoke or an odor to come out of the appliance when it is first used. It is not harmful. To remove any packing oil that may have remained after production, we recommend that you run the appliance on the steak function for 20 minutes and set the thermostat to the maximum temperature (500 ° F).

9. When installing the Maxx Air fryer, always make sure that the sliding crumb tray is in place before starting the cooking process. Rinse and clean the pull-out crumb tray after each use.

10. When cooking foods that may leak crumbs or grease during the cooking process, make sure the baking tray / drip tray is in the lowest slot. This will help keep the device as clean as possible and protect the lower heating elements.

11. Place the baking sheet / drip pan under the grid or the cooking basket, as food may leak during cooking. The baking sheet will help catch any fat or crumbs.

Chapter 2 Breakfasts

Super Easy Bacon Cups

Prep time: 5 minutes | Cook time: 20 minutes | Serves 2

3 slices bacon, cooked, sliced in half
2 slices ham
1 slice tomato
2 eggs
2 teaspoons grated Parmesan cheese
Salt and ground black pepper, to taste

1. Select the BAKE function and preheat MAXX to 375ºF (191ºC). Line 2 greased muffin tins with 3 half-strips of bacon
2. Put one slice of ham and half slice of tomato in each muffin tin on top of the bacon
3. Crack one egg on top of the tomato in each muffin tin and sprinkle each with half a teaspoon of grated Parmesan cheese. Sprinkle with salt and ground black pepper, if desired.
4. Bake in the preheated air fryer oven for 20 minutes. Remove from the air fryer oven and let cool.
5. Serve warm.

Golden Avocado Tempura

Prep time: 5 minutes | Cook time: 10 minutes | Serves 4

½ cup bread crumbs
½ teaspoons salt
1 Haas avocado, pitted, peeled and sliced
Liquid from 1 can white beans

1. Mix the bread crumbs and salt in a shallow bowl until well-incorporated.
2. Dip the avocado slices in the bean liquid, then into the bread crumbs.
3. Put the avocados in the air fryer oven, taking care not to overlap any slices. Select the AIR FRY function and cook at 350ºF (177ºC) for 10 minutes, giving the basket a good shake at the halfway point.
4. Serve immediately.

Classic British Breakfast

Prep time: 5 minutes | Cook time: 25 minutes | Serves 2

1 cup potatoes, sliced and diced
2 cups beans in tomato sauce
2 eggs
1 tablespoon olive oil
1 sausage
Salt, to taste

1. Select the BAKE function and preheat MAXX to 390ºF (199ºC) and allow to warm.
2. Break the eggs onto a baking dish and sprinkle with salt.
3. Lay the beans on the dish, next to the eggs.
4. In a bowl, coat the potatoes with the olive oil. Sprinkle with salt.
5. Transfer the bowl of potato slices to the air fryer oven and bake for 10 minutes.
6. Swap out the bowl of potatoes for the dish containing the eggs and beans. Bake for another 10 minutes. Cover the potatoes with parchment paper.
7. Slice up the sausage and throw the slices on top of the beans and eggs. Bake for another 5 minutes.
8. Serve with the potatoes.

Bacon Hot Dogs

Prep time: 5 minutes | Cook time: 15 minutes | Serves 4

3 brazilian sausages, cut into 3 equal pieces
9 slices bacon
1 tablespoon Italian
herbs
Salt and ground black pepper, to taste

1. Take each slice of bacon and wrap around each piece of sausage. Sprinkle with Italian herbs, salt and pepper.
2. Select the AIR FRY function and cook the sausages in the air fryer oven at 355ºF (179ºC) for 15 minutes.
3. Serve warm.

Kale and Potato Nuggets

Prep time: 10 minutes | Cook time: 18 minutes | Serves 4

1 teaspoon extra virgin olive oil
1 clove garlic, minced
4 cups kale, rinsed and chopped
2 cups potatoes, boiled and mashed
⅛ cup milk
Salt and ground black pepper, to taste
Cooking spray

1. In a skillet over medium heat, sauté the garlic in the olive oil, until it turns golden brown. Sauté with the kale for an additional 3 minutes and remove from the heat.
2. Mix the mashed potatoes, kale and garlic in a bowl. Pour in the milk and sprinkle with salt and pepper.
3. Shape the mixture into nuggets and spritz with cooking spray.
4. Put in the air fryer basket. Select the AIR FRY function and cook at 390ºF (199ºC) for 15 minutes, flip the nuggets halfway through cooking to make sure the nuggets fry evenly.
5. Serve immediately.

Egg and Bacon Muffins

Prep time: 5 minutes | Cook time: 15 minutes | Serves 1

2 eggs
Salt and ground black pepper, to taste
1 tablespoon green pesto
3 ounces (85 g) shredded Cheddar cheese
5 ounces (142 g) cooked bacon
1 scallion, chopped

1. Select the BAKE function and preheat MAXX to 350ºF (177ºC). Line a cupcake tin with parchment paper.
2. Beat the eggs with pepper, salt, and pesto in a bowl. Mix in the cheese.
3. Pour the eggs into the cupcake tin and top with the bacon and scallion.
4. Bake in the preheated air fryer oven for 15 minutes, or until the egg is set.
5. Serve immediately.

Onion Omelet

Prep time: 10 minutes | Cook time: 12 minutes | Serves 2

3 eggs
Salt and ground black pepper, to taste
½ teaspoons soy sauce
1 large onion, chopped
2 tablespoons grated Cheddar cheese
Cooking spray

1. Select the BAKE function and preheat MAXX to 355ºF (179ºC).
2. In a bowl, whisk together the eggs, salt, pepper, and soy sauce.
3. Spritz a small pan with cooking spray. Spread the chopped onion across the bottom of the pan, then transfer the pan to the air fryer oven.
4. Bake in the preheated air fryer oven for 6 minutes or until the onion is translucent.
5. Add the egg mixture on top of the onions to coat well. Add the cheese on top, then continue baking for another 6 minutes.
6. Allow to cool before serving.

Parmesan Sausage Egg Muffins

Prep time: 5 minutes | Cook time: 20 minutes | Serves 4

6 ounces (170 g) Italian sausage, sliced
6 eggs
⅛ cup heavy cream
Salt and ground
black pepper, to taste
3 ounces (85 g) Parmesan cheese, grated
Cooking spray

1. Select the BAKE function and preheat MAXX to 350ºF (177ºC). Spritz a muffin pan with cooking spray.
2. Put the sliced sausage in the muffin pan.
3. Beat the eggs with the cream in a bowl and season with salt and pepper.
4. Pour half of the mixture over the sausages in the pan.
5. Sprinkle with cheese and the remaining egg mixture.
6. Bake in the preheated air fryer oven for 20 minutes or until set.
7. Serve immediately.

Breakfast Sausage and Cauliflower

Prep time: 5 minutes | Cook time: 45 minutes | Serves 4

1 pound (454 g) sausage, cooked and crumbled	Cheddar cheese, plus more for topping
2 cups heavy whipping cream	8 eggs, beaten
1 head cauliflower, chopped	Salt and ground black pepper, to taste
1 cup grated	

1. Select the BAKE function and preheat MAXX to 350ºF (177ºC).
2. In a large bowl, mix the sausage, heavy whipping cream, chopped cauliflower, cheese and eggs. Sprinkle with salt and ground black pepper.
3. Pour the mixture into a greased casserole dish. Bake in the preheated air fryer oven for 45 minutes or until firm.
4. Top with more Cheddar cheese and serve.

Quick and Easy Blueberry Muffins

Prep time: 10 minutes | Cook time: 12 minutes | Makes 8 muffins

1⅓ cups flour	1 egg
½ cup sugar	½ cup milk
2 teaspoons baking powder	⅔ cup blueberries, fresh or frozen and thawed
¼ teaspoon salt	
⅓ cup canola oil	

1. Select the BAKE function and preheat MAXX to 330ºF (166ºC).
2. In a medium bowl, stir together flour, sugar, baking powder, and salt.
3. In a separate bowl, combine oil, egg, and milk and mix well.
4. Add egg mixture to dry ingredients and stir just until moistened.
5. Gently stir in the blueberries.
6. Spoon batter evenly into parchment paper-lined muffin cups.
7. Put 4 muffin cups in air fryer basket and bake for 12 minutes or until tops spring back when touched lightly.
8. Repeat with the remaining muffins.
9. Serve immediately.

Parmesan Ranch Risotto

Prep time: 10 minutes | Cook time: 30 minutes | Serves 2

1 tablespoon olive oil	1 onion, diced
1 clove garlic, minced	¾ cup Arborio rice
1 tablespoon unsalted butter	2 cups chicken stock, boiling
	½ cup Parmesan cheese, grated

1. Select the BAKE function and preheat MAXX to 390ºF (199ºC).
2. Grease a round baking tin with olive oil and stir in the garlic, butter, and onion.
3. Transfer the tin to the air fryer oven and bake for 4 minutes. Add the rice and bake for 4 more minutes.
4. Turn the air fryer oven to 320ºF (160ºC) and pour in the chicken stock. Cover and bake for 22 minutes.
5. Scatter with cheese and serve.

Ham and Corn Muffins

Prep time: 10 minutes | Cook time: 6 minutes | Makes 8 muffins

¾ cup yellow cornmeal	2 tablespoons canola oil
¼ cup flour	½ cup milk
1½ teaspoons baking powder	½ cup shredded sharp Cheddar cheese
¼ teaspoon salt	½ cup diced ham
1 egg, beaten	

1. Select the BAKE function and preheat MAXX to 390ºF (199ºC).
2. In a medium bowl, stir together the cornmeal, flour, baking powder, and salt.
3. Add the egg, oil, and milk to dry ingredients and mix well.
4. Stir in shredded cheese and diced ham.
5. Divide batter among 8 parchment paper-lined muffin cups.
6. Put 4 filled muffin cups in air fryer basket and bake for 5 minutes.
7. Reduce temperature to 330ºF (166ºC) and bake for 1 minute or until a toothpick inserted in center of the muffin comes out clean.
8. Repeat with the remaining muffins.
9. Serve warm.

Sourdough Croutons

Prep time: 5 minutes | Cook time: 6 minutes | Makes 4 cups

4 cups cubed sourdough bread, 1-inch cubes
1 tablespoon olive oil

1 teaspoon fresh thyme leaves
¼ teaspoon salt
Freshly ground black pepper, to taste

1. Combine all ingredients in a bowl.
2. Toss the bread cubes into the air fryer oven. Select the AIR FRY function and cook at 400ºF (204ºC) for 6 minutes, shaking the basket once or twice while they cook.
3. Serve warm.

Hearty Cheddar Biscuits

Prep time: 10 minutes | Cook time: 22 minutes | Makes 8 biscuits

2⅓ cups self-rising flour
2 tablespoons sugar
½ cup butter (1 stick), frozen for 15 minutes
½ cup grated Cheddar cheese,

plus more to melt on top
1⅓ cups buttermilk
1 cup all-purpose flour, for shaping
1 tablespoon butter, melted

1. Line a buttered 7-inch metal cake pan with parchment paper or a silicone liner.
2. Combine the flour and sugar in a large mixing bowl. Grate the butter into the flour. Add the grated cheese and stir to coat the cheese and butter with flour. Then add the buttermilk and stir just until you can no longer see streaks of flour. The dough should be quite wet.
3. Spread the all-purpose (not self-rising) flour out on a small cookie sheet. With a spoon, scoop 8 evenly sized balls of dough into the flour, making sure they don't touch each other. With floured hands, coat each dough ball with flour and toss them gently from hand to hand to shake off any excess flour. Put each floured dough ball into the prepared pan, right up next to the other. This will help the biscuits rise, rather than spreading out.

4. Transfer the cake pan to the air fryer basket. Let the ends of the aluminum foil sling hang across the cake pan before returning the basket to the air fryer oven.
5. Select the AIR FRY function and cook at 380ºF (193ºC) for 20 minutes. Check the biscuits twice to make sure they are not getting too brown on top. If they are, re-arrange the aluminum foil strips to cover any brown parts. After 20 minutes, check the biscuits by inserting a toothpick into the center of the biscuits. It should come out clean. If it needs a little more time, continue to air fry for two extra minutes. Brush the tops of the biscuits with some melted butter and sprinkle a little more grated cheese on top if desired. Pop the basket back into the air fryer oven for another 2 minutes.
6. Remove the cake pan from the air fryer oven. Let the biscuits cool for just a minute or two and then turn them out onto a plate and pull apart. Serve immediately.

Simple Scotch Eggs

Prep time: 5 minutes | Cook time: 25 minutes | Serves 4

4 large hard boiled eggs
1 (12-ounce / 340-g) package pork

sausage
8 slices thick-cut bacon

Special Equipment:
4 wooden toothpicks, soaked in water for at least 30 minutes

1. Slice the sausage into four parts and place each part into a large circle.
2. Put an egg into each circle and wrap it in the sausage. Put in the refrigerator for 1 hour.
3. Make a cross with two pieces of thick-cut bacon. Put a wrapped egg in the center, fold the bacon over top of the egg, and secure with a toothpick.
4. Select the AIR FRY function and cook at 450ºF (235ºC) for 25 minutes.
5. Serve immediately.

All-in-One Toast

Prep time: 10 minutes | Cook time: 10 minutes | Serves 1

1 strip bacon, diced
1 slice 1-inch thick bread
1 egg
Salt and freshly

ground black pepper, to taste
¼ cup grated Colby cheese

1. Select the AIR FRY function and cook the bacon at 400ºF (204ºC) for 3 minutes, shaking the basket once or twice while it cooks. Remove the bacon to a paper towel lined plate and set aside.
2. Use a sharp paring knife to score a large circle in the middle of the slice of bread, cutting halfway through, but not all the way through to the cutting board. Press down on the circle in the center of the bread slice to create an indentation.
3. Transfer the slice of bread, hole side up, to the air fryer basket. Crack the egg into the center of the bread, and season with salt and pepper.
4. Adjust the air fryer oven temperature to 380ºF (193ºC) and air fry for 5 minutes. Sprinkle the grated cheese around the edges of the bread, leaving the center of the yolk uncovered, and top with the cooked bacon. Press the cheese and bacon into the bread lightly to help anchor it to the bread and prevent it from blowing around in the air fryer oven.
5. Air fry for one or two more minutes, just to melt the cheese and finish cooking the egg. Serve immediately.

Potatoes Lyonnaise

Prep time: 10 minutes | Cook time: 31 minutes | Serves 4

1 Vidalia onion, sliced
1 teaspoon butter, melted
1 teaspoon brown sugar
2 large russet potatoes (about 1

pound / 454 g in total), sliced ½-inch thick
1 tablespoon vegetable oil
Salt and freshly ground black pepper, to taste

1. Toss the sliced onions, melted butter and brown sugar together in the air fryer basket. Select the AIR FRY function and cook at 370ºF (188ºC) for 8 minutes, shaking the basket occasionally to help the onions cook evenly.
2. While the onions are cooking, bring a saucepan of salted water to a boil on the stovetop. Par-cook the potatoes in boiling water for 3 minutes. Drain the potatoes and pat them dry with a clean kitchen towel.
3. Add the potatoes to the onions in the air fryer basket and drizzle with vegetable oil. Toss to coat the potatoes with the oil and season with salt and freshly ground black pepper.
4. Increase the air fryer oven temperature to 400ºF (204ºC) and air fry for 20 minutes, tossing the vegetables a few times during the cooking time to help the potatoes brown evenly.
5. Season with salt and freshly ground black pepper and serve warm.

Cornflakes Toast Sticks

Prep time: 10 minutes | Cook time: 6 minutes | Serves 4

2 eggs
½ cup milk
⅛ teaspoon salt
½ teaspoon pure vanilla extract
¾ cup crushed cornflakes

6 slices sandwich bread, each slice cut into 4 strips
Maple syrup, for dipping
Cooking spray

1. In a small bowl, beat together the eggs, milk, salt, and vanilla.
2. Put crushed cornflakes on a plate or in a shallow dish.
3. Dip bread strips in egg mixture, shake off excess, and roll in cornflake crumbs.
4. Spray both sides of bread strips with oil.
5. Put bread strips in air fryer basket in a single layer.
6. Select the AIR FRY function and cook at 390ºF (199ºC) for 6 minutes, or until golden brown.
7. Repeat with the remaining French toast sticks.
8. Serve with maple syrup.

Pita and Pepperoni Pizza

Prep time: 10 minutes | Cook time: 6 minutes | Serves 1

1 teaspoon olive oil
1 tablespoon pizza sauce
1 pita bread
6 pepperoni slices
¼ cup grated

Mozzarella cheese
¼ teaspoon garlic powder
¼ teaspoon dried oregano

1. Select the BAKE function and preheat MAXX to 350ºF (177ºC). Grease the air fryer basket with olive oil.
2. Spread the pizza sauce on top of the pita bread. Put the pepperoni slices over the sauce, followed by the Mozzarella cheese.
3. Season with garlic powder and oregano.
4. Put the pita pizza inside the air fryer oven and place a trivet on top.
5. Bake in the preheated air fryer oven for 6 minutes and serve.

Bacon Eggs on the Go

Prep time: 5 minutes | Cook time: 15 minutes | Serves 1

2 eggs
4 ounces (113 g) bacon, cooked

Salt and ground black pepper, to taste

1. Select the BAKE function and preheat MAXX to 400ºF (204ºC). Put liners in a regular cupcake tin.
2. Crack an egg into each of the cups and add the bacon. Season with some pepper and salt.
3. Bake in the preheated air fryer oven for 15 minutes, or until the eggs are set.
4. Serve warm.

Oat and Chia Porridge

Prep time: 10 minutes | Cook time: 5 minutes | Serves 4

2 tablespoons peanut butter
4 tablespoons honey
1 tablespoon butter,

melted
4 cups milk
2 cups oats
1 cup chia seeds

1. Select the BAKE function and preheat MAXX to 390ºF (199ºC).
2. Put the peanut butter, honey, butter, and milk in a bowl and stir to mix. Add the oats and chia seeds and stir.
3. Transfer the mixture to a bowl and bake in the air fryer oven for 5 minutes. Give another stir before serving.

Easy Sausage Pizza

Prep time: 10 minutes | Cook time: 6 minutes | Serves 4

2 tablespoons ketchup
1 pita bread
⅓ cup sausage
½ pound (227 g)

Mozzarella cheese
1 teaspoon garlic powder
1 tablespoon olive oil

1. Select the BAKE function and preheat MAXX to 340ºF (171ºC).
2. Spread the ketchup over the pita bread.
3. Top with the sausage and cheese. Sprinkle with the garlic powder and olive oil.
4. Put the pizza in the air fryer basket and bake for 6 minutes.
5. Serve warm.

Simple Cinnamon Toasts

Prep time: 5 minutes | Cook time: 4 minutes | Serves 4

1 tablespoon salted butter
2 teaspoons ground cinnamon

4 tablespoons sugar
½ teaspoon vanilla extract
10 bread slices

1. Select the BAKE function and preheat MAXX to 380ºF (193ºC).
2. In a bowl, combine the butter, cinnamon, sugar, and vanilla extract. Spread onto the slices of bread.
3. Put the bread inside the air fryer oven and bake for 4 minutes or until golden brown.
4. Serve warm.

Gold Avocado

Prep time: 5 minutes | Cook time: 6 minutes | Serves 4

2 large avocados, sliced
¼ teaspoon paprika
Salt and ground black pepper, to taste
½ cup flour
2 eggs, beaten
1 cup bread crumbs

1. Sprinkle paprika, salt and pepper on the slices of avocado.
2. Lightly coat the avocados with flour. Dredge them in the eggs, before covering with bread crumbs.
3. Transfer to the air fryer oven. Select the AIR FRY function and cook at 400ºF (204ºC) for 6 minutes.
4. Serve warm.

Mushroom and Squash Toast

Prep time: 10 minutes | Cook time: 10 minutes | Serves 4

1 tablespoon olive oil
1 red bell pepper, cut into strips
2 green onions, sliced
1 cup sliced button or cremini
mushrooms
1 small yellow squash, sliced
2 tablespoons softened butter
4 slices bread
½ cup soft goat cheese

1. Brush the air fryer basket with the olive oil.
2. Put the red pepper, green onions, mushrooms, and squash inside the air fryer oven and give them a stir. Select the AIR FRY function and cook at 350ºF (177ºC) for 7 minutes, or until the vegetables are tender, shaking the basket once throughout the cooking time.
3. Remove the vegetables and set them aside.
4. Spread the butter on the slices of bread and transfer to the air fryer oven, butter-side up. Brown for 3 minutes.
5. Remove the toast from the air fryer oven and top with goat cheese and vegetables. Serve warm.

Fast Coffee Donuts

Prep time: 5 minutes | Cook time: 6 minutes | Serves 6

¼ cup sugar
½ teaspoon salt
1 cup flour
1 teaspoon baking powder
¼ cup coffee
1 tablespoon aquafaba
1 tablespoon sunflower oil

1. In a large bowl, combine the sugar, salt, flour, and baking powder.
2. Add the coffee, aquafaba, and sunflower oil and mix until a dough is formed. Leave the dough to rest in and the refrigerator.
3. Remove the dough from the fridge and divide up, kneading each section into a doughnut.
4. Put the doughnuts inside the air fryer oven. Select the AIR FRY function and cook at 400ºF (204ºC) for 6 minutes.
5. Serve immediately.

Lush Vegetable Omelet

Prep time: 10 minutes | Cook time: 13 minutes | Serves 2

2 teaspoons canola oil
4 eggs, whisked
3 tablespoons plain milk
1 teaspoon melted butter
1 red bell pepper, seeded and chopped
1 green bell pepper, seeded and chopped
1 white onion, finely chopped
½ cup baby spinach leaves, roughly chopped
½ cup Halloumi cheese, shaved
Kosher salt and freshly ground black pepper, to taste

1. Select the BAKE function and preheat MAXX to 350ºF (177ºC).
2. Grease a baking pan with canola oil.
3. Put the remaining ingredients in the baking pan and stir well.
4. Transfer to the air fryer oven and bake for 13 minutes.
5. Serve warm.

English Pumpkin Egg Bake

Prep time: 10 minutes | Cook time: 10 minutes | Serves 2

2 eggs
½ cup milk
2 cups flour
2 tablespoons cider vinegar
2 teaspoons baking powder
1 tablespoon sugar
1 cup pumpkin purée
1 teaspoon cinnamon powder
1 teaspoon baking soda
1 tablespoon olive oil

1. Select the BAKE function and preheat MAXX to 300ºF (149ºC).
2. Crack the eggs into a bowl and beat with a whisk. Combine with the milk, flour, cider vinegar, baking powder, sugar, pumpkin purée, cinnamon powder, and baking soda, mixing well.
3. Grease a baking tray with oil. Add the mixture and transfer into the air fryer oven. Bake for 10 minutes.
4. Serve warm.

Potato Bread Rolls

Prep time: 15 minutes | Cook time: 20 minutes | Serves 5

5 large potatoes, boiled and mashed
Salt and ground black pepper, to taste
½ teaspoon mustard seeds
1 tablespoon olive oil
2 small onions, chopped
2 sprigs curry leaves
½ teaspoon turmeric powder
2 green chilis, seeded and chopped
1 bunch coriander, chopped
8 slices bread, brown sides discarded

1. Put the mashed potatoes in a bowl and sprinkle on salt and pepper. Set to one side.
2. Fry the mustard seeds in olive oil over a medium-low heat in a skillet, stirring continuously, until they sputter.
3. Add the onions and cook until they turn translucent. Add the curry leaves and turmeric powder and stir. Cook for a further 2 minutes until fragrant.
4. Remove the pan from the heat and combine with the potatoes. Mix in the green chilies and coriander.

5. Wet the bread slightly and drain of any excess liquid.
6. Spoon a small amount of the potato mixture into the center of the bread and enclose the bread around the filling, sealing it entirely. Continue until the rest of the bread and filling is used up. Brush each bread roll with some oil and transfer to the air fryer basket.
7. Select the AIR FRY function and cook at 400ºF (204ºC) for 15 minutes, gently shaking the air fryer basket at the halfway point to ensure each roll is cooked evenly.
8. Serve immediately.

Apple and Walnut Muffins

Prep time: 15 minutes | Cook time: 10 minutes | Makes 8 muffins

1 cup flour
$1/_3$ cup sugar
1 teaspoon baking powder
¼ teaspoon baking soda
¼ teaspoon salt
1 teaspoon cinnamon
¼ teaspoon ginger
¼ teaspoon nutmeg
1 egg
2 tablespoons
pancake syrup, plus 2 teaspoons
2 tablespoons melted butter, plus 2 teaspoons
¾ cup unsweetened applesauce
½ teaspoon vanilla extract
¼ cup chopped walnuts
¼ cup diced apple

1. Select the BAKE function and preheat MAXX to 330ºF (166ºC).
2. In a large bowl, stir together the flour, sugar, baking powder, baking soda, salt, cinnamon, ginger, and nutmeg.
3. In a small bowl, beat egg until frothy. Add syrup, butter, applesauce, and vanilla and mix well.
4. Pour egg mixture into dry ingredients and stir just until moistened.
5. Gently stir in nuts and diced apple.
6. Divide batter among 8 parchment paper-lined muffin cups.
7. Put 4 muffin cups in air fryer basket and bake for 10 minutes.
8. Repeat with remaining 4 muffins or until toothpick inserted in center comes out clean.
9. Serve warm.

Creamy Cinnamon Rolls

Prep time: 10 minutes | Cook time: 9 minutes | Serves 8

1 pound (454 g) frozen bread dough, thawed	4 ounces (113 g) cream cheese, softened
¼ cup butter, melted	2 tablespoons butter, softened
¾ cup brown sugar	1¼ cups powdered sugar
1½ tablespoons ground cinnamon	½ teaspoon vanilla extract
Cream Cheese Glaze:	

1. Let the bread dough come to room temperature on the counter. On a lightly floured surface, roll the dough into a 13-inch by 11-inch rectangle. Position the rectangle so the 13-inch side is facing you. Brush the melted butter all over the dough, leaving a 1-inch border uncovered along the edge farthest away from you.
2. Combine the brown sugar and cinnamon in a small bowl. Sprinkle the mixture evenly over the buttered dough, keeping the 1-inch border uncovered. Roll the dough into a log, starting with the edge closest to you. Roll the dough tightly, rolling evenly, and push out any air pockets. When you get to the uncovered edge of the dough, press the dough onto the roll to seal it together.
3. Cut the log into 8 pieces, slicing slowly with a sawing motion so you don't flatten the dough. Turn the slices on their sides and cover with a clean kitchen towel. Let the rolls sit in the warmest part of the kitchen for 1½ to 2 hours to rise.
4. To make the glaze, place the cream cheese and butter in a microwave-safe bowl. Soften the mixture in the microwave for 30 seconds at a time until it is easy to stir. Gradually add the powdered sugar and stir to combine. Add the vanilla extract and whisk until smooth. Set aside.
5. When the rolls have risen, transfer 4 of the rolls to the air fryer basket. Select the AIR FRY function and cook at 350°F (177°C) for 5 minutes. Turn the rolls over and air fry for another 4 minutes. Repeat with the remaining 4 rolls.
6. Let the rolls cool for two minutes before glazing. Spread large dollops of cream cheese glaze on top of the warm cinnamon rolls, allowing some glaze to drip down the side of the rolls. Serve warm.

Tomato and Mozzarella Bruschetta

Prep time: 5 minutes | Cook time: 4 minutes | Serves 1

6 small loaf slices	grated
½ cup tomatoes, finely chopped	1 tablespoon fresh basil, chopped
3 ounces (85 g) Mozzarella cheese,	1 tablespoon olive oil

1. Put the loaf slices inside the air fryer oven. Select the AIR FRY function and cook at 350°F (177°C) for 3 minutes.
2. Add the tomato, Mozzarella, basil, and olive oil on top.
3. Air fry for an additional minute before serving.

Spinach Omelet

Prep time: 10 minutes | Cook time: 10 minutes | Serves 1

1 teaspoon olive oil	cheese
3 eggs	¼ cup chopped spinach
Salt and ground black pepper, to taste	1 tablespoon chopped parsley
1 tablespoon ricotta	

1. Grease the air fryer basket with olive oil. Select the BAKE function and preheat MAXX to 330°F (166°C).
2. In a bowl, beat the eggs with a fork and sprinkle salt and pepper.
3. Add the ricotta, spinach, and parsley and then transfer to the air fryer oven. Bake for 10 minutes or until the egg is set.
4. Serve warm.

Pretzels

Prep time: 10 minutes | Cook time: 6 minutes | Makes 24 pretzels

2 teaspoons yeast
1 cup water, warm
1 teaspoon sugar
1 teaspoon salt
2½ cups all-purpose flour
2 tablespoons

butter, melted, plus more as needed
1 cup boiling water
1 tablespoon baking soda
Coarse sea salt, to taste

1. Combine the yeast and water in a small bowl. Combine the sugar, salt and flour in the bowl of a stand mixer. With the mixer running and using the dough hook, drizzle in the yeast mixture and melted butter and knead dough until smooth and elastic, about 10 minutes. Shape into a ball and let the dough rise for 1 hour.
2. Punch the dough down to release any air and divide the dough into 24 portions.
3. Roll each portion into a skinny rope using both hands on the counter and rolling from the center to the ends of the rope. Spin the rope into a pretzel shape (or tie the rope into a knot) and place the tied pretzels on a parchment lined baking sheet.
4. Combine the boiling water and baking soda in a shallow bowl and whisk to dissolve. Let the water cool so you can put the hands in it. Working in batches, dip the pretzels (top side down) into the baking soda mixture and let them soak for 30 seconds to a minute. Then remove the pretzels carefully and return them (top side up) to the baking sheet. Sprinkle the coarse salt on the top.
5. Select the AIR FRY function and cook at 350ºF (177ºC) for 6 minutes, flipping once halfway. When the pretzels are finished, brush them generously with the melted butter and enjoy them warm.

Banana Churros with Oatmeal

Prep time: 15 minutes | Cook time: 15 minutes | Serves 2

For the Churros:
1 large yellow banana, peeled, cut in half lengthwise, then cut in half widthwise
2 tablespoons whole-wheat pastry flour
⅛ teaspoon sea salt

2 teaspoons oil (sunflower or melted coconut)
1 teaspoon water
Cooking spray
1 tablespoon coconut sugar
½ teaspoon cinnamon

For the Oatmeal:
¾ cup rolled oats

1½ cups water

To make the churros
1. Put the 4 banana pieces in a medium-size bowl and add the flour and salt. Stir gently. Add the oil and water. Stir gently until evenly mixed. You may need to press some coating onto the banana pieces.
2. Spray the air fryer basket with the oil spray. Put the banana pieces in the air fryer basket. Select the AIR FRY function and cook at 340ºF (171ºC) for 5 minutes. Remove, gently turn over, and air fry for another 5 minutes or until browned.
3. In a medium bowl, add the coconut sugar and cinnamon and stir to combine. When the banana pieces are nicely browned, spray with the oil and place in the cinnamon-sugar bowl. Toss gently with a spatula to coat the banana pieces with the mixture.

To make the oatmeal
1. While the bananas are cooking, make the oatmeal. In a medium pot, bring the oats and water to a boil, then reduce to low heat. Simmer, stirring often, until all the water is absorbed, about 5 minutes. Put the oatmeal into two bowls.
2. Top the oatmeal with the coated banana pieces and serve immediately.

PB&J

Prep time: 5 minutes | Cook time: 6 minutes | Serves 4

½ cup cornflakes, crushed	peanut butter
¼ cup shredded coconut	2 medium bananas, cut into ½-inch-thick slices
8 slices oat nut bread or any whole-grain, oversize bread	6 tablespoons pineapple preserves
6 tablespoons	1 egg, beaten
	Cooking spray

1. In a shallow dish, mix the cornflake crumbs and coconut.
2. For each sandwich, spread one bread slice with 1½ tablespoons of peanut butter. Top with banana slices. Spread another bread slice with 1½ tablespoons of preserves. Combine to make a sandwich.
3. Using a pastry brush, brush top of sandwich lightly with beaten egg. Sprinkle with about 1½ tablespoons of crumb coating, pressing it in to make it stick. Spray with cooking spray.
4. Turn sandwich over and repeat to coat and spray the other side.
5. Air frying 2 at a time, place sandwiches in air fryer basket. Select the AIR FRY function and cook at 360ºF (182ºC) for 6 minutes, or until coating is golden brown and crispy.
6. Cut the cooked sandwiches in half and serve warm.

Buttermilk Biscuits

Prep time: 5 minutes | Cook time: 5 minutes | Makes 12 biscuits

2 cups all-purpose flour, plus more for dusting the work surface	2 teaspoons sugar
	1 teaspoon salt
1 tablespoon baking powder	6 tablespoons cold unsalted butter, cut into 1-tablespoon slices
¼ teaspoon baking soda	¾ cup buttermilk

1. Select the BAKE function and preheat MAXX to 360ºF (182ºC). Spray the air fryer basket with olive oil.
2. In a large mixing bowl, combine the flour, baking powder, baking soda, sugar, and salt and mix well.
3. Using a fork, cut in the butter until the mixture resembles coarse meal.
4. Add the buttermilk and mix until smooth.
5. Dust more flour on a clean work surface. Turn the dough out onto the work surface and roll it out until it is about ½ inch thick.
6. Using a 2-inch biscuit cutter, cut out the biscuits. Put the uncooked biscuits in the greased air fryer basket in a single layer.
7. Bake for 5 minutes. Transfer the cooked biscuits from the air fryer oven to a platter.
8. Cut the remaining biscuits. Bake the remaining biscuits.
9. Serve warm.

Spinach with Scrambled Eggs

Prep time: 10 minutes | Cook time: 10 minutes | Serves 2

2 tablespoons olive oil	1 teaspoon fresh lemon juice
4 eggs, whisked	½ teaspoon coarse salt
5 ounces (142 g) fresh spinach, chopped	½ teaspoon ground black pepper
1 medium tomato, chopped	½ cup of fresh basil, roughly chopped

1. Grease a baking pan with the oil, tilting it to spread the oil around. Select the BAKE function and preheat MAXX to 280ºF (138ºC).
2. Mix the remaining ingredients, apart from the basil leaves, whisking well until everything is completely combined.
3. Bake in the air fryer oven for 10 minutes.
4. Top with fresh basil leaves before serving.

Posh Orange Rolls

Prep time: 15 minutes | Cook time: 8 minutes | Makes 8 rolls

3 ounces (85 g) low-fat cream cheese
1 tablespoon low-fat sour cream or plain yogurt
2 teaspoons sugar
¼ teaspoon pure vanilla extract
¼ teaspoon orange extract
1 can (8 count)
organic crescent roll dough
¼ cup chopped walnuts
¼ cup dried cranberries
¼ cup shredded, sweetened coconut
Butter-flavored cooking spray

Orange Glaze:

½ cup powdered sugar
1 tablespoon orange juice
¼ teaspoon orange extract
Dash of salt

1. Cut a circular piece of parchment paper slightly smaller than the bottom of the air fryer basket. Set aside.
2. In a small bowl, combine the cream cheese, sour cream or yogurt, sugar, and vanilla and orange extracts. Stir until smooth.
3. Separate crescent roll dough into 8 triangles and divide cream cheese mixture among them. Starting at wide end, spread cheese mixture to within 1 inch of point.
4. Sprinkle nuts and cranberries evenly over cheese mixture.
5. Starting at wide end, roll up triangles, then sprinkle with coconut, pressing in lightly to make it stick. Spray tops of rolls with butter-flavored cooking spray.
6. Put parchment paper in air fryer basket, and place 4 rolls on top, spaced evenly.
7. Select the AIR FRY function and cook at 300ºF (149ºC) for 8 minutes, until rolls are golden brown and cooked through.
8. Repeat with the remaining 4 rolls. You should be able to use the same piece of parchment paper twice.
9. In a small bowl, stir together ingredients for glaze and drizzle over warm rolls. Serve warm.

Banana Bread

Prep time: 10 minutes | Cook time: 22 minutes | Makes 3 loaves

3 ripe bananas, mashed
1 cup sugar
1 large egg
4 tablespoons (½ stick) unsalted
butter, melted
1½ cups all-purpose flour
1 teaspoon baking soda
1 teaspoon salt

1. Coat the insides of 3 mini loaf pans with cooking spray.
2. In a large mixing bowl, mix the bananas and sugar.
3. In a separate large mixing bowl, combine the egg, butter, flour, baking soda, and salt and mix well.
4. Add the banana mixture to the egg and flour mixture. Mix well.
5. Divide the batter evenly among the prepared pans.
6. Select the BAKE function and preheat MAXX to 310ºF (154ºC). Set the mini loaf pans into the air fryer basket.
7. Bake in the preheated air fryer oven for 22 minutes. Insert a toothpick into the center of each loaf; if it comes out clean, they are done.
8. When the loaves are cooked through, remove the pans from the air fryer basket. Turn out the loaves onto a wire rack to cool.
9. Serve warm.

Grit and Ham Fritters

Prep time: 15 minutes | Cook time: 20 minutes | Serves 6 to 8

4 cups water
1 cup quick-cooking grits
¼ teaspoon salt
2 tablespoons butter
2 cups grated Cheddar cheese, divided
1 cup finely diced ham

1 tablespoon chopped chives
Salt and freshly ground black pepper, to taste
1 egg, beaten
2 cups panko bread crumbs
Cooking spray

1. Bring the water to a boil in a saucepan. Whisk in the grits and ¼ teaspoon of salt, and cook for 7 minutes until the grits are soft. Remove the pan from the heat and stir in the butter and 1 cup of the grated Cheddar cheese. Transfer the grits to a bowl and let them cool for 10 to 15 minutes.
2. Stir the ham, chives and the rest of the cheese into the grits and season with salt and pepper to taste. Add the beaten egg and refrigerate the mixture for 30 minutes.
3. Put the panko bread crumbs in a shallow dish. Measure out ¼-cup portions of the grits mixture and shape them into patties. Coat all sides of the patties with the panko bread crumbs, patting them with the hands so the crumbs adhere to the patties. You should have about 16 patties. Spritz both sides of the patties with cooking spray.
4. In batches of 5 or 6, select the AIR FRY function and cook at 400°F (204°C) for 8 minutes. Using a flat spatula, flip the fritters over and air fry for another 4 minutes.
5. Serve hot.

Nut and Seed Muffins

Prep time: 15 minutes | Cook time: 10 minutes | Makes 8 muffins

½ cup whole-wheat flour, plus 2 tablespoons
¼ cup oat bran
2 tablespoons flaxseed meal
¼ cup brown sugar
½ teaspoon baking soda
½ teaspoon baking powder
¼ teaspoon salt
½ teaspoon cinnamon
½ cup buttermilk

2 tablespoons melted butter
1 egg
½ teaspoon pure vanilla extract
½ cup grated carrots
¼ cup chopped pecans
¼ cup chopped walnuts
1 tablespoon pumpkin seeds
1 tablespoon sunflower seeds
Cooking spray

Special Equipment:
16 foil muffin cups, paper liners removed

1. Select the BAKE function and preheat MAXX to 330°F (166°C).
2. In a large bowl, stir together the flour, bran, flaxseed meal, sugar, baking soda, baking powder, salt, and cinnamon.
3. In a medium bowl, beat together the buttermilk, butter, egg, and vanilla. Pour into flour mixture and stir just until dry ingredients moisten. Do not beat.
4. Gently stir in carrots, nuts, and seeds.
5. Double up the foil cups so you have 8 total and spritz with cooking spray.
6. Put 4 foil cups in air fryer basket and divide half the batter among them.
7. Bake for 10 minutes or until a toothpick inserted in center comes out clean.
8. Repeat with the remaining 4 muffins.
9. Serve warm.

Avocado Quesadillas

Prep time: 10 minutes | Cook time: 11 minutes | Serves 4

4 eggs
2 tablespoons skim milk
Salt and ground black pepper, to taste
Cooking spray
4 flour tortillas

4 tablespoons salsa
2 ounces (57 g) Cheddar cheese, grated
½ small avocado, peeled and thinly sliced

1. Select the BAKE function and preheat MAXX to 270ºF (132ºC).
2. Beat together the eggs, milk, salt, and pepper.
3. Spray a baking pan lightly with cooking spray and add egg mixture.
4. Bake for 8 minutes, stirring every 1 to 2 minutes, until eggs are scrambled to the liking. Remove and set aside.
5. Spray one side of each tortilla with cooking spray. Flip over.
6. Divide eggs, salsa, cheese, and avocado among the tortillas, covering only half of each tortilla.
7. Fold each tortilla in half and press down lightly. Increase the temperature of the air fryer oven to 390ºF (199ºC) and switch from BAKE to AIR FRY.
8. Put 2 tortillas in air fryer basket and air fry for 3 minutes or until cheese melts and outside feels slightly crispy. Repeat with remaining two tortillas.
9. Cut each cooked tortilla into halves. Serve warm.

Soufflé

Prep time: 10 minutes | Cook time: 22 minutes | Serves 4

⅓ cup butter, melted
¼ cup flour
1 cup milk
1 ounce (28 g) sugar
4 egg yolks

1 teaspoon vanilla extract
6 egg whites
1 teaspoon cream of tartar
Cooking spray

1. In a bowl, mix the butter and flour until a smooth consistency is achieved.
2. Pour the milk into a saucepan over medium-low heat. Add the sugar and allow to dissolve before raising the heat to boil the milk.
3. Pour in the flour and butter mixture and stir rigorously for 7 minutes to eliminate any lumps. Make sure the mixture thickens. Take off the heat and allow to cool for 15 minutes.
4. Select the BAKE function and preheat MAXX to 320ºF (160ºC). Spritz 6 soufflé dishes with cooking spray.
5. Put the egg yolks and vanilla extract in a separate bowl and beat them together with a fork. Pour in the milk and combine well to incorporate everything.
6. In a smaller bowl mix the egg whites and cream of tartar with a fork. Fold into the egg yolks-milk mixture before adding in the flour mixture. Transfer equal amounts to the 6 soufflé dishes.
7. Put the dishes in the air fryer oven and bake for 15 minutes.
8. Serve warm.

Bacon and Broccoli Bread Pudding

Prep time: 15 minutes | Cook time: 48 minutes | Serves 2 to 4

½ pound (227 g) thick cut bacon, cut into
¼-inch pieces
3 cups brioche bread, cut into ½-inch cubes
2 tablespoons butter, melted
3 eggs
1 cup milk

½ teaspoon salt
Freshly ground black pepper, to taste
1 cup frozen broccoli florets, thawed and
chopped
1½ cups grated Swiss cheese

1. Select the AIR FRY function and cook the bacon at 400ºF (204ºC) for 8 minutes, or until crispy, shaking the basket a few times to help it air fry evenly. Remove the bacon and set it aside on a paper towel.
2. Air fry the brioche bread cubes for 2 minutes to dry and toast lightly.
3. Butter a cake pan. Combine all the remaining ingredients in a large bowl and toss well. Transfer the mixture to the buttered cake pan, cover with aluminum foil and refrigerate the bread pudding overnight, or for at least 8 hours.
4. Remove the cake pan from the refrigerator an hour before you plan to bake and let it sit on the countertop to come to room temperature.
5. Switch from AIR FRY to BAKE and preheat MAXX to 330ºF (166ºC). Transfer the covered cake pan to the air fryer basket, lowering the pan into the basket. Fold the ends of the aluminum foil over the top of the pan before returning the basket to the air fryer oven.
6. Bake for 20 minutes. Remove the foil and air fry for an additional 20 minutes. If the top browns a little too much before the custard has set, simply return the foil to the pan. The bread pudding has cooked through when a skewer inserted into the center comes out clean.
7. Serve warm.

Chapter 3 Vegetables

Vegan and Vegetarian

Super Veg Rolls

Prep time: 20 minutes | Cook time: 10 minutes | Serves 6

2 potatoes, mashed
¼ cup peas
¼ cup mashed carrots
1 small cabbage, sliced
¼ cups beans
2 tablespoons
sweetcorn
1 small onion, chopped
½ cup bread crumbs
1 packet spring roll sheets
½ cup cornstarch slurry

1. Boil all the vegetables in water over a low heat. Rinse and allow to dry.
2. Unroll the spring roll sheets and spoon equal amounts of vegetable onto the center of each one. Fold into spring rolls and coat each one with the slurry and bread crumbs.
3. Select the AIR FRY function and cook the rolls in the air fryer oven at 390ºF (199ºC) for 10 minutes.
4. Serve warm.

Green Beans with Shallot

Prep time: 10 minutes | Cook time: 10 minutes | Serves 4

1½ pounds (680 g) French green beans, stems removed and blanched
1 tablespoon salt
½ pound (227 g)
shallots, peeled and cut into quarters
½ teaspoon ground white pepper
2 tablespoons olive oil

1. Coat the vegetables with the rest of the ingredients in a bowl.
2. Transfer to the air fryer basket. Select the AIR FRY function and cook at 400ºF (204ºC) for 10 minutes, making sure the green beans achieve a light brown color.
3. Serve hot.

Mediterranean Air Fried Veggies

Prep time: 10 minutes | Cook time: 6 minutes | Serves 4

1 large zucchini, sliced
1 cup cherry tomatoes, halved
1 parsnip, sliced
1 green pepper, sliced
1 carrot, sliced
1 teaspoon mixed
herbs
1 teaspoon mustard
1 teaspoon garlic purée
6 tablespoons olive oil
Salt and ground black pepper, to taste

1. Combine all the ingredients in a bowl, making sure to coat the vegetables well.
2. Transfer to the air fryer oven. Select the AIR FRY function and cook at 400ºF (204ºC) for 6 minutes, ensuring the vegetables are tender and browned.
3. Serve immediately.

Mushroom and Pepper Pizza Squares

Prep time: 10 minutes | Cook time: 10 minutes | Serves 10

1 pizza dough, cut into squares
1 cup chopped oyster mushrooms
1 shallot, chopped
¼ red bell pepper,
chopped
2 tablespoons parsley
Salt and ground black pepper, to taste

1. Select the BAKE function and preheat MAXX to 400ºF (204ºC).
2. In a bowl, combine the oyster mushrooms, shallot, bell pepper and parsley. Sprinkle some salt and pepper as desired.
3. Spread this mixture on top of the pizza squares.
4. Bake in the air fryer oven for 10 minutes.
5. Serve warm.

Russet Potato Gratin

Prep time: 10 minutes | Cook time: 35 minutes | Serves 6

½ cup milk
7 medium russet potatoes, peeled
Salt, to taste
1 teaspoon black pepper

½ cup heavy whipping cream
½ cup grated semi-mature cheese
½ teaspoon nutmeg

1. Select the BAKE function and preheat MAXX to 390ºF (199ºC).
2. Cut the potatoes into wafer-thin slices.
3. In a bowl, combine the milk and cream and sprinkle with salt, pepper, and nutmeg.
4. Use the milk mixture to coat the slices of potatoes. Put in a baking dish. Top the potatoes with the rest of the milk mixture.
5. Put the baking dish into the air fryer basket and bake for 25 minutes.
6. Pour the cheese over the potatoes.
7. Bake for an additional 10 minutes, ensuring the top is nicely browned before serving.

Lush Vegetables Roast

Prep time: 15 minutes | Cook time: 20 minutes | Serves 6

1⅓ cups small parsnips, peeled and cubed
1⅓ cups celery
2 red onions, sliced
1⅓ cups small butternut squash, cut in half, deseeded

and cubed
1 tablespoon fresh thyme needles
1 tablespoon olive oil
Salt and ground black pepper, to taste

1. Select the ROAST function and preheat MAXX to 390ºF (199ºC).
2. Combine the cut vegetables with the thyme, olive oil, salt and pepper.
3. Put the vegetables in the basket and transfer the basket to the air fryer oven.
4. Roast for 20 minutes, stirring once throughout the roasting time, until the vegetables are nicely browned and cooked through.
5. Serve warm.

Potato and Broccoli with Tofu Scramble

Prep time: 15 minutes | Cook time: 30 minutes | Serves 3

2½ cups chopped red potato
2 tablespoons olive oil, divided
1 block tofu, chopped finely
2 tablespoons tamari
1 teaspoon turmeric

powder
½ teaspoon onion powder
½ teaspoon garlic powder
½ cup chopped onion
4 cups broccoli florets

1. Toss together the potatoes and 1 tablespoon of the olive oil.
2. Select the AIR FRY function and cook the potatoes in a baking dish at 400ºF (204ºC) for 15 minutes, shaking once during the cooking time to ensure they fry evenly.
3. Combine the tofu, the remaining 1 tablespoon of the olive oil, turmeric, onion powder, tamari, and garlic powder together, stirring in the onions, followed by the broccoli.
4. Top the potatoes with the tofu mixture and air fry for an additional 15 minutes. Serve warm.

Balsamic Brussels Sprouts

Prep time: 5 minutes | Cook time: 13 minutes | Serves 2

2 cups Brussels sprouts, halved
1 tablespoon olive oil
1 tablespoon

balsamic vinegar
1 tablespoon maple syrup
¼ teaspoon sea salt

1. Evenly coat the Brussels sprouts with the olive oil, balsamic vinegar, maple syrup, and salt.
2. Transfer to the air fryer basket. Select the AIR FRY function and cook at 375ºF (191ºC) for 5 minutes.
3. Give the basket a good shake, turn the heat to 400ºF (204ºC) and continue to air fry for another 8 minutes.
4. Serve hot.

Ratatouille

Prep time: 20 minutes | Cook time: 25 minutes | Serves 4

1 sprig basil
1 sprig flat-leaf parsley
1 sprig mint
1 tablespoon coriander powder
1 teaspoon capers
½ lemon, juiced
Salt and ground black pepper, to taste
2 eggplants, sliced crosswise
2 red onions, chopped

4 cloves garlic, minced
2 red peppers, sliced crosswise
1 fennel bulb, sliced crosswise
3 large zucchinis, sliced crosswise
5 tablespoons olive oil
4 large tomatoes, chopped
2 teaspoons herbs de Provence

1. Blend the basil, parsley, coriander, mint, lemon juice and capers, with a little salt and pepper. Make sure all ingredients are well-incorporated.
2. Coat the eggplant, onions, garlic, peppers, fennel, and zucchini with olive oil.
3. Transfer the vegetables into a baking dish and top with the tomatoes and herb purée. Sprinkle with more salt and pepper, and the herbs de Provence.
4. Select the AIR FRY function and cook at 400ºF (204ºC) for 25 minutes.
5. Serve immediately.

Mascarpone Mushrooms

Prep time: 10 minutes | Cook time: 15 minutes | Serves 4

Vegetable oil spray
4 cups sliced mushrooms
1 medium yellow onion, chopped
2 cloves garlic, minced
¼ cup heavy whipping cream or half-and-half
8 ounces (227 g) mascarpone cheese
1 teaspoon dried

thyme
1 teaspoon kosher salt
1 teaspoon black pepper
½ teaspoon red pepper flakes
4 cups cooked konjac noodles, for serving
½ cup grated Parmesan cheese

1. Select the BAKE function and preheat MAXX to 350ºF (177ºC). Spray a heatproof pan with vegetable oil spray.
2. In a medium bowl, combine the mushrooms, onion, garlic, cream, mascarpone, thyme, salt, black pepper, and red pepper flakes. Stir to combine. Transfer the mixture to the prepared pan.
3. Put the pan in the air fryer basket. Bake for 15 minutes, stirring halfway through the baking time.
4. Divide the pasta among four shallow bowls. Spoon the mushroom mixture evenly over the pasta. Sprinkle with Parmesan cheese and serve.

Sweet Potatoes with Tofu

Prep time: 15 minutes | Cook time: 35 minutes | Serves 8

8 sweet potatoes, scrubbed
2 tablespoons olive oil
1 large onion, chopped
2 green chilies, deseeded and chopped
8 ounces (227 g)

tofu, crumbled
2 tablespoons Cajun seasoning
1 cup chopped tomatoes
1 can kidney beans, drained and rinsed
Salt and ground black pepper, to taste

1. With a knife, pierce the skin of the sweet potatoes. Select the AIR FRY function and cook the sweet potatoes in the air fryer oven at 400ºF (204ºC) for 30 minutes, or until soft.
2. Remove from the air fryer oven, halve each potato, and set to one side.
3. Over a medium heat, fry the onions and chilies in the olive oil in a skillet for 2 minutes until fragrant.
4. Add the tofu and Cajun seasoning and air fry for a further 3 minutes before incorporating the kidney beans and tomatoes. Sprinkle some salt and pepper as desire.
5. Top each sweet potato halve with a spoonful of the tofu mixture and serve.

Sweet Potatoes with Zucchini

Prep time: 20 minutes | Cook time: 20 minutes | Serves 4

2 large-sized sweet potatoes, peeled and quartered
1 medium zucchini, sliced
1 Serrano pepper, deseeded and thinly sliced
1 bell pepper, deseeded and thinly sliced
1 to 2 carrots, cut into matchsticks
¼ cup olive oil
1½ tablespoons

maple syrup
½ teaspoon porcini powder
¼ teaspoon mustard powder
½ teaspoon fennel seeds
1 tablespoon garlic powder
½ teaspoon fine sea salt
¼ teaspoon ground black pepper
Tomato ketchup, for serving

1. Put the sweet potatoes, zucchini, peppers, and the carrot into the air fryer basket. Coat with a drizzling of olive oil.
2. Select the AIR FRY function and cook at 350ºF (177ºC) for 15 minutes.
3. In the meantime, prepare the sauce by vigorously combining the other ingredients, except for the tomato ketchup, with a whisk.
4. Lightly grease a baking dish.
5. Transfer the cooked vegetables to the baking dish, pour over the sauce and coat the vegetables well.
6. Increase the temperature to 390ºF (199ºC) and air fry the vegetables for an additional 5 minutes.
7. Serve warm with a side of ketchup.

Lush Summer Rolls

Prep time: 15 minutes | Cook time: 15 minutes | Serves 4

1 cup shiitake mushroom, sliced thinly
1 celery stalk, chopped
1 medium carrot, shredded
½ teaspoon finely chopped ginger

1 teaspoon sugar
1 tablespoon soy sauce
1 teaspoon nutritional yeast
8 spring roll sheets
1 teaspoon corn starch
2 tablespoons water

1. In a bowl, combine the ginger, soy sauce, nutritional yeast, carrots, celery, mushroom, and sugar.
2. Mix the cornstarch and water to create an adhesive for the spring rolls.
3. Scoop a tablespoonful of the vegetable mixture into the middle of the spring roll sheets. Brush the edges of the sheets with the cornstarch adhesive and enclose around the filling to make spring rolls.
4. Place the rolls in the air fryer basket. Select the AIR FRY function and cook at 400ºF (204ºC) for 15 minutes, or until crisp.
5. Serve hot.

Blistered Shishito Peppers

Prep time: 10 minutes | Cook time: 6 minutes | Serves 4

Dipping Sauce:
1 cup sour cream
2 tablespoons fresh lemon juice
1 clove garlic,

minced
1 green onion (white and green parts), finely chopped

Peppers:
8 ounces (227 g) shishito peppers
1 tablespoon vegetable oil
1 teaspoon toasted sesame oil
Kosher salt and

black pepper, to taste
¼ to ½ teaspoon red pepper flakes
½ teaspoon toasted sesame seeds

1. In a small bowl, stir all the ingredients for the dipping sauce to combine. Cover and refrigerate until serving time.
2. In a medium bowl, toss the peppers with the vegetable oil. Put the peppers in the air fryer basket. Select the AIR FRY function and cook at 400ºF (204ºC) for 6 minutes, or until peppers are lightly charred in spots, stirring the peppers halfway through the cooking time.
3. Transfer the peppers to a serving bowl. Drizzle with the sesame oil and toss to coat. Season with salt and pepper. Sprinkle with the red pepper and sesame seeds and toss again.
4. Serve immediately with the dipping sauce.

Rice and Eggplant Bowl

Prep time: 15 minutes | Cook time: 10 minutes | Serves 4

¼ cup sliced cucumber
1 teaspoon salt
1 tablespoon sugar
7 tablespoons Japanese rice vinegar
3 medium eggplants, sliced

3 tablespoons sweet white miso paste
1 tablespoon mirin rice wine
4 cups cooked sushi rice
4 spring onions
1 tablespoon toasted sesame seeds

1. Coat the cucumber slices with the rice wine vinegar, salt, and sugar.
2. Put a dish on top of the bowl to weight it down completely.
3. In a bowl, mix the eggplants, mirin rice wine, and miso paste. Allow to marinate for half an hour.
4. Put the eggplant slices in the air fryer oven. Select the AIR FRY function and cook at 400°F (204°C) for 10 minutes.
5. Fill the bottom of a serving bowl with rice and top with the eggplants and pickled cucumbers.
6. Add the spring onions and sesame seeds for garnish. Serve immediately.

Super Vegetable Burger

Prep time: 15 minutes | Cook time: 12 minutes | Serves 8

½ pound (227 g) cauliflower, steamed and diced, rinsed and drained
2 teaspoons coconut oil, melted
2 teaspoons minced garlic
¼ cup desiccated coconut
½ cup oats
3 tablespoons flour
1 tablespoon

flaxseeds plus 3 tablespoons water, divided
1 teaspoon mustard powder
2 teaspoons thyme
2 teaspoons parsley
2 teaspoons chives
Salt and ground black pepper, to taste
1 cup bread crumbs

1. Combine the cauliflower with all the ingredients, except for the bread crumbs, incorporating everything well.

2. Using the hands, shape 8 equal-sized amounts of the mixture into burger patties. Coat the patties in bread crumbs before putting them in the air fryer basket in a single layer.
3. Select the AIR FRY function and cook at 390°F (199°C) for 12 minutes, or until crispy.
4. Serve hot.

Cauliflower Faux Rice

Prep time: 15 minutes | Cook time: 40 minutes | Serves 8

1 large head cauliflower, rinsed and drained, cut into florets
½ lemon, juiced
2 garlic cloves, minced
2 (8-ounce / 227-g) cans mushrooms
1 (8-ounce / 227-g) can water chestnuts

¾ cup peas
1 egg, beaten
4 tablespoons soy sauce
1 tablespoon peanut oil
1 tablespoon sesame oil
1 tablespoon minced fresh ginger
Cooking spray

1. Mix the peanut oil, soy sauce, sesame oil, minced ginger, lemon juice, and minced garlic to combine well.
2. In a food processor, pulse the florets in small batches to break them down to resemble rice grains. Pour into the air fryer basket.
3. Drain the chestnuts and roughly chop them. Pour into the basket. Select the AIR FRY function and cook at 350°F (177°C) for 20 minutes.
4. In the meantime, drain the mushrooms. Add the mushrooms and the peas to the air fryer oven and continue to air fry for another 15 minutes.
5. Lightly spritz a frying pan with cooking spray. Prepare an omelet with the beaten egg, ensuring it is firm. Lay on a cutting board and slice it up.
6. When the cauliflower is ready, throw in the omelet. Switch from AIR FRY to BAKE and bake for an additional 5 minutes. Serve hot.

Chermoula Beet Roast

Prep time: 15 minutes | Cook time: 25 minutes | Serves 4

Chermoula:

1 cup packed fresh cilantro leaves
½ cup packed fresh parsley leaves
6 cloves garlic, peeled
2 teaspoons smoked paprika
2 teaspoons ground cumin

1 teaspoon ground coriander
½ to 1 teaspoon cayenne pepper
Pinch of crushed saffron (optional)
½ cup extra-virgin olive oil
Kosher salt, to taste

Beets:

3 medium beets, trimmed, peeled, and cut into 1-inch chunks
2 tablespoons

chopped fresh cilantro
2 tablespoons chopped fresh parsley

1. In a food processor, combine the cilantro, parsley, garlic, paprika, cumin, coriander, and cayenne. Pulse until coarsely chopped. Add the saffron, if using, and process until combined. With the food processor running, slowly add the olive oil in a steady stream; process until the sauce is uniform. Season with salt.
2. Select the ROAST function and preheat MAXX to 375ºF (191ºC).
3. In a large bowl, drizzle the beets with ½ cup of the chermoula to coat. Arrange the beets in the air fryer basket. Roast for 25 to minutes, or until the beets are tender.
4. Transfer the beets to a serving platter. Sprinkle with the chopped cilantro and parsley and serve.

Basmati Risotto

Prep time: 10 minutes | Cook time: 30 minutes | Serves 2

1 onion, diced
1 small carrot, diced
2 cups vegetable broth, boiling
½ cup grated Cheddar cheese
1 clove garlic,

minced
¾ cup long-grain basmati rice
1 tablespoon olive oil
1 tablespoon unsalted butter

1. Select the BAKE function and preheat MAXX to 390ºF (199ºC).
2. Grease a baking tin with oil and stir in the butter, garlic, carrot, and onion.
3. Put the tin in the air fryer oven and bake for 4 minutes.
4. Pour in the rice and bake for a further 4 minutes, stirring three times throughout the baking time.
5. Turn the temperature down to 320ºF (160ºC).
6. Add the vegetable broth and give the dish a gentle stir. Bake for 22 minutes, leaving the air fryer oven uncovered.
7. Pour in the cheese, stir once more and serve.

Spicy Cauliflower Roast

Prep time: 15 minutes | Cook time: 20 minutes | Serves 4

Cauliflower:

5 cups cauliflower florets
3 tablespoons vegetable oil
½ teaspoon ground

cumin
½ teaspoon ground coriander
½ teaspoon kosher salt

Sauce:

½ cup Greek yogurt or sour cream
¼ cup chopped fresh cilantro
1 jalapeño, coarsely chopped

4 cloves garlic, peeled
½ teaspoon kosher salt
2 tablespoons water

1. Select the ROAST function and preheat MAXX to 400ºF (204ºC).
2. In a large bowl, combine the cauliflower, oil, cumin, coriander, and salt. Toss to coat.
3. Put the cauliflower in the air fryer basket. Roast for 20 minutes, stirring halfway through the roasting time.
4. Meanwhile, in a blender, combine the yogurt, cilantro, jalapeño, garlic, and salt. Blend, adding the water as needed to keep the blades moving and to thin the sauce.
5. At the end of roasting time, transfer the cauliflower to a large serving bowl. Pour the sauce over and toss gently to coat. Serve immediately.

Cauliflower, Chickpea, and Avocado Mash

Prep time: 10 minutes | Cook time: 25 minutes | Serves 4

1 medium head cauliflower, cut into florets
1 can chickpeas, drained and rinsed
1 tablespoon extra-virgin olive oil
2 tablespoons lemon

juice
Salt and ground black pepper, to taste
4 flatbreads, toasted
2 ripe avocados, mashed

1. In a bowl, mix the chickpeas, cauliflower, lemon juice and olive oil. Sprinkle salt and pepper as desired.
2. Put inside the air fryer basket. Select the AIR FRY function and cook at 425°F (218°C) for 25 minutes.
3. Spread on top of the flatbread along with the mashed avocado. Sprinkle with more pepper and salt and serve.

Black Bean and Tomato Chili

Prep time: 15 minutes | Cook time: 23 minutes | Serves 6

1 tablespoon olive oil
1 medium onion, diced
3 garlic cloves, minced
1 cup vegetable broth
3 cans black beans, drained and rinsed

2 cans diced tomatoes
2 chipotle peppers, chopped
2 teaspoons cumin
2 teaspoons chili powder
1 teaspoon dried oregano
½ teaspoon salt

1. Over a medium heat, fry the garlic and onions in the olive oil for 3 minutes.
2. Add the remaining ingredients, stirring constantly and scraping the bottom to prevent sticking.
3. Select the BAKE function and preheat MAXX to 400°F (204°C).
4. Take a dish and place the mixture inside. Put a sheet of aluminum foil on top.
5. Transfer to the air fryer oven and bake for 20 minutes.
6. When ready, plate up and serve immediately.

Creamy and Cheesy Spinach

Prep time: 10 minutes | Cook time: 15 minutes | Serves 4

Vegetable oil spray
1 (10-ounce / 283-g) package frozen spinach, thawed and squeezed dry
½ cup chopped onion
2 cloves garlic, minced
4 ounces (113 g)

cream cheese, diced
½ teaspoon ground nutmeg
1 teaspoon kosher salt
1 teaspoon black pepper
½ cup grated Parmesan cheese

1. Select the BAKE function and preheat MAXX to 350°F (177°C). Spray a heatproof pan with vegetable oil spray.
2. In a medium bowl, combine the spinach, onion, garlic, cream cheese, nutmeg, salt, and pepper. Transfer to the prepared pan.
3. Put the pan in the air fryer basket. Bake for 10 minutes. Open and stir to thoroughly combine the cream cheese and spinach.
4. Sprinkle the Parmesan cheese on top. Bake for 5 minutes, or until the cheese has melted and browned.
5. Serve hot.

Potatoes with Zucchinis

Prep time: 10 minutes | Cook time: 45 minutes | Serves 4

2 potatoes, peeled and cubed
4 carrots, cut into chunks
1 head broccoli, cut into florets
4 zucchinis, sliced

thickly
Salt and ground black pepper, to taste
¼ cup olive oil
1 tablespoon dry onion powder

1. Select the BAKE function and preheat MAXX to 400°F (204°C).
2. In a baking dish, add all the ingredients and combine well.
3. Bake for 45 minutes in the air fryer oven, ensuring the vegetables are soft and the sides have browned before serving.

Gold Ravioli

Prep time: 10 minutes | Cook time: 6 minutes | Serves 4

½ cup panko bread crumbs
2 teaspoons nutritional yeast
1 teaspoon dried basil
1 teaspoon dried oregano
1 teaspoon garlic powder
Salt and ground black pepper, to taste
¼ cup aquafaba
8 ounces (227 g) ravioli
Cooking spray

1. Cover the air fryer basket with aluminum foil and coat with a light brushing of oil.
2. Combine the panko bread crumbs, nutritional yeast, basil, oregano, and garlic powder. Sprinkle with salt and pepper to taste.
3. Put the aquafaba in a separate bowl. Dip the ravioli in the aquafaba before coating it in the panko mixture. Spritz with cooking spray and transfer to the air fryer oven.
4. Select the AIR FRY function and cook at 400ºF (204ºC) for 6 minutes. Shake the air fryer basket halfway.
5. Serve hot.

Vegetable Sides

Easy Rosemary Green Beans

Prep time: 5 minutes | Cook time: 5 minutes | Serves 1

1 tablespoon butter, melted
2 tablespoons rosemary
½ teaspoon salt
3 cloves garlic, minced
¾ cup chopped green beans

1. Combine the melted butter with the rosemary, salt, and minced garlic. Toss in the green beans, coating them well.
2. Select the AIR FRY function and cook at 390ºF (199ºC) for 5 minutes.
3. Serve immediately.

Herbed Radishes

Prep time: 5 minutes | Cook time: 10 minutes | Serves 2

1 pound (454 g) radishes
2 tablespoons unsalted butter, melted
¼ teaspoon dried oregano
½ teaspoon dried parsley
½ teaspoon garlic powder

1. Prepare the radishes by cutting off their tops and bottoms and quartering them.
2. In a bowl, combine the butter, dried oregano, dried parsley, and garlic powder. Toss with the radishes to coat.
3. Transfer the radishes to the air fryer oven. Select the AIR FRY function and cook at 350ºF (177ºC) for 10 minutes, shaking the basket at the halfway point to ensure the radishes air fry evenly through. The radishes are ready when they turn brown.
4. Serve immediately.

Easy Potato Croquettes

Prep time: 15 minutes | Cook time: 15 minutes | Serves 10

¼ cup nutritional yeast
2 cups boiled potatoes, mashed
1 flax egg
1 tablespoon flour
2 tablespoons
chopped chives
Salt and ground black pepper, to taste
2 tablespoons vegetable oil
¼ cup bread crumbs

1. In a bowl, combine the nutritional yeast, potatoes, flax egg, flour, and chives. Sprinkle with salt and pepper as desired.
2. In a separate bowl, mix the vegetable oil and bread crumbs to achieve a crumbly consistency.
3. Shape the potato mixture into small balls and dip each one into the bread crumb mixture.
4. Put the croquettes inside the air fryer oven. Select the AIR FRY function and cook at 400ºF (204ºC) for 15 minutes, ensuring the croquettes turn golden brown.
5. Serve immediately.

Crispy Jicama Fries

Prep time: 5 minutes | Cook time: 20 minutes | Serves 1

1 small jicama, peeled
¼ teaspoon onion powder
¾ teaspoon chili
powder
¼ teaspoon garlic powder
¼ teaspoon ground black pepper

1. To make the fries, cut the jicama into matchsticks of the desired thickness.
2. In a bowl, toss them with the onion powder, chili powder, garlic powder, and black pepper to coat. Transfer the fries into the air fryer basket.
3. Select the AIR FRY function and cook at 350ºF (177ºC) for 20 minutes, giving the basket an occasional shake throughout the cooking process. The fries are ready when they are hot and golden.
4. Serve immediately.

Tofu Bites

Prep time: 15 minutes | Cook time: 30 minutes | Serves 4

1 packaged firm tofu, cubed and pressed to remove excess water
1 tablespoon soy sauce
1 tablespoon ketchup
1 tablespoon maple syrup
½ teaspoon vinegar
1 teaspoon liquid
smoke
1 teaspoon hot sauce
2 tablespoons sesame seeds
1 teaspoon garlic powder
Salt and ground black pepper, to taste
Cooking spray

1. Spritz a baking dish with cooking spray.
2. Combine all the ingredients to coat the tofu completely and allow the marinade to absorb for half an hour.
3. Transfer the tofu to the baking dish. Select the AIR FRY function and cook at 375ºF (191ºC) for 15 minutes. Flip the tofu over and air fry for another 15 minutes on the other side.
4. Serve immediately.

Cauliflower Tater Tots

Prep time: 15 minutes | Cook time: 16 minutes | Serves 12

1 pound (454 g) cauliflower, steamed and chopped
½ cup nutritional yeast
1 tablespoon oats
1 tablespoon desiccated coconuts
3 tablespoons flaxseed meal
3 tablespoons water
1 onion, chopped
1 teaspoon minced garlic
1 teaspoon chopped parsley
1 teaspoon chopped oregano
1 teaspoon chopped chives
Salt and ground black pepper, to taste
½ cup bread crumbs

1. Drain any excess water out of the cauliflower by wringing it with a paper towel.
2. In a bowl, combine the cauliflower with the remaining ingredients, save the bread crumbs. Using the hands, shape the mixture into several small balls.
3. Coat the balls in the bread crumbs and transfer to the air fryer basket. Select the AIR FRY function and cook at 390ºF (199ºC) for 6 minutes. Then raise the temperature to 400ºF (204ºC) and then air fry for an additional 10 minutes.
4. Serve immediately.

Zucchini Balls

Prep time: 5 minutes | Cook time: 10 minutes | Serves 4

4 zucchinis
1 egg
½ cup grated Parmesan cheese
1 tablespoon Italian herbs
1 cup grated coconut

1. Thinly grate the zucchinis and dry with a cheesecloth, ensuring to remove all the moisture.
2. In a bowl, combine the zucchinis with the egg, Parmesan, Italian herbs, and grated coconut, mixing well to incorporate everything. Using the hands, mold the mixture into balls.
3. Lay the zucchini balls in the air fryer basket. Select the AIR FRY function and cook at 400ºF (204ºC) for 10 minutes.
4. Serve hot.

Golden Pickles

Prep time: 10 minutes | Cook time: 15 minutes | Serves 4

14 dill pickles, sliced
¼ cup flour
⅛ teaspoon baking powder
Pinch of salt
2 tablespoons

cornstarch plus 3 tablespoons water
6 tablespoons panko bread crumbs
½ teaspoon paprika
Cooking spray

1. Drain any excess moisture out of the dill pickles on a paper towel.
2. In a bowl, combine the flour, baking powder and salt.
3. Throw in the cornstarch and water mixture and combine well with a whisk.
4. Put the panko bread crumbs in a shallow dish along with the paprika. Mix thoroughly.
5. Dip the pickles in the flour batter, before coating in the bread crumbs. Spritz all the pickles with the cooking spray.
6. Transfer to the air fryer basket. Select the AIR FRY function and cook at 400ºF (204ºC) for 15 minutes, or until golden brown.
7. Serve immediately.

Saltine Wax Beans

Prep time: 10 minutes | Cook time: 7 minutes | Serves 4

½ cup flour
1 teaspoon smoky chipotle powder
½ teaspoon ground black pepper
1 teaspoon sea salt flakes

2 eggs, beaten
½ cup crushed saltines
10 ounces (283 g) wax beans
Cooking spray

1. Combine the flour, chipotle powder, black pepper, and salt in a bowl. Put the eggs in a second bowl. Put the crushed saltines in a third bowl.
2. Wash the beans with cold water and discard any tough strings.
3. Coat the beans with the flour mixture, before dipping them into the beaten egg. Cover them with the crushed saltines.
4. Spritz the beans with cooking spray.

5. Select the AIR FRY function and cook at 360ºF (182ºC) for 4 minutes. Give the air fryer basket a good shake and continue to air fry for 3 minutes. Serve hot.

Crispy Chickpeas

Prep time: 5 minutes | Cook time: 15 minutes | Serves 4

1 (15-ounces / 425-g) can chickpeas, drained but not rinsed
2 tablespoons olive

oil
1 teaspoon salt
2 tablespoons lemon juice

1. Add all the ingredients together in a bowl and mix. Transfer this mixture to the air fryer basket.
2. Select the AIR FRY function and cook at 400ºF (204ºC) for 15 minutes, ensuring the chickpeas become nice and crispy.
3. Serve immediately.

Lush Vegetable Salad

Prep time: 15 minutes | Cook time: 10 minutes | Serves 4

6 plum tomatoes, halved
2 large red onions, sliced
4 long red pepper, sliced
2 yellow pepper, sliced
6 cloves garlic, crushed

1 tablespoon extra-virgin olive oil
1 teaspoon paprika
½ lemon, juiced
Salt and ground black pepper, to taste
1 tablespoon baby capers

1. Put the tomatoes, onions, peppers, and garlic in a large bowl and cover with the extra-virgin olive oil, paprika, and lemon juice. Sprinkle with salt and pepper as desired.
2. Line the inside of the air fryer basket with aluminum foil. Put the vegetables inside. Select the AIR FRY function and cook at 420ºF (216ºC) for 10 minutes, ensuring the edges turn brown.
3. Serve in a salad bowl with the baby capers.

Sweet and Sour Tofu 20

Prep time: 15 minutes | Cook time: 20 minutes | Serves 2

2 teaspoons apple cider vinegar
1 tablespoon sugar
1 tablespoon soy sauce
3 teaspoons lime juice
1 teaspoon ground ginger
1 teaspoon garlic powder

½ block firm tofu, pressed to remove excess liquid and cut into cubes
1 teaspoon cornstarch
2 green onions, chopped
Toasted sesame seeds, for garnish

1. In a bowl, thoroughly combine the apple cider vinegar, sugar, soy sauce, lime juice, ground ginger, and garlic powder.
2. Cover the tofu with this mixture and leave to marinate for at least 30 minutes.
3. Transfer the tofu to the air fryer oven, keeping any excess marinade for the sauce. Select the AIR FRY function and cook at 400ºF (204ºC) for 20 minutes, or until crispy.
4. In the meantime, thicken the sauce with the cornstarch over a medium-low heat.
5. Serve the cooked tofu with the sauce, green onions, and sesame seeds.

Simple Buffalo Cauliflower

Prep time: 5 minutes | Cook time: 5 minutes | Serves 1

½ packet dry ranch seasoning
2 tablespoons salted butter, melted

1 cup cauliflower florets
¼ cup buffalo sauce

1. Select the ROAST function and preheat MAXX to 400ºF (204ºC).
2. In a bowl, combine the dry ranch seasoning and butter. Toss with the cauliflower florets to coat and transfer them to the air fryer oven.
3. Roast for 5 minutes, shaking the basket occasionally to ensure the florets roast evenly.
4. Remove the cauliflower from the air fryer oven, pour the buffalo sauce over it, and serve.

Roasted Potatoes and Asparagus

Prep time: 5 minutes | Cook time: 23 minutes | Serves 4

4 medium potatoes
1 bunch asparagus
⅓ cup cottage cheese
⅓ cup low-fat crème fraiche

1 tablespoon wholegrain mustard
Salt and pepper, to taste
Cooking spray

1. Spritz the air fryer basket with cooking spray.
2. Place the potatoes in the basket. Select the AIR FRY function and cook at 390ºF (199ºC) for 20 minutes.
3. Boil the asparagus in salted water for 3 minutes.
4. Remove the potatoes and mash them with rest of ingredients. Sprinkle with salt and pepper.
5. Serve immediately.

Lemony Falafel

Prep time: 15 minutes | Cook time: 15 minutes | Serves 8

1 teaspoon cumin seeds
½ teaspoon coriander seeds
2 cups chickpeas, drained and rinsed
½ teaspoon red pepper flakes
3 cloves garlic
¼ cup chopped

parsley
¼ cup chopped coriander
½ onion, diced
1 tablespoon juice from freshly squeezed lemon
3 tablespoons flour
½ teaspoon salt
Cooking spray

1. Fry the cumin and coriander seeds over medium heat until fragrant.
2. Grind using a mortar and pestle.
3. Put all of ingredients, except for the cooking spray, in a food processor and blend until a fine consistency is achieved.
4. Use the hands to mold the mixture into falafels and spritz with the cooking spray.
5. Transfer the falafels to the air fryer basket in one layer.
6. Select the AIR FRY function and cook at 400ºF (204ºC) for 15 minutes, serving when they turn golden brown.

Sesame Taj Tofu

Prep time: 5 minutes | Cook time: 25 minutes | Serves 4

1 block firm tofu, pressed and cut into 1-inch thick cubes
2 tablespoons soy sauce
2 teaspoons toasted

sesame seeds
1 teaspoon rice vinegar
1 tablespoon cornstarch

1. Add the tofu, soy sauce, sesame seeds, and rice vinegar in a bowl together and mix well to coat the tofu cubes. Then cover the tofu in cornstarch and put it in the air fryer basket.
2. Select the AIR FRY function and cook at 400ºF (204ºC) for 25 minutes, giving the basket a shake at five-minute intervals to ensure the tofu cooks evenly.
3. Serve immediately.

Sweet Potato Fries

Prep time: 5 minutes | Cook time: 25 minutes | Serves 4

2 pounds (907 g) sweet potatoes, rinsed, sliced into matchsticks
1 teaspoon curry

powder
2 tablespoons olive oil
Salt, to taste

1. Select the BAKE function and preheat MAXX to 390ºF (199ºC).
2. Drizzle the oil in the baking pan, place the fries inside and bake for 25 minutes.
3. Sprinkle with the curry powder and salt before serving.

Potato with Creamy Cheese

Prep time: 5 minutes | Cook time: 15 minutes | Serves 2

2 medium potatoes
1 teaspoon butter
3 tablespoons sour cream

1 teaspoon chives
1½ tablespoons grated Parmesan cheese

1. Pierce the potatoes with a fork and boil them in water until they are cooked.

2. Transfer to the air fryer oven. Select the AIR FRY function and cook at 350ºF (177ºC) for 15 minutes.
3. In the meantime, combine the sour cream, cheese and chives in a bowl. Cut the potatoes halfway to open them up and fill with the butter and sour cream mixture.
4. Serve immediately.

Chili Fingerling Potatoes

Prep time: 10 minutes | Cook time: 16 minutes | Serves 4

1 pound (454 g) fingerling potatoes, rinsed and cut into wedges
1 teaspoon olive oil
1 teaspoon salt
1 teaspoon black

pepper
1 teaspoon cayenne pepper
1 teaspoon nutritional yeast
½ teaspoon garlic powder

1. Coat the potatoes with the rest of the ingredients.
2. Transfer to the air fryer basket. Select the AIR FRY function and cook at 400ºF (204ºC) for 16 minutes, shaking the basket at the halfway point.
3. Serve immediately.

Roasted Lemony Broccoli

Prep time: 5 minutes | Cook time: 15 minutes | Serves 6

2 heads broccoli, cut into florets
2 teaspoons extra-virgin olive oil, plus more for coating
1 teaspoon salt

½ teaspoon black pepper
1 clove garlic, minced
½ teaspoon lemon juice

1. Cover the air fryer basket with aluminum foil and coat with a light brushing of oil.
2. Select the ROAST function and preheat MAXX to 375ºF (191ºC).
3. In a bowl, combine all ingredients, save for the lemon juice, and transfer to the air fryer basket. Roast for 15 minutes.
4. Serve with the lemon juice.

Air Fried Asparagus

Prep time: 5 minutes | Cook time: 5 minutes | Serves 4

1 pound (454 g) fresh asparagus spears, trimmed	oil
	Salt and ground black pepper, to taste
1 tablespoon olive	

1. Combine all the ingredients and transfer to the air fryer basket.
2. Select the AIR FRY function and cook at 375ºF (191ºC) for 5 minutes, or until soft.
3. Serve hot.

Simple Pesto Gnocchi

Prep time: 10 minutes | Cook time: 15 minutes | Serves 4

1 (1-pound / 454-g) package gnocchi	1 tablespoon extra-virgin olive oil
1 medium onion, chopped	1 (8-ounce / 227-g) jar pesto
3 cloves garlic, minced	1/3 cup grated Parmesan cheese

1. In a large bowl combine the onion, garlic, and gnocchi, and drizzle with the olive oil. Mix thoroughly.
2. Transfer the mixture to the air fryer oven. Select the AIR FRY function and cook at 340ºF (171ºC) for 15 minutes, stirring occasionally, making sure the gnocchi become light brown and crispy.
3. Add the pesto and Parmesan cheese, and give everything a good stir before serving.

Air Fried Potatoes with Olives

Prep time: 15 minutes | Cook time: 40 minutes | Serves 1

1 medium russet potatoes, scrubbed and peeled	Dollop of butter
	Dollop of cream cheese
1 teaspoon olive oil	1 tablespoon Kalamata olives
1/4 teaspoon onion powder	
1/8 teaspoon salt	1 tablespoon chopped chives

1. In a bowl, coat the potatoes with the onion powder, salt, olive oil, and butter.
2. Transfer to the air fryer oven. Select the AIR FRY function and cook at 400ºF (204ºC) for 40 minutes, turning the potatoes over at the halfway point.
3. Take care when removing the potatoes from the air fryer oven and serve with the cream cheese, Kalamata olives and chives on top.

Roasted Eggplant Slices

Prep time: 5 minutes | Cook time: 15 minutes | Serves 1

1 large eggplant, sliced	1/4 teaspoon salt
	1/2 teaspoon garlic powder
2 tablespoons olive oil	

1. Select the ROAST function and preheat MAXX to 390ºF (199ºC).
2. Apply the olive oil to the slices with a brush, coating both sides. Season each side with sprinklings of salt and garlic powder.
3. Put the slices in the air fryer oven and roast for 15 minutes.
4. Serve immediately.

Air Fried Brussels Sprouts

Prep time: 5 minutes | Cook time: 10 minutes | Serves 1

1 pound (454 g) Brussels sprouts	1 tablespoon unsalted butter, melted
1 tablespoon coconut oil, melted	

1. Prepare the Brussels sprouts by halving them, discarding any loose leaves.
2. Combine with the melted coconut oil and transfer to the air fryer oven.
3. Select the AIR FRY function and cook at 400ºF (204ºC) for 10 minutes, giving the basket a good shake throughout the air frying time to brown them up if desired.
4. The sprouts are ready when they are partially caramelized. Remove them from the air fryer oven and serve with a topping of melted butter before serving.

Fig, Chickpea, and Arugula Salad

Prep time: 15 minutes | Cook time: 20 minutes | Serves 4

8 fresh figs, halved
1½ cups cooked chickpeas
1 teaspoon crushed roasted cumin seeds
4 tablespoons balsamic vinegar
2 tablespoons extra-
virgin olive oil, plus more for greasing
Salt and ground black pepper, to taste
3 cups arugula rocket, washed and dried

1. Cover the air fryer basket with aluminum foil and grease lightly with oil. Put the figs in the air fryer basket. Select the AIR FRY function and cook at 375ºF (191ºC) for 10 minutes.
2. In a bowl, combine the chickpeas and cumin seeds.
3. Remove the air fried figs from the air fryer oven and replace with the chickpeas. Air fry for 10 minutes. Leave to cool.
4. In the meantime, prepare the dressing. Mix the balsamic vinegar, olive oil, salt and pepper.
5. In a salad bowl, combine the arugula rocket with the cooled figs and chickpeas.
6. Toss with the sauce and serve.

Sriracha Golden Cauliflower

Prep time: 5 minutes | Cook time: 17 minutes | Serves 4

¼ cup vegan butter, melted
¼ cup sriracha sauce
4 cups cauliflower florets
1 cup bread crumbs
1 teaspoon salt

1. Mix the sriracha and vegan butter in a bowl and pour this mixture over the cauliflower, taking care to cover each floret entirely.
2. In a separate bowl, combine the bread crumbs and salt.
3. Dip the cauliflower florets in the bread crumbs, coating each one well. Select the AIR FRY function and cook the florets in the air fryer oven at 375ºF (191ºC) for 17 minutes.
4. Serve hot.

Cheesy Macaroni Balls

Prep time: 10 minutes | Cook time: 10 minutes | Serves 2

2 cups leftover macaroni
1 cup shredded Cheddar cheese
½ cup flour
1 cup bread crumbs
3 large eggs
1 cup milk
½ teaspoon salt
¼ teaspoon black pepper

1. In a bowl, combine the leftover macaroni and shredded cheese.
2. Pour the flour in a separate bowl. Put the bread crumbs in a third bowl. Finally, in a fourth bowl, mix the eggs and milk with a whisk.
3. With an ice-cream scoop, create balls from the macaroni mixture. Coat them the flour, then in the egg mixture, and lastly in the bread crumbs.
4. Arrange the balls in the air fryer basket. Select the AIR FRY function and cook at 365ºF (185ºC) for 10 minutes, giving them an occasional stir. Ensure they crisp up nicely.
5. Serve hot.

Corn Pakodas

Prep time: 10 minutes | Cook time: 8 minutes | Serves 5

1 cup flour
¼ teaspoon baking soda
¼ teaspoon salt
½ teaspoon curry powder
½ teaspoon red chili
powder
¼ teaspoon turmeric powder
¼ cup water
10 cobs baby corn, blanched
Cooking spray

1. Cover the air fryer basket with aluminum foil and spritz with the cooking spray.
2. In a bowl, combine all the ingredients, save for the corn. Stir with a whisk until well combined.
3. Coat the corn in the batter and put inside the air fryer oven.
4. Select the AIR FRY function and cook at 425ºF (218ºC) for 8 minutes, or until a golden brown color is achieved.
5. Serve hot.

Stuffed Vegetables

Jalapeño Poppers

Prep time: 5 minutes | Cook time: 33 minutes | Serves 4

8 medium jalapeño peppers
5 ounces (142 g) cream cheese
¼ cup grated
Mozzarella cheese
½ teaspoon Italian seasoning mix
8 slices bacon

1. Select the BAKE function and preheat MAXX to 400ºF (204ºC).
2. Cut the jalapeños in half.
3. Use a spoon to scrape out the insides of the peppers.
4. In a bowl, add together the cream cheese, Mozzarella cheese and Italian seasoning.
5. Pack the cream cheese mixture into the jalapeño halves and place the other halves on top.
6. Wrap each pepper in 1 slice of bacon, starting from the bottom and working up.
7. Bake for 33 minutes.
8. Serve!

Golden Garlicky Mushrooms

Prep time: 10 minutes | Cook time: 10 minutes | Serves 4

6 small mushrooms
1 tablespoon bread crumbs
1 tablespoon olive oil
1 ounce (28 g) onion, peeled and
diced
1 teaspoon parsley
1 teaspoon garlic purée
Salt and ground black pepper, to taste

1. Combine the bread crumbs, oil, onion, parsley, salt, pepper and garlic in a bowl. Cut out the mushrooms' stalks and stuff each cap with the crumb mixture.
2. Select the AIR FRY function and cook the mushrooms in the air fryer oven at 350ºF (177ºC) for 10 minutes.
3. Serve hot.

Cashew Stuffed Mushrooms

Prep time: 10 minutes | Cook time: 15 minutes | Serves 6

1 cup basil
½ cup cashew, soaked overnight
½ cup nutritional yeast
1 tablespoon lemon juice
2 cloves garlic
1 tablespoon olive oil
Salt, to taste
1 pound (454 g) baby Bella mushroom, stems removed

1. Prepare the pesto. In a food processor, blend the basil, cashew nuts, nutritional yeast, lemon juice, garlic and olive oil to combine well. Sprinkle with salt as desired.
2. Turn the mushrooms cap-side down and spread the pesto on the underside of each cap.
3. Transfer to the air fryer oven. Select the AIR FRY function and cook at 400ºF (204ºC) for 15 minutes.
4. Serve warm.

Kidney Beans Oatmeal in Peppers

Prep time: 15 minutes | Cook time: 6 minutes | Serves 2 to 4

2 large bell peppers, halved lengthwise, deseeded
2 tablespoons cooked kidney beans
2 tablespoons cooked chick peas
2 cups cooked oatmeal
1 teaspoon ground cumin
½ teaspoon paprika
½ teaspoon salt or to taste
¼ teaspoon black pepper powder
¼ cup yogurt

1. Put the bell peppers, cut-side down, in the air fryer basket. Select the AIR FRY function and cook at 355ºF (179ºC) for 2 minutes.
2. Take the peppers out of the air fryer oven and let cool.
3. In a bowl, combine the rest of the ingredients.
4. Divide the mixture evenly and use each portion to stuff a pepper.
5. Return the stuffed peppers to the air fryer oven and continue to air fry for 4 minutes. Serve hot.

Ricotta Potatoes

Prep time: 15 minutes | Cook time: 15 minutes | Serves 4

4 potatoes
2 tablespoons olive oil
½ cup Ricotta cheese, at room temperature
2 tablespoons chopped scallions
1 tablespoon roughly chopped fresh parsley
1 tablespoon minced coriander

2 ounces (57 g) Cheddar cheese, preferably freshly grated
1 teaspoon celery seeds
½ teaspoon salt
½ teaspoon garlic pepper

1. Pierce the skin of the potatoes with a knife. Transfer to the air fryer basket.
2. Select the AIR FRY function and cook at 350ºF (177ºC) for 13 minutes. If they are not cooked through by this time, leave for 2 to 3 minutes longer.
3. In the meantime, make the stuffing by combining all the other ingredients.
4. Cut halfway into the cooked potatoes to open them.
5. Spoon equal amounts of the stuffing into each potato and serve hot.

Marinara Pepperoni Mushroom Pizza

Prep time: 5 minutes | Cook time: 18 minutes | Serves 4

4 large portobello mushrooms, stems removed
4 teaspoons olive oil

1 cup marinara sauce
1 cup shredded Mozzarella cheese
10 slices sugar-free pepperoni

1. Select the BAKE function and preheat MAXX to 375ºF (191ºC).
2. Brush each mushroom cap with the olive oil, one teaspoon for each cap.
3. Put on a baking sheet and bake, stem-side down, for 8 minutes.
4. Take out of the air fryer oven and divide the marinara sauce, Mozzarella cheese and pepperoni evenly among the caps.
5. Switch from BAKE to AIR FRY. Air fry for another 10 minutes until browned.
6. Serve hot.

Beef Stuffed Bell Peppers

Prep time: 10 minutes | Cook time: 30 minutes | Serves 4

1 pound (454 g) ground beef
1 tablespoon taco seasoning mix
1 can diced tomatoes and green chilis

4 green bell peppers
1 cup shredded Monterey jack cheese, divided

1. Set a skillet over a high heat and cook the ground beef for 8 minutes. Make sure it is cooked through and browned all over. Drain the fat.
2. Stir in the taco seasoning mix, and the diced tomatoes and green chilis. Allow the mixture to cook for a further 4 minutes.
3. In the meantime, slice the tops off the green peppers and remove the seeds and membranes.
4. When the meat mixture is fully cooked, spoon equal amounts of it into the peppers and top with the Monterey jack cheese. Then place the peppers into the air fryer oven. Select the AIR FRY function and cook at 350ºF (177ºC) for 15 minutes.
5. The peppers are ready when they are soft, and the cheese is bubbling and brown. Serve warm.

Gorgonzola Mushrooms with Horseradish Mayo

Prep time: 15 minutes | Cook time: 10 minutes | Serves 5

½ cup bread crumbs
2 cloves garlic, pressed
2 tablespoons chopped fresh coriander
1/3 teaspoon kosher salt
½ teaspoon crushed red pepper flakes
1½ tablespoons olive oil

20 medium mushrooms, stems removed
½ cup grated Gorgonzola cheese
¼ cup low-fat mayonnaise
1 teaspoon prepared horseradish, well-drained
1 tablespoon finely chopped fresh parsley

1. Combine the bread crumbs together with the garlic, coriander, salt, red pepper, and olive oil.
2. Take equal-sized amounts of the bread crumb mixture and use them to stuff the mushroom caps. Add the grated Gorgonzola on top of each.
3. Put the mushrooms in a baking pan and transfer to the air fryer oven.
4. Select the AIR FRY function and cook at 380ºF (193ºC) for 10 minutes, ensuring the stuffing is warm throughout.
5. In the meantime, prepare the horseradish mayo. Mix the mayonnaise, horseradish and parsley.
6. When the mushrooms are ready, serve with the mayo.

Prosciutto Mini Mushroom Pizza

Prep time: 10 minutes | Cook time: 5 minutes | Serves 3

3 portobello mushroom caps, cleaned and scooped
3 tablespoons olive oil
Pinch of salt

Pinch of dried Italian seasonings
3 tablespoons tomato sauce
3 tablespoons shredded Mozzarella cheese
12 slices prosciutto

1. Season both sides of the portobello mushrooms with a drizzle of olive oil, then sprinkle salt and the Italian seasonings on the insides.
2. With a knife, spread the tomato sauce evenly over the mushroom, before adding the Mozzarella on top.
3. Put the portobello in the air fryer basket and place in the air fryer oven.
4. Select the AIR FRY function and cook at 330ºF (166ºC) for 1 minute, before taking the air fryer basket out of the air fryer oven and putting the prosciutto slices on top.
5. Air fry for another 4 minutes.
6. Serve warm.

Chapter 4 Fish and Seafood

air fryer oven Fish Sticks

Prep time: 10 minutes | Cook time: 10 to 12 minutes | Serves 4

Salt and pepper, to taste
1½ pounds (680g) skinless haddock fillets, ¾ inch thick, sliced into 4-inch strips
2 cups panko bread crumbs
1 tablespoon vegetable oil
¼ cup all-purpose flour
¼ cup mayonnaise
2 large eggs
1 tablespoon Old Bay seasoning
Vegetable oil spray

1. Dissolve ¼ cup salt in 2 quarts cold water in a large container. Add the haddock, cover, and let sit for 15 minutes.
2. Toss the panko with the oil in a bowl until evenly coated. Microwave, stirring frequently, until light golden brown, 2 to 4 minutes; transfer to a shallow dish. Whisk the flour, mayonnaise, eggs, Old Bay, ⅛ teaspoon salt, and ⅛ teaspoon pepper together in a second shallow dish.
3. Set a wire rack in a rimmed baking sheet and spray with vegetable oil spray. Remove the haddock from the brine and thoroughly pat dry with paper towels. Working with 1 piece at a time, dredge the haddock in the egg mixture, letting excess drip off, then coat with the panko mixture, pressing gently to adhere. Transfer the fish sticks to the prepared rack and freeze until firm, about 1 hour.
4. Lightly spray the air fryer basket with vegetable oil spray. Arrange up to 5 fish sticks in the prepared basket, spaced evenly apart.
5. Select the AIR FRY function and cook at 400ºF (204ºC) for 10 to 12 minutes, or until fish sticks are golden and register 140ºF (60ºC), flipping and rotating fish sticks halfway through cooking.
6. Serve warm.

Cornmeal-Crusted Trout Fingers

Prep time: 15 minutes | Cook time: 6 minutes | Serves 2

½ cup yellow cornmeal, medium or finely ground (not coarse)
⅓ cup all-purpose flour
1½ teaspoons baking powder
1 teaspoon kosher salt, plus more as needed
½ teaspoon freshly ground black pepper, plus more as needed
⅛ teaspoon cayenne pepper
¾ pound (340 g)
skinless trout fillets, cut into strips 1 inch wide and 3 inches long
3 large eggs, lightly beaten
Cooking spray
½ cup mayonnaise
2 tablespoons capers, rinsed and finely chopped
1 tablespoon fresh tarragon
1 teaspoon fresh lemon juice, plus lemon wedges, for serving

1. In a large bowl, whisk together the cornmeal, flour, baking powder, salt, black pepper, and cayenne. Dip the trout strips in the egg, then toss them in the cornmeal mixture until fully coated. Transfer the trout to a rack set over a baking sheet and liberally spray all over with cooking spray.
2. Transfer half the fish to the air fryer oven. Select the AIR FRY function and cook at 400ºF (204ºC) for 6 minutes, or until the fish is cooked through and golden brown. Transfer the fish sticks to a plate and repeat with the remaining fish.
3. Meanwhile, in a bowl, whisk together the mayonnaise, capers, tarragon, and lemon juice. Season the tartar sauce with salt and black pepper.
4. Serve the trout fingers hot along with the tartar sauce and lemon wedges.

Tandoori-Spiced Salmon and Potatoes

Prep time: 10 minutes | Cook time: 28 minutes | Serves 2

1 pound (454 g) fingerling potatoes
2 tablespoons vegetable oil, divided
Kosher salt and freshly ground black pepper, to taste
1 teaspoon ground turmeric
1 teaspoon ground cumin
1 teaspoon ground ginger
½ teaspoon smoked paprika
¼ teaspoon cayenne pepper
2 (6-ounce / 170-g) skin-on salmon fillets

1. In a bowl, toss the potatoes with 1 tablespoon of the oil until evenly coated. Season with salt and pepper. Transfer the potatoes to the air fryer oven. Select the AIR FRY function and cook at 375ºF (191ºC) for 20 minutes.
2. Meanwhile, in a bowl, combine the remaining 1 tablespoon oil, the turmeric, cumin, ginger, paprika, and cayenne. Add the salmon fillets and turn in the spice mixture until fully coated all over.
3. After the potatoes have cooked for 20 minutes, place the salmon fillets, skin-side up, on top of the potatoes, and continue cooking until the potatoes are tender, the salmon is cooked, and the salmon skin is slightly crisp.
4. Transfer the salmon fillets to two plates and serve with the potatoes while both are warm.

Roasted Cod with Lemon-Garlic Potatoes

Prep time: 10 minutes | Cook time: 28 minutes | Serves 2

3 tablespoons unsalted butter, softened, divided
2 garlic cloves, minced
1 lemon, grated to yield 2 teaspoons zest and sliced ¼ inch thick
Salt and pepper, to taste
1 large russet potato (12 ounce / 340-g), unpeeled, sliced ¼ inch thick
1 tablespoon minced fresh parsley, chives, or tarragon
2 (8-ounce / 227-g) skinless cod fillets,
1¼ inches thick
Vegetable oil spray

1. Make foil sling for air fryer basket by folding 1 long sheet of aluminum foil so it is 4 inches wide. Lay sheet of foil widthwise across basket, pressing foil into and up sides of basket. Fold excess foil as needed so that edges of foil are flush with top of basket. Lightly spray the foil and basket with vegetable oil spray.
2. Microwave 1 tablespoon butter, garlic, 1 teaspoon lemon zest, ¼ teaspoon salt, and ⅛ teaspoon pepper in a medium bowl, stirring once, until the butter is melted and the mixture is fragrant, about 30 seconds. Add the potato slices and toss to coat. Shingle the potato slices on sling in prepared basket to create 2 even layers.
3. Select the AIR FRY function and cook at 400ºF (204ºC) for 16 to 18 minutes, or until potato slices are spotty brown and just tender, using a sling to rotate potatoes halfway through cooking.
4. Combine the remaining 2 tablespoons butter, remaining 1 teaspoon lemon zest, and parsley in a small bowl. Pat the cod dry with paper towels and season with salt and pepper. Place the fillets, skinned-side down, on top of potato slices, spaced evenly apart. (Tuck thinner tail ends of fillets under themselves as needed to create uniform pieces.) Dot the fillets with the butter mixture and top with the lemon slices. Return the basket to the air fryer oven and air fry until the cod flakes apart when gently prodded with a paring knife and registers 140ºF (60ºC), 12 to 15 minutes, using a sling to rotate the potato slices and cod halfway through cooking.
5. Using a sling, carefully remove potatoes and cod from air fryer oven. Cut the potato slices into 2 portions between fillets using fish spatula. Slide spatula along underside of potato slices and transfer with cod to individual plates. Serve.

Moroccan Spiced Halibut with Chickpea Salad

Prep time: 15 minutes | Cook time: 12 minutes | Serves 2

¾ teaspoon ground coriander
½ teaspoon ground cumin
¼ teaspoon ground ginger
⅛ teaspoon ground cinnamon
Salt and pepper, to taste
2 (8-ounce / 227-g) skinless halibut fillets, 1¼ inches thick
4 teaspoons extra-virgin olive oil,
divided, plus extra for drizzling
1 (15-ounce / 425-g) can chickpeas, rinsed
1 tablespoon lemon juice, plus lemon wedges for serving
1 teaspoon harissa
½ teaspoon honey
2 carrots, peeled and shredded
2 tablespoons chopped fresh mint, divided
Vegetable oil spray

1. Select the BAKE function and preheat MAXX to 300ºF (149ºC).
2. Make foil sling for air fryer basket by folding 1 long sheet of aluminum foil so it is 4 inches wide. Lay sheet of foil widthwise across basket, pressing foil into and up sides of basket. Fold excess foil as needed so that edges of foil are flush with top of basket. Lightly spray foil and basket with vegetable oil spray.
3. Combine coriander, cumin, ginger, cinnamon, ⅛ teaspoon salt, and ⅛ teaspoon pepper in a small bowl. Pat halibut dry with paper towels, rub with 1 teaspoon oil, and sprinkle all over with spice mixture. Arrange fillets skinned side down on sling in prepared basket, spaced evenly apart. Bake until halibut flakes apart when gently prodded with a paring knife and registers 140ºF (60ºC), 12 to 16 minutes, using the sling to rotate fillets halfway through cooking.
4. Meanwhile, microwave chickpeas in medium bowl until heated through, about 2 minutes. Stir in remaining 1 tablespoon oil, lemon juice, harissa, honey, ⅛ teaspoon salt, and ⅛ teaspoon pepper. Add carrots and 1 tablespoon mint and toss to combine. Season with salt and pepper, to taste.
5. Using sling, carefully remove halibut from air fryer oven and transfer to individual plates. Sprinkle with remaining 1 tablespoon mint and drizzle with extra oil to taste. Serve with salad and lemon wedges.

Trout Amandine with Lemon Butter Sauce

Prep time: 20 minutes | Cook time:8 minutes | Serves 4

Trout Amandine:
⅔ cup toasted almonds
⅓ cup grated Parmesan cheese
1 teaspoon salt
½ teaspoon freshly ground black pepper
2 tablespoons butter, melted
4 (4-ounce / 113-g) trout fillets, or salmon fillets
Cooking spray

Lemon Butter Sauce:
8 tablespoons (1 stick) butter, melted
2 tablespoons freshly squeezed lemon juice
½ teaspoon Worcestershire
sauce
½ teaspoon salt
½ teaspoon freshly ground black pepper
¼ teaspoon hot sauce

1. In a blender or food processor, pulse the almonds for 5 to 10 seconds until finely processed. Transfer to a shallow bowl and whisk in the Parmesan cheese, salt, and pepper. Place the melted butter in another shallow bowl.
2. One at a time, dip the fish in the melted butter, then the almond mixture, coating thoroughly.
3. Select the BAKE function and preheat MAXX to 300ºF (149ºC). Line the air fryer basket with parchment paper.
4. Place the coated fish on the parchment and spritz with oil.
5. Bake for 4 minutes. Flip the fish, spritz it with oil, and bake for 4 minutes more until the fish flakes easily with a fork.
6. In a small bowl, whisk the butter, lemon juice, Worcestershire sauce, salt, pepper, and hot sauce until blended.
7. Serve with the fish.

Sole and Asparagus Bundles

Prep time: 10 minutes | Cook time: 14 minutes | Serves 2

8 ounces (227 g) asparagus, trimmed
1 teaspoon extra-virgin olive oil, divided
Salt and pepper, to taste
4 (3-ounce / 85-g) skinless sole or flounder fillets, ⅛ to ¼ inch thick
4 tablespoons
unsalted butter, softened
1 small shallot, minced
1 tablespoon chopped fresh tarragon
¼ teaspoon lemon zest plus ½ teaspoon juice
Vegetable oil spray

1. Select the BAKE function and preheat MAXX to 300ºF (149ºC).
2. Toss asparagus with ½ teaspoon oil, pinch salt, and pinch pepper in a bowl. Cover and microwave until bright green and just tender, about 3 minutes, tossing halfway through microwaving. Uncover and set aside to cool slightly.
3. Make foil sling for air fryer basket by folding 1 long sheet of aluminum foil so it is 4 inches wide. Lay sheet of foil widthwise across basket, pressing foil into and up sides of basket. Fold excess foil as needed so that edges of foil are flush with top of basket. Lightly spray foil and basket with vegetable oil spray.
4. Pat sole dry with paper towels and season with salt and pepper. Arrange fillets skinned side up on cutting board, with thicker ends closest to you. Arrange asparagus evenly across base of each fillet, then tightly roll fillets away from you around asparagus to form tidy bundles.
5. Rub bundles evenly with remaining ½ teaspoon oil and arrange seam side down on sling in prepared basket. Bake until asparagus is tender and sole flakes apart when gently prodded with a paring knife, 14 to 18 minutes, using a sling to rotate bundles halfway through cooking.
6. Combine butter, shallot, tarragon, and lemon zest and juice in a bowl. Using sling, carefully remove sole bundles from air fryer oven and transfer to individual plates. Top evenly with butter mixture and serve.

Crab Cakes with Lettuce and Apple Salad

Prep time: 10 minutes | Cook time: 13 minutes | Serves 2

8 ounces (227 g) lump crab meat, picked over for shells
2 tablespoons panko bread crumbs
1 scallion, minced
1 large egg
1 tablespoon mayonnaise
1½ teaspoons Dijon mustard
Pinch of cayenne pepper
2 shallots, sliced
thin
1 tablespoon extra-virgin olive oil, divided
1 teaspoon lemon juice, plus lemon wedges for serving
⅛ teaspoon salt
Pinch of pepper
½ (3-ounce / 85-g) small head Bibb lettuce, torn into bite-size pieces
½ apple, cored and sliced thin

1. Line large plate with triple layer of paper towels. Transfer crab meat to prepared plate and pat dry with additional paper towels. Combine panko, scallion, egg, mayonnaise, mustard, and cayenne in a bowl. Using a rubber spatula, gently fold in crab meat until combined; discard paper towels. Divide crab mixture into 4 tightly packed balls, then flatten each into 1-inch-thick cake (cakes will be delicate). Transfer cakes to plate and refrigerate until firm, about 10 minutes.
2. Toss shallots with ½ teaspoon oil in separate bowl; transfer to air fryer basket. Select the AIR FRY function and cook at 400ºF (204ºC) for 5 to 7 minutes, or until shallots are browned, tossing once halfway through cooking. Return shallots to now-empty bowl and set aside.
3. Arrange crab cakes in air fryer basket, spaced evenly apart. Return basket to air fryer oven and air fry until crab cakes are light golden brown on both sides, 8 to 10 minutes, flipping and rotating cakes halfway through cooking.
4. Meanwhile, whisk remaining 2½ teaspoons oil, lemon juice, salt, and pepper together in large bowl. Add lettuce, apple, and shallots and toss to coat. Serve crab cakes with salad, passing lemon wedges separately.

Orange-Mustard Glazed Salmon

Prep time: 10 minutes | Cook time: 10 minutes | Serves 2

1 tablespoon orange marmalade
¼ teaspoon grated orange zest plus 1 tablespoon juice
2 teaspoons whole-grain mustard
2 (8-ounce / 227 -g) skin-on salmon fillets, 1½ inches thick
Salt and pepper, to taste
Vegetable oil spray

1. Make foil sling for air fryer basket by folding 1 long sheet of aluminum foil so it is 4 inches wide. Lay sheet of foil widthwise across basket, pressing foil into and up sides of basket. Fold excess foil as needed so that edges of foil are flush with top of basket. Lightly spray foil and basket with vegetable oil spray.
2. Combine marmalade, orange zest and juice, and mustard in bowl. Pat salmon dry with paper towels and season with salt and pepper. Brush tops and sides of fillets evenly with glaze. Arrange fillets skin side down on sling in prepared basket, spaced evenly apart.
3. Select the AIR FRY function and cook at 400ºF (204ºC) for 10 to 14 minutes, or until center is still translucent when checked with the tip of a paring knife and registers 125ºF (52ºC) (for medium-rare), using sling to rotate fillets halfway through cooking.
4. Using the sling, carefully remove salmon from air fryer oven. Slide fish spatula along underside of fillets and transfer to individual serving plates, leaving skin behind. Serve.

Swordfish Skewers with Caponata

Prep time: 15 minutes | Cook time: 20 minutes | Serves 2

1 (10-ounce / 283- g) small Italian eggplant, cut into 1-inch pieces
6 ounces (170 g) cherry tomatoes
3 scallions, cut into 2 inches long
2 tablespoons extra-virgin olive oil, divided
Salt and pepper, to taste
12 ounces (340 g) skinless swordfish steaks, 1¼ inches thick, cut into 1-inch pieces
2 teaspoons honey, divided
2 teaspoons ground coriander, divided
1 teaspoon grated lemon zest, divided
1 teaspoon juice
4 (6-inch) wooden skewers
1 garlic clove, minced
½ teaspoon ground cumin
1 tablespoon chopped fresh basil

1. Toss eggplant, tomatoes, and scallions with 1 tablespoon oil, ¼ teaspoon salt, and ⅛ teaspoon pepper in bowl; transfer to air fryer basket.
2. Select the AIR FRY function and cook at 400ºF (204ºC) for 14 minutes, or until eggplant is softened and browned and tomatoes have begun to burst, tossing halfway through cooking. Transfer vegetables to cutting board and set aside to cool slightly.
3. Pat swordfish dry with paper towels. Combine 1 teaspoon oil, 1 teaspoon honey, 1 teaspoon coriander, ½ teaspoon lemon zest, ⅛ teaspoon salt, and pinch pepper in a clean bowl. Add swordfish and toss to coat. Thread swordfish onto skewers, leaving about ¼ inch between each piece (3 or 4 pieces per skewer).
4. Arrange skewers in air fryer basket, spaced evenly apart. (Skewers may overlap slightly.) Return basket to air fryer oven and air fry until swordfish is browned and registers 140ºF (60ºC), 6 to 8 minutes, flipping and rotating skewers halfway through cooking.
5. Meanwhile, combine remaining 2 teaspoons oil, remaining 1 teaspoon honey, remaining 1 teaspoon coriander, remaining ½ teaspoon lemon zest, lemon juice, garlic, cumin, ¼ teaspoon salt, and ⅛ teaspoon pepper in large bowl. Microwave, stirring once, until fragrant, about 30 seconds. Coarsely chop the cooked vegetables, transfer to bowl with dressing, along with any accumulated juices, and gently toss to combine. Stir in basil and season with salt and pepper to taste. Serve skewers with caponata.

Crunchy Air Fried Cod Fillets

Prep time: 10 minutes | Cook time: 12 minutes | Serves 2

⅓ cup panko bread crumbs
1 teaspoon vegetable oil
1 small shallot, minced
1 small garlic clove, minced
½ teaspoon minced fresh thyme
Salt and pepper, to taste
1 tablespoon minced

fresh parsley
1 tablespoon mayonnaise
1 large egg yolk
¼ teaspoon grated lemon zest, plus lemon wedges for serving
2 (8-ounce / 227-g) skinless cod fillets, 1¼ inches thick
Vegetable oil spray

1. Select the BAKE function and preheat MAXX to 300ºF (149ºC).
2. Make foil sling for air fryer basket by folding 1 long sheet of aluminum foil so it is 4 inches wide. Lay sheet of foil widthwise across basket, pressing foil into and up sides of basket. Fold excess foil as needed so that edges of foil are flush with top of basket. Lightly spray the foil and basket with vegetable oil spray.
3. Toss the panko with the oil in a bowl until evenly coated. Stir in the shallot, garlic, thyme, ¼ teaspoon salt, and ⅛ teaspoon pepper. Microwave, stirring frequently, until the panko is light golden brown, about 2 minutes. Transfer to a shallow dish and let cool slightly; stir in the parsley. Whisk the mayonnaise, egg yolk, lemon zest, and ⅛ teaspoon pepper together in another bowl.
4. Pat the cod dry with paper towels and season with salt and pepper. Arrange the fillets, skinned-side down, on plate and brush tops evenly with mayonnaise mixture. (Tuck thinner tail ends of fillets under themselves as needed to create uniform pieces.) Working with 1 fillet at a time, dredge the coated side in panko mixture, pressing gently to adhere. Arrange the fillets, crumb-side up, on sling in the prepared basket, spaced evenly apart.
5. Bake for 12 to 16 minutes, using a sling to rotate fillets halfway through cooking. Using a sling, carefully remove cod from air fryer oven. Serve with the lemon wedges.

Remoulade Crab Cakes

Prep time: 15 minutes | Cook time: 10 minutes | Serves 4

Remoulade:
¾ cup mayonnaise
2 teaspoons Dijon mustard
1½ teaspoons yellow mustard
1 teaspoon vinegar
¼ teaspoon hot

sauce
1 teaspoon tiny capers, drained and chopped
¼ teaspoon salt
⅛ teaspoon ground black pepper

Crab Cakes:
1 cup bread crumbs, divided
2 tablespoons mayonnaise
1 scallion, finely chopped
6 ounces (170 g) crab meat
2 tablespoons pasteurized egg

product (liquid eggs in a carton)
2 teaspoons lemon juice
½ teaspoon red pepper flakes
½ teaspoon Old Bay seasoning
Cooking spray

1. In a small bowl, whisk to combine the mayonnaise, Dijon mustard, yellow mustard, vinegar, hot sauce, capers, salt, and pepper.
2. Refrigerate for at least 1 hour before serving.
3. Place a parchment liner in the air fryer basket.
4. In a large bowl, mix to combine ½ cup of bread crumbs with the mayonnaise and scallion. Set the other ½ cup of bread crumbs aside in a small bowl.
5. Add the crab meat, egg product, lemon juice, red pepper flakes, and Old Bay seasoning to the large bowl, and stir to combine.
6. Divide the crab mixture into 4 portions, and form into patties.
7. Dredge each patty in the remaining bread crumbs to coat.
8. Place the prepared patties on the liner in the air fryer oven in a single layer.
9. Spray lightly with cooking spray. Select the AIR FRY function and cook at 400ºF (204ºC) for 5 minutes. Flip the crab cakes over, air fry for another 5 minutes, until golden, and serve.

Pecan-Crusted Tilapia

Prep time: 10minutes | Cook time: 10 minutes | Serves 4

1¼ cups pecans
¾ cup panko bread crumbs
½ cup all-purpose flour
2 tablespoons Cajun seasoning
2 eggs, beaten with

2 tablespoons water
4 (6-ounce/ 170-g) tilapia fillets
Vegetable oil, for spraying
Lemon wedges, for serving

1. Grind the pecans in the food processor until they resemble coarse meal. Combine the ground pecans with the panko on a plate. On a second plate, combine the flour and Cajun seasoning. Dry the tilapia fillets using paper towels and dredge them in the flour mixture, shaking off any excess. Dip the fillets in the egg mixture and then dredge them in the pecan and panko mixture, pressing the coating onto the fillets. Place the breaded fillets on a plate or rack.
2. Spray both sides of the breaded fillets with oil. Carefully transfer 2 of the fillets to the air fryer basket. Select the AIR FRY function and cook at 375ºF (191ºC) for 9 to 10 minutes, flipping once halfway through, until the flesh is opaque and flaky. Repeat with the remaining fillets.
3. Serve immediately with lemon wedges.

Roasted Salmon Fillets

Prep time: 5 minutes | Cook time: 10 minutes | Serves 2

2 (8-ounce / 227 -g) skin-on salmon fillets, 1½ inches thick
1 teaspoon

vegetable oil
Salt and pepper, to taste
Vegetable oil spray

1. Make foil sling for air fryer basket by folding 1 long sheet of aluminum foil so it is 4 inches wide. Lay sheet of foil widthwise across basket, pressing foil into and up sides of basket. Fold excess foil as needed so that edges of foil are flush with top of basket. Lightly spray foil and basket with vegetable oil spray.
2. Pat salmon dry with paper towels, rub with oil, and season with salt and pepper. Arrange fillets skin side down on sling in prepared basket, spaced evenly apart.
3. Select the AIR FRY function and cook at 400ºF (204ºC) for 10 to 14 minutes, or until center is still translucent when checked with the tip of a paring knife and registers 125ºF (52ºC) (for medium-rare), using sling to rotate fillets halfway through cooking.
4. Using the sling, carefully remove salmon from air fryer oven. Slide fish spatula along underside of fillets and transfer to individual serving plates, leaving skin behind. Serve.

Confetti Salmon Burgers

Prep time: 10 minutes | Cook time: 12 minutes | Serves 4

14 ounces (397 g) cooked fresh or canned salmon, flaked with a fork
¼ cup minced scallion, white and light green parts only
¼ cup minced red bell pepper
¼ cup minced celery
2 small lemons

1 teaspoon crab boil seasoning such as Old Bay
½ teaspoon kosher salt
½ teaspoon black pepper
1 egg, beaten
½ cup fresh bread crumbs
Vegetable oil, for spraying

1. In a large bowl, combine the salmon, vegetables, the zest and juice of 1 of the lemons, crab boil seasoning, salt, and pepper. Add the egg and bread crumbs and stir to combine. Form the mixture into 4 patties weighing approximately 5 ounces (142 g) each. Chill until firm, about 15 minutes.
2. Spray the salmon patties with oil on all sides and spray the air fryer basket to prevent sticking.
3. Select the AIR FRY function and cook at 400ºF (204ºC) for 12 minutes, flipping halfway through, until the burgers are browned and cooked through. Cut the remaining lemon into 4 wedges and serve with the burgers.

Bacon-Wrapped Scallops

Prep time: 10 minutes | Cook time: 12 minutes | Serves 4

12 slices bacon
24 large sea scallops, tendons removed
1 teaspoon plus 2 tablespoons extra-virgin olive oil, divided
Salt and pepper, to taste
6 (6-inch) wooden skewers
1 tablespoon cider vinegar
1 teaspoon Dijon mustard
5 ounces (142 g) baby spinach
1 fennel bulb, stalks discarded, bulb halved, cored, and sliced thin
5 ounces (142 g) raspberries

1. Select the BAKE function and preheat MAXX to 350°F (177°C).
2. Line large plate with 4 layers of paper towels and arrange 6 slices bacon over towels in a single layer. Top with 4 more layers of paper towels and remaining 6 slices bacon. Cover with 2 layers of paper towels, place a second large plate on top, and press gently to flatten. Microwave until fat begins to render but bacon is still pliable, about 5 minutes.
3. Pat scallops dry with paper towels and toss with 1 teaspoon oil, ⅛ teaspoon salt, and ⅛ teaspoon pepper in a bowl until evenly coated. Arrange 2 scallops side to side, flat side down, on the cutting board. Starting at narrow end, wrap 1 slice bacon tightly around sides of scallop bundle. (Bacon should overlap slightly; trim excess as needed.) Thread scallop bundle onto skewer through bacon. Repeat with remaining scallops and bacon, threading 2 bundles onto each skewer.
4. Arrange 3 skewers in air fryer basket, parallel to each other and spaced evenly apart. Arrange remaining 3 skewers on top, perpendicular to the bottom layer. Bake until bacon is crisp and scallops are firm and centers are opaque, 12 to 16 minutes, flipping and rotating skewers halfway through cooking.
5. Meanwhile, whisk remaining 2 tablespoons oil, vinegar, mustard, ⅛ teaspoon salt, and ⅛ teaspoon pepper in large serving bowl until combined. Add spinach, fennel, and raspberries and gently toss to coat. Serve skewers with salad.

Shrimp Dejonghe Skewers

Prep time: 10 minutes | Cook time: 15 minutes | Serves 4

2 teaspoons sherry
3 tablespoons unsalted butter, melted
1 cup panko bread crumbs
3 cloves garlic, minced
⅓ cup minced flat-leaf parsley, plus more for garnish
1 teaspoon kosher salt
Pinch of cayenne pepper
1½ pounds (680 g) shrimp, peeled and deveined
Vegetable oil, for spraying
Lemon wedges, for serving

1. Stir the sherry and melted butter together in a shallow bowl or pie plate and whisk until combined. Set aside. Whisk together the panko, garlic, parsley, salt, and cayenne pepper on a large plate or shallow bowl.
2. Thread the shrimp onto metal skewers designed for the air fryer oven or bamboo skewers, 3 to 4 per skewer. Dip 1 shrimp skewer in the butter mixture, then dredge in the panko mixture until each shrimp is lightly coated. Place the skewer on a plate or rimmed baking sheet and repeat the process with the remaining skewers.
3. Arrange 4 skewers in the air fryer basket. Spray the skewers with oil. Select the AIR FRY function and cook at 350°F (177°C) for 8 minutes, until the bread crumbs are golden brown and the shrimp are cooked through. Transfer the cooked skewers to a serving plate and keep warm while cooking the remaining 4 skewers in the air fryer oven.
4. Sprinkle the cooked skewers with additional fresh parsley and serve with lemon wedges if desired.

Baja Fish Tacos

Prep time: 15 minutes | Cook time: 10 minutes | Serves 4

Fried Fish:

1 pound (454 g) tilapia fillets (or other mild white fish)
½ cup all-purpose flour
1 teaspoon garlic powder
1 teaspoon kosher

salt
¼ teaspoon cayenne pepper
½ cup mayonnaise
3 tablespoons milk
1¾ cups panko bread crumbs
Vegetable oil, for spraying

Tacos:

8 corn tortillas
¼ head red or green cabbage, shredded
1 ripe avocado, halved and each half cut into 4 slices
12 ounces (340

g) pico de gallo or other fresh salsa
Dollop of Mexican crema
1 lime, cut into wedges

1. To make the fish, cut the fish fillets into strips 3 to 4 inches long and 1 inch wide. Combine the flour, garlic powder, salt, and cayenne pepper on a plate and whisk to combine. In a shallow bowl, whisk the mayonnaise and milk together. Place the panko on a separate plate. Dredge the fish strips in the seasoned flour, shaking off any excess. Dip the strips in the mayonnaise mixture, coating them completely, then dredge in the panko, shaking off any excess. Place the fish strips on a plate or rack.
2. Working in batches, spray half the fish strips with oil and arrange them in the air fryer basket, taking care not to crowd them. Select the AIR FRY function and cook at 400°F (204°C) for 4 minutes, then flip and air fry for another 3 to 4 minutes until the outside is brown and crisp and the inside is opaque and flakes easily with a fork. Repeat with the remaining strips.
3. Heat the tortillas in the microwave or on the stovetop. To assemble the tacos, place 2 fish strips inside each tortilla. Top with shredded cabbage, a slice of avocado, pico de gallo, and a dollop of crema. Serve with a lime wedge on the side.

Tuna-Stuffed Quinoa Patties

Prep time: 10 minutes | Cook time: 15 minutes | Serves 4

12 ounces (340 g) quinoa
4 slices white bread with crusts removed
½ cup milk
3 eggs
10 ounces (283 g) tuna packed in olive oil, drained

2 to 3 lemons
Kosher salt and pepper, to taste
1¼ cups panko bread crumbs
Vegetable oil, for spraying
Lemon wedges, for serving

1. Rinse the quinoa in a fine-mesh sieve until the water runs clear. Bring 4 cups of salted water to a boil. Add the quinoa, cover, and reduce heat to low. Simmer the quinoa covered until most of the water is absorbed and the quinoa is tender, 15 to 20 minutes. Drain and allow to cool to room temperature. Meanwhile, soak the bread in the milk.
2. Mix the drained quinoa with the soaked bread and 2 of the eggs in a large bowl and mix thoroughly. In a medium bowl, combine the tuna, the remaining egg, and the juice and zest of 1 of the lemons. Season well with salt and pepper. Spread the panko on a plate.
3. Scoop up approximately ½ cup of the quinoa mixture and flatten into a patty. Place a heaping tablespoon of the tuna mixture in the center of the patty and close the quinoa around the tuna. Flatten the patty slightly to create an oval-shaped croquette. Dredge both sides of the croquette in the panko. Repeat with the remaining quinoa and tuna.
4. Spray the air fryer basket with oil to prevent sticking. Arrange 4 or 5 of the croquettes in the basket, taking care to avoid overcrowding. Spray the tops of the croquettes with oil.
5. Select the AIR FRY function and cook at 400°F (204°C) for 8 minutes, or until the top side is browned and crispy. Carefully turn the croquettes over and spray the second side with oil. Air fry until the second side is browned and crispy, another 7 minutes. Repeat with the remaining croquettes.
6. Serve the croquetas warm with plenty of lemon wedges for spritzing.

Jalea

Prep time: 20 minutes | Cook time: 10 minutes | Serves 4

Salsa Criolla:

½ red onion, thinly sliced
2 tomatoes, diced
1 serrano or jalapeño pepper, deseeded and diced

1 clove garlic, minced
¼ cup chopped fresh cilantro
Pinch of kosher salt
3 limes

Fried Seafood:

1 pound (454 g) firm, white-fleshed fish such as cod (add an extra ½-pound /227-g fish if not using shrimp)
20 large or jumbo shrimp, shelled and deveined
¼ cup all-purpose flour
¼ cup cornstarch
1 teaspoon garlic powder

1 teaspoon kosher salt
¼ teaspoon cayenne pepper
2 cups panko bread crumbs
2 eggs, beaten with 2 tablespoons water
Vegetable oil, for spraying
Mayonnaise or tartar sauce, for serving (optional)

1. To make the Salsa Criolla, combine the red onion, tomatoes, pepper, garlic, cilantro, and salt in a medium bowl. Add the juice and zest of 2 of the limes. Refrigerate the salad while you make the fish.
2. To make the seafood, cut the fish fillets into strips approximately 2 inches long and 1 inch wide. Place the flour, cornstarch, garlic powder, salt, and cayenne pepper on a plate and whisk to combine. Place the panko on a separate plate. Dredge the fish strips in the seasoned flour mixture, shaking off any excess. Dip the strips in the egg mixture, coating them completely, then dredge in the panko, shaking off any excess. Place the fish strips on a plate or rack. Repeat with the shrimp, if using.
3. Spray the air fryer basket with oil. Working in 2 or 3 batches, arrange the fish and shrimp in a single layer in the basket, taking care not to crowd the basket. Spray with oil.
4. Select the AIR FRY function and cook at 400ºF (204ºC) for 5 minutes, then flip and air fry for another 4 to 5 minutes until the outside is brown and crisp and the inside of the fish is opaque and flakes easily with a fork. Repeat with the remaining seafood.
5. Place the fried seafood on a platter. Use a slotted spoon to remove the salsa criolla from the bowl, leaving behind any liquid that has accumulated. Place the salsa criolla on top of the fried seafood. Serve immediately with the remaining lime, cut into wedges, and mayonnaise or tartar sauce as desired.

Oyster Po'Boy

Prep time: 20 minutes | Cook time: 5 minutes | Serves 4

¾ cup all-purpose flour
¼ cup yellow cornmeal
1 tablespoon Cajun seasoning
1 teaspoon salt
2 large eggs, beaten
1 teaspoon hot sauce
1 pound (454 g) pre-shucked oysters

1 (12-inch) French baguette, quartered and sliced horizontally
Tartar Sauce, as needed
2 cups shredded lettuce, divided
2 tomatoes, cut into slices
Cooking spray

1. In a shallow bowl, whisk the flour, cornmeal, Cajun seasoning, and salt until blended. In a second shallow bowl, whisk together the eggs and hot sauce.
2. One at a time, dip the oysters in the cornmeal mixture, the eggs, and again in the cornmeal, coating thoroughly.
3. Line the air fryer basket with parchment paper.
4. Place the oysters on the parchment and spritz with oil.
5. Select the AIR FRY function and cook at 400ºF (204ºC) for 2 minutes. Shake the basket, spritz the oysters with oil, and air fry for 3 minutes more until lightly browned and crispy.
6. Spread each sandwich half with Tartar Sauce. Assemble the po'boys by layering each sandwich with fried oysters, ½ cup shredded lettuce, and 2 tomato slices.
7. Serve immediately.

Salmon Patties

Prep time: 10 minutes | Cook time: 8 minutes | Serves 4

2 (5-ounce / 142 g) cans salmon, flaked
2 large eggs, beaten
1/3 cup minced onion
2/3 cup panko bread crumbs

1½ teaspoons Italian-Style seasoning
1 teaspoon garlic powder
Cooking spray

1. In a medium bowl, stir together the salmon, eggs, and onion.
2. In a small bowl, whisk the bread crumbs, Italian-Style seasoning, and garlic powder until blended. Add the bread crumb mixture to the salmon mixture and stir until blended. Shape the mixture into 8 patties.
3. Select the BAKE function and preheat MAXX to 350ºF (177ºC). Line the air fryer basket with parchment paper.
4. Working in batches as needed, place the patties on the parchment and spritz with oil.
5. Bake for 4 minutes. Flip, spritz the patties with oil, and bake for 4 to 8 minutes more, until browned and firm. Serve.

Thai Shrimp Skewers with Peanut Dipping Sauce

Prep time: 15 minutes | Cook time: 6 minutes | Serves 2

Salt and pepper, to taste
12 ounces (340 g) extra-large shrimp, peeled and deveined
1 tablespoon vegetable oil
1 teaspoon honey
½ teaspoon grated lime zest plus 1 tablespoon juice, plus lime wedges for serving

6 (6-inch) wooden skewers
3 tablespoons creamy peanut butter
3 tablespoons hot tap water
1 tablespoon chopped fresh cilantro
1 teaspoon fish sauce

1. Dissolve 2 tablespoons salt in 1 quart cold water in a large container. Add shrimp, cover, and refrigerate for 15 minutes.
2. Remove shrimp from brine and pat dry with paper towels. Whisk oil, honey, lime zest, and ¼ teaspoon pepper together in a large bowl. Add shrimp and toss to coat. Thread shrimp onto skewers, leaving about ¼ inch between each shrimp (3 or 4 shrimp per skewer).
3. Arrange 3 skewers in air fryer basket, parallel to each other and spaced evenly apart. Arrange remaining 3 skewers on top, perpendicular to the bottom layer.
4. Select the AIR FRY function and cook at 400ºF (204ºC) for 6 to 8 minutes, or until shrimp are opaque throughout, flipping and rotating skewers halfway through cooking.
5. Whisk peanut butter, hot tap water, lime juice, cilantro, and fish sauce together in a bowl until smooth. Serve skewers with peanut dipping sauce and lime wedges.

Fried Shrimp

Prep time: 15 minutes | Cook time: 5 minutes | Serves 4

½ cup self-rising flour
1 teaspoon paprika
1 teaspoon salt
½ teaspoon freshly ground black pepper
1 large egg, beaten

1 cup finely crushed panko bread crumbs
20 frozen large shrimp (about 1-pound / 907-g), peeled and deveined
Cooking spray

1. In a shallow bowl, whisk the flour, paprika, salt, and pepper until blended. Add the beaten egg to a second shallow bowl and the bread crumbs to a third.
2. One at a time, dip the shrimp into the flour, the egg, and the bread crumbs, coating thoroughly.
3. Line the air fryer basket with parchment paper.
4. Place the shrimp on the parchment and spritz with oil.
5. Select the AIR FRY function and cook at 400ºF (204ºC) for 2 minutes. Shake the basket, spritz the shrimp with oil, and air fry for 3 minutes more until lightly browned and crispy. Serve hot.

Crab Cakes with Sriracha Mayonnaise

Prep time: 15 minutes | Cook time: 10 minutes | Serves 4

Sriracha Mayonnaise:

1 cup mayonnaise	1½ teaspoons
1 tablespoon sriracha	freshly squeezed lemon juice

Crab Cakes:

1 teaspoon extra-virgin olive oil	1 egg
¼ cup finely diced red bell pepper	1½ teaspoons freshly squeezed lemon juice
¼ cup diced onion	1¾ cups panko bread crumbs, divided
¼ cup diced celery	
1 pound (454 g) lump crab meat	Vegetable oil, for spraying
1 teaspoon Old Bay seasoning	

1. Mix the mayonnaise, sriracha, and lemon juice in a small bowl. Place ⅔ cup of the mixture in a separate bowl to form the base of the crab cakes. Cover the remaining sriracha mayonnaise and refrigerate. (This will become dipping sauce for the crab cakes once they are cooked.)
2. Heat the olive oil in a heavy-bottomed, medium skillet over medium-high heat. Add the bell pepper, onion, and celery and sauté for 3 minutes. Transfer the vegetables to the bowl with the reserved ⅔ cup of sriracha mayonnaise. Mix in the crab, Old Bay seasoning, egg, and lemon juice. Add 1 cup of the panko. Form the crab mixture into 8 cakes. Dredge the cakes in the remaining ¾ cup of panko, turning to coat. Place on a baking sheet. Cover and refrigerate for at least 1 hour and up to 8 hours.
3. Select the BAKE function and preheat MAXX to 375°F (191°C). Spray the air fryer basket with oil. Working in batches as needed so as not to overcrowd the basket, place the chilled crab cakes in a single layer in the basket. Spray the crab cakes with oil. Bake until golden brown, 8 to 10 minutes, carefully turning halfway through cooking. Remove to a platter and keep warm. Repeat with the remaining crab cakes as needed. Serve the crab cakes immediately with sriracha mayonnaise dipping sauce.

Salmon Burgers

Prep time: 15 minutes | Cook time: 12 minutes | Serves 5

Lemon-Caper Rémoulade:

½ cup mayonnaise	chopped fresh parsley
2 tablespoons minced drained capers	2 teaspoons fresh lemon juice
2 tablespoons	

Salmon Patties:

1 pound (454 g) wild salmon fillet, skinned and pin bones removed	1 large egg, lightly beaten
	1 tablespoon Dijon mustard
6 tablespoons panko bread crumbs	1 teaspoon fresh lemon juice
¼ cup minced red onion plus ¼ cup slivered for serving	1 tablespoon chopped fresh parsley
1 garlic clove, minced	½ teaspoon kosher salt

For Serving:

5 whole wheat potato buns or gluten-free buns	10 butter lettuce leaves

1. For the lemon-caper rémoulade: In a small bowl, combine the mayonnaise, capers, parsley, and lemon juice and mix well.
2. For the salmon patties: Cut off a 4-ounce / 113-g piece of the salmon and transfer to a food processor. Pulse until it becomes pasty. With a sharp knife, chop the remaining salmon into small cubes.
3. In a medium bowl, combine the chopped and processed salmon with the panko, minced red onion, garlic, egg, mustard, lemon juice, parsley, and salt. Toss gently to combine. Form the mixture into 5 patties about ¾ inch thick. Refrigerate for at least 30 minutes.
4. Working in batches, place the patties in the air fryer basket. Select the AIR FRY function and cook at 400°F (204°C) for 12 minutes, gently flipping halfway, until golden and cooked through.
5. To serve, transfer each patty to a bun. Top each with 2 lettuce leaves, 2 tablespoons of the rémoulade, and the slivered red onions.

Cajun Fish Fillets

Prep time: 15 minutes | Cook time: 6 minutes | Serves 4

¾ cup all-purpose flour
¼ cup yellow cornmeal
1 large egg, beaten

¼ cup Cajun seasoning
4 (4-ounce / 113-g) catfish fillets
Cooking spray

1. In a shallow bowl, whisk the flour and cornmeal until blended. Place the egg in a second shallow bowl and the Cajun seasoning in a third shallow bowl.
2. One at a time, dip the catfish fillets in the breading, the egg, and the Cajun seasoning, coating thoroughly.
3. Select the BAKE function and preheat MAXX to 300ºF (149ºC). Line the air fryer basket with parchment paper.
4. Place the coated fish on the parchment and spritz with oil.
5. Bake for 3 minutes. Flip the fish, spritz it with oil, and bake for 3 to 5 minutes more until the fish flakes easily with a fork and reaches an internal temperature of 145ºF (63ºC). Serve warm.

Tortilla Shrimp Tacos

Prep time: 10 minutes | Cook time: 6 minutes | Serves 4

Spicy Mayo:
3 tablespoons mayonnaise
1 tablespoon

Louisiana-style hot pepper sauce

Cilantro-Lime Slaw:
2 cups shredded green cabbage
½ small red onion, thinly sliced
1 small jalapeño, thinly sliced

2 tablespoons chopped fresh cilantro
Juice of 1 lime
¼ teaspoon kosher salt

Shrimp:
1 large egg, beaten
1 cup crushed tortilla chips
24 jumbo shrimp (about 1 pound / 454 g), peeled and

deveined
⅛ teaspoon kosher salt
Cooking spray
8 corn tortillas, for serving

1. For the spicy mayo: In a small bowl, mix the mayonnaise and hot pepper sauce.
2. For the cilantro-lime slaw: In a large bowl, toss together the cabbage, onion, jalapeño, cilantro, lime juice, and salt to combine. Cover and refrigerate to chill.
3. For the shrimp: Place the egg in a shallow bowl and the crushed tortilla chips in another. Season the shrimp with the salt. Dip the shrimp in the egg, then in the crumbs, pressing gently to adhere. Place on a work surface and spray both sides with oil.
4. Working in batches, arrange a single layer of the shrimp in the air fryer basket. Select the AIR FRY function and cook at 360ºF (182ºC) for 6 minutes, flipping halfway, until golden and cooked through in the center.
5. To serve, place 2 tortillas on each plate and top each with 3 shrimp. Top each taco with ¼ cup slaw, then drizzle with spicy mayo.

Blackened Fish

Prep time: 15 minutes | Cook time: 8 minutes | Serves 4

1 large egg, beaten
Blackened seasoning, as needed
2 tablespoons light

brown sugar
4 (4-ounce / 113- g) tilapia fillets
Cooking spray

1. In a shallow bowl, place the beaten egg. In a second shallow bowl, stir together the Blackened seasoning and the brown sugar.
2. One at a time, dip the fish fillets in the egg, then the brown sugar mixture, coating thoroughly.
3. Select the BAKE function and preheat MAXX to 300ºF (149ºC). Line the air fryer basket with parchment paper.
4. Place the coated fish on the parchment and spritz with oil.
5. Bake for 4 minutes. Flip the fish, spritz it with oil, and bake for 4 to 6 minutes more until the fish is white inside and flakes easily with a fork.
6. Serve immediately.

New Orleans-Style Crab Cakes

Prep time: 10 minutes | Cook time: 8 to 10 minutes | Serves 4

1¼ cups bread crumbs
2 teaspoons Creole Seasoning
1 teaspoon dry mustard
1 teaspoon salt
1 teaspoon freshly ground black pepper

1½ cups crab meat
2 large eggs, beaten
1 teaspoon butter, melted
⅓ cup minced onion
Cooking spray
Pecan Tartar Sauce, for serving

1. Line the air fryer basket with parchment paper.
2. In a medium bowl, whisk the bread crumbs, Creole Seasoning, dry mustard, salt, and pepper until blended. Add the crab meat, eggs, butter, and onion. Stir until blended. Shape the crab mixture into 8 patties.
3. Place the crab cakes on the parchment and spritz with oil.
4. Select the AIR FRY function and cook at 350ºF (177ºC) for 4 minutes. Flip the cakes, spritz them with oil, and air fry for 4 to 6 minutes more until the outsides are firm and a fork inserted into the center comes out clean. Serve with the Pecan Tartar Sauce.

Crawfish Creole Casserole

Prep time: 20 minutes | Cook time: 25 minutes | Serves 4

1½ cups crawfish meat
½ cup chopped celery
½ cup chopped onion
½ cup chopped green bell pepper
2 large eggs, beaten
1 cup half-and-half
1 tablespoon butter,

melted
1 tablespoon cornstarch
1 teaspoon Creole seasoning
¾ teaspoon salt
½ teaspoon freshly ground black pepper
1 cup shredded Cheddar cheese
Cooking spray

1. In a medium bowl, stir together the crawfish, celery, onion, and green pepper.

2. In another medium bowl, whisk the eggs, half-and-half, butter, cornstarch, Creole seasoning, salt, and pepper until blended. Stir the egg mixture into the crawfish mixture. Add the cheese and stir to combine.
3. Select the BAKE function and preheat MAXX to 300ºF (149ºC). Spritz a baking pan with oil.
4. Transfer the crawfish mixture to the prepared pan and place it in the air fryer basket.
5. Bake for 25 minutes, stirring every 10 minutes, until a knife inserted into the center comes out clean.
6. Serve immediately.

Vegetable and Fish Tacos

Prep time: 10 minutes | Cook time: 9 to 12 minutes | Serves 4

1 pound (454 g) white fish fillets
2 teaspoons olive oil
3 tablespoons freshly squeezed lemon juice, divided
1½ cups chopped red cabbage
1 large carrot,

grated
½ cup low-sodium salsa
⅓ cup low-fat Greek yogurt
4 soft low-sodium whole-wheat tortillas

1. Brush the fish with the olive oil and sprinkle with 1 tablespoon of lemon juice. Transfer to the air fryer basket.
2. Select the AIR FRY function and cook at 400ºF (204ºC) for 9 to 12 minutes, or until the fish just flakes when tested with a fork.
3. Meanwhile, in a medium bowl, stir together the remaining 2 tablespoons of lemon juice, the red cabbage, carrot, salsa, and yogurt.
4. When the fish is cooked, remove it from the air fryer basket and break it up into large pieces.
5. Offer the fish, tortillas, and the cabbage mixture, and let each person assemble a taco.
6. Serve immediately.

Spicy Orange Shrimp

Prep time: 20 minutes | Cook time: 10 to 15 minutes | Serves 4

⅓ cup orange juice
3 teaspoons minced garlic
1 teaspoon Old Bay seasoning
¼ to ½ teaspoon cayenne pepper

1 pound (454 g) medium shrimp, peeled and deveined, with tails off
Cooking spray

1. In a medium bowl, combine the orange juice, garlic, Old Bay seasoning, and cayenne pepper.
2. Dry the shrimp with paper towels to remove excess water.
3. Add the shrimp to the marinade and stir to evenly coat. Cover with plastic wrap and place in the refrigerator for 30 minutes so the shrimp can soak up the marinade.
4. Spray the air fryer basket lightly with cooking spray.
5. Place the shrimp into the air fryer basket. Select the AIR FRY function and cook at 400ºF (204ºC) for 5 minutes. Shake the basket and lightly spray with olive oil. Air fry until the shrimp are opaque and crisp, 5 to 10 more minutes.
6. Serve immediately.

Crispy Coconut Shrimp

Prep time: 15 minutes | Cook time: 8 minutes | Serves 4

Sweet Chili Mayo:
3 tablespoons mayonnaise
3 tablespoons Thai

sweet chili sauce
1 tablespoon Sriracha sauce

Shrimp:
⅔ cup sweetened shredded coconut
⅔ cup panko bread crumbs
Kosher salt, to taste
2 tablespoons all-purpose or gluten-

free flour
2 large eggs
24 extra-jumbo shrimp (about 1 pound / 454 g), peeled and deveined
Cooking spray

1. In a medium bowl, combine the mayonnaise, Thai sweet chili sauce, and Sriracha and mix well.

2. In a medium bowl, combine the coconut, panko, and ¼ teaspoon salt. Place the flour in a shallow bowl. Whisk the eggs in another shallow bowl.
3. Season the shrimp with ⅛ teaspoon salt. Dip the shrimp in the flour, shaking off any excess, then into the egg. Coat in the coconut-panko mixture, gently pressing to adhere, then transfer to a large plate. Spray both sides of the shrimp with oil.
4. Working in batches, arrange a single layer of the shrimp in the air fryer basket. Select the AIR FRY function and cook at 360ºF (182ºC) for 8 minutes, flipping halfway, until the crust is golden brown and the shrimp are cooked through.
5. Serve with the sweet chili mayo for dipping.

Blackened Shrimp Tacos

Prep time: 10 minutes | Cook time: 10 to 15 minutes | Serves 4

12 ounces (340 g) medium shrimp, deveined, with tails off
1 teaspoon olive oil
1 to 2 teaspoons Blackened seasoning

8 corn tortillas, warmed
1 (14-ounce / 397-g) bag coleslaw mix
2 limes, cut in half
Cooking spray

1. Spray the air fryer basket lightly with cooking spray.
2. Dry the shrimp with a paper towel to remove excess water.
3. In a medium bowl, toss the shrimp with olive oil and Blackened seasoning.
4. Place the shrimp in the air fryer basket. Select the AIR FRY function and cook at 400ºF (204ºC) for 5 minutes. Shake the basket, lightly spray with cooking spray, and cook until the shrimp are cooked through and starting to brown, 5 to 10 more minutes.
5. Fill each tortilla with the coleslaw mix and top with the blackened shrimp. Squeeze fresh lime juice over top and serve.

Fish Croquettes with Lemon-Dill Aioli

Prep time: 15 minutes | Cook time: 10 minutes | Serves 4

Croquettes:

3 large eggs, divided
12 ounces (340 g) raw cod fillet, flaked apart with two forks
¼ cup 1% milk
½ cup boxed instant mashed potatoes
2 teaspoons olive oil
⅓ cup chopped fresh dill
1 shallot, minced
1 large garlic clove, minced

¾ cup plus 2 tablespoons bread crumbs, divided
1 teaspoon fresh lemon juice
1 teaspoon kosher salt
½ teaspoon dried thyme
¼ teaspoon freshly ground black pepper
Cooking spray

Lemon-Dill Aioli:

5 tablespoons mayonnaise
Juice of ½ lemon

1 tablespoon chopped fresh dill

1. For the croquettes: In a medium bowl, lightly beat 2 of the eggs. Add the fish, milk, instant mashed potatoes, olive oil, dill, shallot, garlic, 2 tablespoons of the bread crumbs, lemon juice, salt, thyme, and pepper. Mix to thoroughly combine. Place in the refrigerator for 30 minutes.
2. For the lemon-dill aioli: In a small bowl, combine the mayonnaise, lemon juice, and dill. Set aside.
3. Measure out about 3½ tablespoons of the fish mixture and gently roll in your hands to form a log about 3 inches long. Repeat to make a total of 12 logs.
4. Beat the remaining egg in a small bowl. Place the remaining ¾ cup bread crumbs in a separate bowl. Dip the croquettes in the egg, then coat in the bread crumbs, gently pressing to adhere. Place on a work surface and spray both sides with cooking spray.
5. Working in batches, arrange a single layer of the croquettes in the air fryer basket. Select the AIR FRY function and cook at 350°F (177°C) for 10 minutes, flipping halfway, until golden.
6. Serve with the aioli for dipping.

Crab Cake Sandwich

Prep time: 15 minutes | Cook time: 10 minutes | Serves 4

Crab Cakes:

½ cup panko bread crumbs
1 large egg, beaten
1 large egg white
1 tablespoon mayonnaise
1 teaspoon Dijon mustard
¼ cup minced fresh parsley
1 tablespoon fresh lemon juice

½ teaspoon Old Bay seasoning
⅛ teaspoon sweet paprika
⅛ teaspoon kosher salt
Freshly ground black pepper, to taste
10 ounces (283 g) lump crab meat
Cooking spray

Cajun Mayo:

¼ cup mayonnaise
1 tablespoon minced dill pickle
1 teaspoon fresh

lemon juice
¾ teaspoon Cajun seasoning

For Serving:

4 Boston lettuce leaves
4 whole wheat

potato buns or gluten-free buns

1. For the crab cakes: In a large bowl, combine the panko, whole egg, egg white, mayonnaise, mustard, parsley, lemon juice, Old Bay, paprika, salt, and pepper to taste and mix well. Fold in the crab meat, being careful not to over mix. Gently shape into 4 round patties, about ½ cup each, ¾ inch thick. Spray both sides with oil.
2. Working in batches, place the crab cakes in the air fryer basket. Select the AIR FRY function and cook at 370°F (188°C) for 10 minutes, flipping halfway, until the edges are golden.
3. Meanwhile, for the Cajun mayo: In a small bowl, combine the mayonnaise, pickle, lemon juice, and Cajun seasoning.
4. To serve: Place a lettuce leaf on each bun bottom and top with a crab cake and a generous tablespoon of Cajun mayonnaise. Add the bun top and serve.

Roasted Cod with Sesame Seeds

Prep time: 5 minutes | Cook time: 7 to 9 minutes | Makes 1 fillet

1 tablespoon reduced-sodium soy sauce
2 teaspoons honey
Cooking spray
6 ounces (170 g) fresh cod fillet
1 teaspoon sesame seeds

1. Select the ROAST function and preheat MAXX to 360ºF (182ºC).
2. In a small bowl, combine the soy sauce and honey.
3. Spray the air fryer basket with cooking spray, then place the cod in the basket, brush with the soy mixture, and sprinkle sesame seeds on top. Roast for 7 to 9 minutes or until opaque.
4. Remove the fish and allow to cool on a wire rack for 5 minutes before serving.

Blackened Salmon

Prep time: 10 minutes | Cook time: 5 to 7 minutes | Serves 4

Salmon:
1 tablespoon sweet paprika
½ teaspoon cayenne pepper
1 teaspoon garlic powder
1 teaspoon dried oregano
1 teaspoon dried thyme
¾ teaspoon kosher salt
⅛ teaspoon freshly ground black pepper
Cooking spray
4 (6 ounces / 170 g each) wild salmon fillets

Cucumber-Avocado Salsa:
2 tablespoons chopped red onion
1½ tablespoons fresh lemon juice
1 teaspoon extra-virgin olive oil
¼ teaspoon plus ⅛ teaspoon kosher salt
Freshly ground black pepper, to taste
4 Persian cucumbers, diced
6 ounces (170 g) Hass avocado, diced

1. For the salmon: In a small bowl, combine the paprika, cayenne, garlic powder, oregano, thyme, salt, and black pepper. Spray both sides of the fish with oil and rub all over. Coat the fish all over with the spices.
2. For the cucumber-avocado salsa: In a medium bowl, combine the red onion, lemon juice, olive oil, salt, and pepper. Let stand for 5 minutes, then add the cucumbers and avocado.
3. Working in batches, arrange the salmon fillets skin side down in the air fryer basket. Select the AIR FRY function and cook at 400ºF (204ºC) for 5 to 7 minutes, or until the fish flakes easily with a fork, depending on the thickness of the fish.
4. Serve topped with the salsa.

Fried Catfish with Dijon Sauce

Prep time: 20 minutes | Cook time: 7 minutes | Serves 4

4 tablespoons butter, melted
2 teaspoons Worcestershire sauce, divided
1 teaspoon lemon pepper
1 cup panko bread crumbs
4 (4-ounce / 113-g) catfish fillets
Cooking spray
½ cup sour cream
1 tablespoon Dijon mustard

1. In a shallow bowl, stir together the melted butter, 1 teaspoon of Worcestershire sauce, and the lemon pepper. Place the bread crumbs in another shallow bowl.
2. One at a time, dip both sides of the fillets in the butter mixture, then the bread crumbs, coating thoroughly.
3. Select the BAKE function and preheat MAXX to 300ºF (149ºC). Line the air fryer basket with parchment paper.
4. Place the coated fish on the parchment and spritz with oil.
5. Bake for 4 minutes. Flip the fish, spritz it with oil, and bake for 3 to 6 minutes more, depending on the thickness of the fillets, until the fish flakes easily with a fork.
6. In a small bowl, stir together the sour cream, Dijon, and remaining 1 teaspoon of Worcestershire sauce. This sauce can be made 1 day in advance and refrigerated before serving. Serve with the fried fish.

Lime-Chili Shrimp Bowl

Prep time: 10 minutes | Cook time: 10 to 15 minutes | Serves 4

2 teaspoons lime juice
1 teaspoon olive oil
1 teaspoon honey
1 teaspoon minced garlic
1 teaspoon chili powder
Salt, to taste
12 ounces (340 g) medium shrimp, peeled and deveined

2 cups cooked brown rice
1 (15-ounce / 425-g) can seasoned black beans, warmed
1 large avocado, chopped
1 cup sliced cherry tomatoes
Cooking spray

1. Spray the air fryer basket lightly with cooking spray.
2. In a medium bowl, mix together the lime juice, olive oil, honey, garlic, chili powder, and salt to make a marinade.
3. Add the shrimp and toss to coat evenly in the marinade.
4. Place the shrimp in the air fryer basket. Select the AIR FRY function and cook at 400ºF (204ºC) for 5 minutes. Shake the basket and air fry until the shrimp are cooked through and starting to brown, an additional 5 to 10 minutes.
5. To assemble the bowls, spoon ¼ of the rice, black beans, avocado, and cherry tomatoes into each of four bowls. Top with the shrimp and serve.

Country Shrimp

Prep time: 10 minutes | Cook time: 15 to 20 minutes | Serves 4

1 pound (454 g) large shrimp, deveined, with tails on
1 pound (454 g) smoked turkey sausage, cut into thick slices
2 corn cobs, quartered

1 zucchini, cut into bite-sized pieces
1 red bell pepper, cut into chunks
1 tablespoon Old Bay seasoning
2 tablespoons olive oil
Cooking spray

1. Spray the air fryer basket lightly with cooking spray.

2. In a large bowl, mix the shrimp, turkey sausage, corn, zucchini, bell pepper, and Old Bay seasoning, and toss to coat with the spices. Add the olive oil and toss again until evenly coated.
3. Spread the mixture in the air fryer basket in a single layer. You will need to cook in batches.
4. Select the AIR FRY function and cook at 400ºF (204ºC) for 15 to 20 minutes, or until cooked through, shaking the basket every 5 minutes for even cooking.
5. Serve immediately.

Roasted Fish with Almond-Lemon Crumbs

Prep time: 10 minutes | Cook time: 7 to 8 minutes | Serves 4

½ cup raw whole almonds
1 scallion, finely chopped
Grated zest and juice of 1 lemon
½ tablespoon extra-virgin olive oil
¾ teaspoon kosher

salt, divided
Freshly ground black pepper, to taste
4 (6 ounces / 170 g each) skinless fish fillets
Cooking spray
1 teaspoon Dijon mustard

1. In a food processor, pulse the almonds to coarsely chop. Transfer to a small bowl and add the scallion, lemon zest, and olive oil. Season with ¼ teaspoon of the salt and pepper to taste and mix to combine.
2. Spray the top of the fish with oil and squeeze the lemon juice over the fish. Season with the remaining ½ teaspoon salt and pepper to taste. Spread the mustard on top of the fish. Dividing evenly, press the almond mixture onto the top of the fillets to adhere.
3. Working in batches, place the fillets in the air fryer basket in a single layer. Select the AIR FRY function and cook at 375ºF (191ºC) for 7 to 8 minutes, until the crumbs start to brown and the fish is cooked through.
4. Serve immediately.

Lemony Shrimp and Zucchini

Prep time: 15 minutes | Cook time: 7 to 8 minutes | Serves 4

1¼ pounds (567 g) extra-large raw shrimp, peeled and deveined
2 medium zucchini (about 8 ounces / 227 g each), halved lengthwise and cut into ½-inch-thick slices
1½ tablespoons olive oil

½ teaspoon garlic salt
1½ teaspoons dried oregano
⅛ teaspoon crushed red pepper flakes (optional)
Juice of ½ lemon
1 tablespoon chopped fresh mint
1 tablespoon chopped fresh dill

1. In a large bowl, combine the shrimp, zucchini, oil, garlic salt, oregano, and pepper flakes (if using) and toss to coat.
2. Working in batches, arrange a single layer of the shrimp and zucchini in the air fryer basket. Select the AIR FRY function and cook at 350ºF (177ºC) for 7 to 8 minutes, shaking the basket halfway, until the zucchini is golden and the shrimp are cooked through.
3. Transfer to a serving dish and tent with foil while you air fry the remaining shrimp and zucchini.
4. Top with the lemon juice, mint, and dill and serve.

Seasoned Breaded Shrimp

Prep time: 15 minutes | Cook time: 10 to 15 minutes | Serves 4

2 teaspoons Old Bay seasoning, divided
½ teaspoon garlic powder
½ teaspoon onion powder
1 pound (454

g) large shrimp, deveined, with tails on
2 large eggs
½ cup whole-wheat panko bread crumbs
Cooking spray

1. Spray the air fryer basket lightly with cooking spray.
2. In a medium bowl, mix together 1 teaspoon of Old Bay seasoning, garlic powder, and onion powder. Add the shrimp and toss with the seasoning mix to lightly coat.
3. In a separate small bowl, whisk the eggs with 1 teaspoon water.
4. In a shallow bowl, mix together the remaining 1 teaspoon Old Bay seasoning and the panko bread crumbs.
5. Dip each shrimp in the egg mixture and dredge in the bread crumb mixture to evenly coat.
6. Place the shrimp in the air fryer basket, in a single layer. Lightly spray the shrimp with cooking spray. You many need to cook the shrimp in batches.
7. Select the AIR FRY function and cook at 380ºF (193ºC) for 10 to 15 minutes, or until the shrimp is cooked through and crispy, shaking the basket at 5-minute intervals to redistribute and evenly cook.
8. Serve immediately.

Cajun-Style Salmon Burgers

Prep time: 10 minutes | Cook time: 10 to 15 minutes | Serves 4

4 (5-ounce / 142-g) cans pink salmon in water, any skin and bones removed, drained
2 eggs, beaten
1 cup whole-wheat bread crumbs

4 tablespoons light mayonnaise
2 teaspoons Cajun seasoning
2 teaspoons dry mustard
4 whole-wheat buns
Cooking spray

1. In a medium bowl, mix the salmon, egg, bread crumbs, mayonnaise, Cajun seasoning, and dry mustard. Cover with plastic wrap and refrigerate for 30 minutes.
2. Spray the air fryer basket lightly with cooking spray.
3. Shape the mixture into four ½-inch-thick patties about the same size as the buns.
4. Place the salmon patties in the air fryer basket in a single layer and lightly spray the tops with cooking spray. You may need to cook them in batches.
5. Select the AIR FRY function and cook at 360ºF (182ºC) for 6 to 8 minutes. Turn the patties over and lightly spray with cooking spray. Air fry until crispy on the outside, 4 to 7 more minutes.
6. Serve on whole-wheat buns.

Spanish Garlic Shrimp

Prep time: 10 minutes | Cook time: 10 to 15 minutes | Serves 4

2 teaspoons minced garlic
2 teaspoons lemon juice
2 teaspoons olive oil
½ to 1 teaspoon

crushed red pepper
12 ounces (340 g) medium shrimp, deveined, with tails on
Cooking spray

1. In a medium bowl, mix together the garlic, lemon juice, olive oil, and crushed red pepper to make a marinade.
2. Add the shrimp and toss to coat in the marinade. Cover with plastic wrap and place the bowl in the refrigerator for 30 minutes.
3. Spray the air fryer basket lightly with cooking spray. Place the shrimp in the air fryer basket.
4. Select the AIR FRY function and cook at 400°F (204°C) for 5 minutes. Shake the basket and air fry until the shrimp are cooked through and nicely browned, an additional 5 to 10 minutes.
5. Cool for 5 minutes before serving.

Garlic-Lemon Tilapia

Prep time: 5 minutes | Cook time: 10 to 15 minutes | Serves 4

1 tablespoon lemon juice
1 tablespoon olive oil
1 teaspoon minced

garlic
½ teaspoon chili powder
4 (6-ounce / 170-g) tilapia fillets

1. Line the air fryer basket with parchment paper.
2. In a large, shallow bowl, mix together the lemon juice, olive oil, garlic, and chili powder to make a marinade. Place the tilapia fillets in the bowl and coat evenly.
3. Place the fillets in the basket in a single layer, leaving space between each fillet. You may need to cook in more than one batch.
4. Select the AIR FRY function and cook at 380°F (193°C) for 10 to 15 minutes, or until the fish is cooked and flakes easily with a fork.Serve hot.

Air Fried Spring Rolls

Prep time: 10 minutes | Cook time: 17 to 22 minutes | Serves 4

2 teaspoons minced garlic
2 cups finely sliced cabbage
1 cup matchstick cut carrots
2 (4-ounce / 113-g) cans tiny shrimp, drained

4 teaspoons soy sauce
Salt and freshly ground black pepper, to taste
16 square spring roll wrappers
Cooking spray

1. Spray the air fryer basket lightly with cooking spray. Spray a medium sauté pan with cooking spray.
2. Add the garlic to the sauté pan and cook over medium heat until fragrant, 30 to 45 seconds. Add the cabbage and carrots and sauté until the vegetables are slightly tender, about 5 minutes.
3. Add the shrimp and soy sauce and season with salt and pepper, then stir to combine. Sauté until the moisture has evaporated, 2 more minutes. Set aside to cool.
4. Place a spring roll wrapper on a work surface so it looks like a diamond. Place 1 tablespoon of the shrimp mixture on the lower end of the wrapper.
5. Roll the wrapper away from you halfway, then fold in the right and left sides, like an envelope. Continue to roll to the very end, using a little water to seal the edge. Repeat with the remaining wrappers and filling.
6. Place the spring rolls in the air fryer basket in a single layer, leaving room between each roll. Lightly spray with cooking spray. You may need to cook them in batches.
7. Select the AIR FRY function and cook at 370°F (188°C) for 5 minutes. Turn the rolls over, lightly spray with cooking spray, and air fry until heated through and the rolls start to brown, 5 to 10 more minutes. Cool for 5 minutes before serving.

Garlic Scallops

Prep time: 10 minutes | Cook time: 10 to 15 minutes | Serves 4

2 teaspoons olive oil
1 packet dry zesty Italian dressing mix
1 teaspoon minced garlic

16 ounces (454 g) small scallops, patted dry
Cooking spray

1. Spray the air fryer basket lightly with cooking spray.
2. In a large zip-top plastic bag, combine the olive oil, Italian dressing mix, and garlic.
3. Add the scallops, seal the zip-top bag, and coat the scallops in the seasoning mixture.
4. Place the scallops in the air fryer basket and lightly spray with cooking spray.
5. Select the AIR FRY function and cook at 400ºF (204ºC) for 5 minutes. Shake the basket, and air fry for 5 to 10 more minutes, or until the scallops reach an internal temperature of 120ºF (49ºC).
6. Serve immediately.

Homemade Fish Sticks

Prep time: 15 minutes | Cook time: 10 to 15 minutes | Serves 4

4 fish fillets
½ cup whole-wheat flour
1 teaspoon seasoned salt
2 eggs

1½ cups whole-wheat panko bread crumbs
½ tablespoon dried parsley flakes
Cooking spray

1. Spray the air fryer basket lightly with cooking spray.
2. Cut the fish fillets lengthwise into "sticks."
3. In a shallow bowl, mix the whole-wheat flour and seasoned salt.
4. In a small bowl, whisk the eggs with 1 teaspoon of water.
5. In another shallow bowl, mix the panko bread crumbs and parsley flakes.
6. Coat each fish stick in the seasoned flour, then in the egg mixture, and dredge them in the panko bread crumbs.

7. Place the fish sticks in the air fryer basket in a single layer and lightly spray the fish sticks with cooking spray. You may need to cook them in batches.
8. Select the AIR FRY function and cook at 400ºF (204ºC) for 5 to 8 minutes. Flip the fish sticks over and lightly spray with the cooking spray. Air fry until golden brown and crispy, 5 to 7 more minutes.
9. Serve warm.

Traditional Tuna Melt

Prep time: 10 minutes | Cook time: 12 minutes | Serves 2

2 cans unsalted albacore tuna, drained
½ cup mayonnaise
½ teaspoon salt
¼ teaspoon ground black pepper
4 slices sourdough

bread
4 pieces sliced Cheddar cheese
2 tablespoons crispy fried onions
Cooking spray
¼ teaspoon granulated garlic

1. In a medium bowl, combine the tuna, mayonnaise, salt, and pepper, and mix well. Set aside.
2. Assemble the sandwiches by laying out the bread and then adding 1 slice of cheese on top of each piece.
3. Sprinkle the fried onions on top of the cheese on 2 of the slices of bread.
4. Divide the tuna between the 2 slices of bread with the onions.
5. Take the remaining 2 slices of bread that have only cheese on them, and place them cheese-side down on top of the tuna.
6. Place one sandwich in the air fryer basket and spray with cooking spray. Select the AIR FRY function and cook at 390ºF (199ºC) for 6 minutes.
7. Using a spatula, flip the sandwich over, spray it again, and air fry for another 6 minutes, or until golden brown. Sprinkle with the garlic immediately after removing from the air fryer basket. Repeat with the other sandwich.
8. Allow the sandwiches to sit for 1 to 2 minutes before cutting and serving.

Crispy Catfish Strips

Prep time: 5 minutes | Cook time: 16 to 18 minutes | Serves 4

1 cup buttermilk	1 cup cornmeal
5 catfish fillets, cut into 1½-inch strips	1 tablespoon Creole, Cajun, or Old Bay seasoning
Cooking spray	

1. Pour the buttermilk into a shallow baking dish. Place the catfish in the dish and refrigerate for at least 1 hour to help remove any fishy taste.
2. Spray the air fryer basket lightly with cooking spray.
3. In a shallow bowl, combine cornmeal and Creole seasoning.
4. Shake any excess buttermilk off the catfish. Place each strip in the cornmeal mixture and coat completely. Press the cornmeal into the catfish gently to help it stick.
5. Place the strips in the air fryer basket in a single layer. Lightly spray the catfish with cooking spray. You may need to cook the catfish in more than one batch.
6. Select the AIR FRY function and cook at 400ºF (204ºC) for 8 minutes. Turn the catfish strips over and lightly spray with cooking spray. Air fry until golden brown and crispy, 8 to 10 more minutes.
7. Serve warm.

Tuna Patty Sliders

Prep time: 15 minutes | Cook time: 10 to 15 minutes | Serves 4

3 (5-ounce / 142-g) cans tuna, packed in water	1 tablespoon sriracha
⅔ cup whole-wheat panko bread crumbs	¾ teaspoon black pepper
⅓ cup shredded Parmesan cheese	10 whole-wheat slider buns
	Cooking spray

1. Spray the air fryer basket lightly with cooking spray.
2. In a medium bowl combine the tuna, bread crumbs, Parmesan cheese, sriracha, and black pepper and stir to combine.
3. Form the mixture into 10 patties.
4. Place the patties in the air fryer basket in a single layer. Spray the patties lightly with cooking spray. You may need to cook them in batches.
5. Select the AIR FRY function and cook at 350ºF (177ºC) for 6 to 8 minutes. Turn the patties over and lightly spray with cooking spray. Air fry until golden brown and crisp, another 4 to 7 more minutes. Serve warm.

Sesame Glazed Salmon

Prep time: 5 minutes | Cook time: 12 to 16 minutes | Serves 4

3 tablespoons soy sauce	garlic
1 tablespoon rice wine or dry sherry	¼ teaspoon minced ginger
1 tablespoon brown sugar	4 (6-ounce / 170-g) salmon fillets, skin-on
1 tablespoon toasted sesame oil	½ tablespoon sesame seeds
1 teaspoon minced	Cooking spray

1. In a small bowl, mix the soy sauce, rice wine, brown sugar, toasted sesame oil, garlic, and ginger.
2. Place the salmon in a shallow baking dish and pour the marinade over the fillets. Cover and refrigerate for at least 1 hour, turning the fillets occasionally to coat in the marinade.
3. Spray the air fryer basket lightly with cooking spray.
4. Shake off as much marinade as possible and place the fillets, skin-side down, in the air fryer basket in a single layer. Reserve the marinade. You may need to cook them in batches.
5. Select the AIR FRY function and cook at 370ºF (188ºC) for 8 to 10 minutes. Brush the tops of the salmon fillets with the reserved marinade and sprinkle with sesame seeds.
6. Increase the temperature to 400ºF (204ºC) and air fry for 2 to 5 more minutes for medium, 1 to 3 minutes for medium rare, or 4 to 6 minutes for well done.
7. Serve warm.

Green Curry Shrimp

Prep time: 15 minutes | Cook time: 5 minutes | Serves 4

1 to 2 tablespoons Thai green curry paste
2 tablespoons coconut oil, melted
1 tablespoon half-and-half or coconut milk
1 teaspoon fish sauce
1 teaspoon soy sauce
1 teaspoon minced fresh ginger
1 clove garlic, minced
1 pound (454 g) jumbo raw shrimp, peeled and deveined
¼ cup chopped fresh Thai basil or sweet basil
¼ cup chopped fresh cilantro

1. In a baking pan, combine the curry paste, coconut oil, half-and-half, fish sauce, soy sauce, ginger, and garlic. Whisk until well combined.
2. Add the shrimp and toss until well coated. Marinate at room temperature for 15 to 30 minutes.
3. Place the pan in the air fryer basket. Select the AIR FRY function and cook at 400°F (204°C) for 5 minutes, stirring halfway through the cooking time.
4. Transfer the shrimp to a serving bowl or platter. Garnish with the basil and cilantro. Serve immediately.

Marinated Salmon Fillets

Prep time: 10 minutes | Cook time: 15 to 20 minutes | Serves 4

¼ cup soy sauce
¼ cup rice wine vinegar
1 tablespoon brown sugar
1 tablespoon olive oil
1 teaspoon mustard powder
1 teaspoon ground ginger
½ teaspoon freshly ground black pepper
½ teaspoon minced garlic
4 (6-ounce / 170-g) salmon fillets, skin-on
Cooking spray

1. In a small bowl, combine the soy sauce, rice wine vinegar, brown sugar, olive oil, mustard powder, ginger, black pepper, and garlic to make a marinade.
2. Place the fillets in a shallow baking dish and pour the marinade over them. Cover the baking dish and marinate for at least 1 hour in the refrigerator, turning the fillets occasionally to keep them coated in the marinade.
3. Spray the air fryer basket lightly with cooking spray.
4. Shake off as much marinade as possible from the fillets and place them, skin-side down, in the air fryer basket in a single layer. You may need to cook the fillets in batches.
5. Select the AIR FRY function and cook at 370°F (188°C) for 15 to 20 minutes. The minimum internal temperature should be 145°F (63°C) at the thickest part of the fillets.
6. Serve hot.

Simple Salmon Patty Bites

Prep time: 15 minutes | Cook time: 10 to 15 minutes | Serves 4

4 (5-ounce / 142-g) cans pink salmon, skinless, boneless in water, drained
2 eggs, beaten
1 cup whole-wheat panko bread crumbs
4 tablespoons finely minced red bell pepper
2 tablespoons parsley flakes
2 teaspoons Old Bay seasoning
Cooking spray

1. Spray the air fryer basket lightly with cooking spray.
2. In a medium bowl, mix the salmon, eggs, panko bread crumbs, red bell pepper, parsley flakes, and Old Bay seasoning.
3. Using a small cookie scoop, form the mixture into 20 balls.
4. Place the salmon bites in the air fryer basket in a single layer and spray lightly with cooking spray. You may need to cook them in batches.
5. Select the AIR FRY function and cook at 360°F (182°C) for 10 to 15 minutes, shaking the basket a couple of times for even cooking.
6. Serve immediately.

Crispy Cod Cakes with Salad Greens

Prep time: 15 minutes | Cook time: 12 minutes | Serves 4

1 pound (454 g) cod fillets, cut into chunks
⅓ cup packed fresh basil leaves
3 cloves garlic, crushed
½ teaspoon smoked paprika
¼ teaspoon salt
¼ teaspoon pepper
1 large egg, beaten
1 cup panko bread crumbs
Cooking spray
Salad greens, for serving

1. In a food processor, pulse cod, basil, garlic, smoked paprika, salt, and pepper until cod is finely chopped, stirring occasionally. Form into 8 patties, about 2 inches in diameter. Dip each first into the egg, then into the panko, patting to adhere. Spray with oil on one side.
2. Working in batches, place half the cakes in the basket, oil-side down; spray with oil. Select the AIR FRY function and cook at 400°F (204°C) for 12 minutes, until golden brown and cooked through.
3. Serve cod cakes with salad greens.

Fish Sandwich with Tartar Sauce

Prep time: 10 minutes | Cook time: 17 minutes | Serves 2

Tartar Sauce:
½ cup mayonnaise
2 tablespoons dried minced onion
1 dill pickle spear, finely chopped
2 teaspoons pickle juice
¼ teaspoon salt
⅛ teaspoon ground black pepper

Fish:
2 tablespoons all-purpose flour
1 egg, lightly beaten
1 cup panko
2 teaspoons lemon
pepper
2 tilapia fillets
Cooking spray
2 hoagie rolls

1. In a small bowl, combine the mayonnaise, dried minced onion, pickle, pickle juice, salt, and pepper.
2. Whisk to combine and chill in the refrigerator while you make the fish.

3. Place a parchment liner in the air fryer basket.
4. Scoop the flour out onto a plate; set aside.
5. Put the beaten egg in a medium shallow bowl.
6. On another plate, mix to combine the panko and lemon pepper.
7. Dredge the tilapia fillets in the flour, then dip in the egg, and then press into the panko mixture.
8. Place the prepared fillets on the liner in the air fryer oven in a single layer.
9. Spray lightly with cooking spray. Select the AIR FRY function and cook at 400°F (204°C) for 8 minutes. Carefully flip the fillets, spray with more cooking spray, and air fry for an additional 9 minutes, until golden and crispy.
10. Place each cooked fillet in a hoagie roll, top with a little bit of tartar sauce, and serve.

Cajun-Style Fish Tacos

Prep time: 5 minutes | Cook time: 10 to 15 minutes | Serves 6

2 teaspoons avocado oil
1 tablespoon Cajun seasoning
4 tilapia fillets
1 (14-ounce / 397-
g) package coleslaw mix
12 corn tortillas
2 limes, cut into wedges

1. Line the air fryer basket with parchment paper.
2. In a medium, shallow bowl, mix the avocado oil and the Cajun seasoning to make a marinade. Add the tilapia fillets and coat evenly.
3. Place the fillets in the basket in a single layer, leaving room between each fillet. You may need to cook in batches.
4. Select the AIR FRY function and cook at 380°F (193°C) for 10 to 15 minutes, or until the fish is cooked and easily flakes with a fork.
5. Assemble the tacos by placing some of the coleslaw mix in each tortilla. Add ⅓ of a tilapia fillet to each tortilla. Squeeze some lime juice over the top of each taco and serve.

Classic Shrimp Empanadas

Prep time: 10 minutes | Cook time: 8 minutes | Serves 5

½ pound (227g) raw shrimp, peeled, deveined and chopped
¼ cup chopped red onion
1 scallion, chopped
2 garlic cloves, minced
2 tablespoons minced red bell pepper
2 tablespoons chopped fresh cilantro
½ tablespoon fresh lime juice

¼ teaspoon sweet paprika
⅛ teaspoon kosher salt
⅛ teaspoon crushed red pepper flakes (optional)
1 large egg, beaten
10 frozen Goya Empanada Discos, thawed
Cooking spray

1. In a medium bowl, combine the shrimp, red onion, scallion, garlic, bell pepper, cilantro, lime juice, paprika, salt, and pepper flakes (if using).
2. In a small bowl, beat the egg with 1 teaspoon water until smooth.
3. Place an empanada disc on a work surface and put 2 tablespoons of the shrimp mixture in the center. Brush the outer edges of the disc with the egg wash. Fold the disc over and gently press the edges to seal. Use a fork and press around the edges to crimp and seal completely. Brush the tops of the empanadas with the egg wash.
4. Spray the bottom of the air fryer basket with cooking spray to prevent sticking. Working in batches, arrange a single layer of the empanadas in the air fryer basket. Select the AIR FRY function and cook at 380ºF (193ºC) for 8 minutes, flipping halfway, until golden brown and crispy.
5. Serve hot.

Chapter 5 Poultry

Herb-Buttermilk Chicken Breast

Prep time: 5 minutes | Cook time: 40 minutes | Serves 2

1 large bone-in, skin-on chicken breast
1 cup buttermilk
1½ teaspoons dried parsley
1½ teaspoons dried chives
¾ teaspoon kosher salt
½ teaspoon dried dill
½ teaspoon onion powder
¼ teaspoon garlic powder
¼ teaspoon dried tarragon
Cooking spray

1. Place the chicken breast in a bowl and pour over the buttermilk, turning the chicken in it to make sure it's completely covered. Let the chicken stand at room temperature for at least 20 minutes or in the refrigerator for up to 4 hours.
2. Meanwhile, in a bowl, stir together the parsley, chives, salt, dill, onion powder, garlic powder, and tarragon.
3. Select the BAKE function and preheat MAXX to 300ºF (149ºC).
4. Remove the chicken from the buttermilk, letting the excess drip off, then place the chicken skin-side up directly in the air fryer oven. Sprinkle the seasoning mix all over the top of the chicken breast, then let stand until the herb mix soaks into the buttermilk, at least 5 minutes.
5. Spray the top of the chicken with cooking spray. Bake for 10 minutes, then increase the temperature to 350ºF (177ºC) and bake until an instant-read thermometer inserted into the thickest part of the breast reads 160ºF (71ºC) and the chicken is deep golden brown, 30 to 35 minutes.
6. Transfer the chicken breast to a cutting board, let rest for 10 minutes, then cut the meat off the bone and cut into thick slices for serving.

Paprika Indian Fennel Chicken

Prep time: 10 minutes | Cook time: 15 minutes | Serves 4

1 pound (454 g) boneless, skinless chicken thighs, cut crosswise into thirds
1 yellow onion, cut into 1½-inch-thick slices
1 tablespoon coconut oil, melted
2 teaspoons minced fresh ginger
2 teaspoons minced garlic
1 teaspoon smoked paprika
1 teaspoon ground fennel
1 teaspoon garam masala
1 teaspoon ground turmeric
1 teaspoon kosher salt
½ to 1 teaspoon cayenne pepper
Vegetable oil spray
2 teaspoons fresh lemon juice
¼ cup chopped fresh cilantro or parsley

1. Use a fork to pierce the chicken all over to allow the marinade to penetrate better.
2. In a large bowl, combine the onion, coconut oil, ginger, garlic, paprika, fennel, garam masala, turmeric, salt, and cayenne. Add the chicken, toss to combine, and marinate at room temperature for 30 minutes, or cover and refrigerate for up to 24 hours.
3. Place the chicken and onion in the air fryer basket. (Discard remaining marinade.) Spray with some vegetable oil spray.
4. Select the AIR FRY function and cook at 350ºF (177ºC) for 15 minutes. Halfway through the cooking time, remove the basket, spray the chicken and onion with more vegetable oil spray, and toss gently to coat. At the end of the cooking time, use a meat thermometer to ensure the chicken has reached an internal temperature of 165ºF (74ºC).
5. Transfer the chicken and onion to a serving platter. Sprinkle with the lemon juice and cilantro and serve.

Lemon Chicken and Spinach Salad

Prep time: 10 minutes | Cook time: 16 to 20 minutes | Serves 4

3 (5-ounce / 142-g) low-sodium boneless, skinless chicken breasts, cut into 1-inch cubes
5 teaspoons olive oil
½ teaspoon dried thyme
1 medium red onion, sliced
1 red bell pepper, sliced
1 small zucchini, cut into strips
3 tablespoons freshly squeezed lemon juice
6 cups fresh baby spinach

1. Select the ROAST function and preheat MAXX to 400ºF (204ºC).
2. In a large bowl, mix the chicken with the olive oil and thyme. Toss to coat. Transfer to a medium metal bowl and roast for 8 minutes in the air fryer oven.
3. Add the red onion, red bell pepper, and zucchini. Roast for 8 to 12 minutes more, stirring once during cooking, or until the chicken reaches an internal temperature of 165ºF (74ºC) on a meat thermometer.
4. Remove the bowl from the air fryer oven and stir in the lemon juice.
5. Put the spinach in a serving bowl and top with the chicken mixture. Toss to combine and serve immediately.

Almond-Crusted Chicken Nuggets

Prep time: 10 minutes | Cook time: 10 to 13 minutes | Serves 4

1 egg white
1 tablespoon freshly squeezed lemon juice
½ teaspoon dried basil
½ teaspoon ground paprika
1 pound (454 g) low-sodium boneless, skinless chicken breasts, cut into 1½-inch cubes
½ cup ground almonds
2 slices low-sodium whole-wheat bread, crumbled

1. Select the BAKE function and preheat MAXX to 400ºF (204ºC).
2. In a shallow bowl, beat the egg white, lemon juice, basil, and paprika with a fork until foamy.
3. Add the chicken and stir to coat.
4. On a plate, mix the almonds and bread crumbs.
5. Toss the chicken cubes in the almond and bread crumb mixture until coated.
6. Bake the nuggets in the air fryer oven, in two batches, for 10 to 13 minutes, or until the chicken reaches an internal temperature of 165ºF (74ºC) on a meat thermometer. Serve immediately.

Chicken with Pineapple and Peach

Prep time: 10 minutes | Cook time: 14 to 15 minutes | Serves 4

1 pound (454 g) low-sodium boneless, skinless chicken breasts, cut into 1-inch pieces
1 medium red onion, chopped
1 (8-ounce / 227-g) can pineapple chunks, drained, ¼ cup juice reserved
1 tablespoon peanut oil or safflower oil
1 peach, peeled, pitted, and cubed
1 tablespoon cornstarch
½ teaspoon ground ginger
¼ teaspoon ground allspice
Brown rice, cooked (optional)

1. Select the BAKE function and preheat MAXX to 380ºF (193ºC).
2. In a medium metal bowl, mix the chicken, red onion, pineapple, and peanut oil. Bake in the air fryer oven for 9 minutes. Remove and stir.
3. Add the peach and return the bowl to the air fryer oven. Bake for 3 minutes more. Remove and stir again.
4. In a small bowl, whisk the reserved pineapple juice, the cornstarch, ginger, and allspice well. Add to the chicken mixture and stir to combine.
5. Bake for 2 to 3 minutes more, or until the chicken reaches an internal temperature of 165ºF (74ºC) on a meat thermometer and the sauce is slightly thickened.
6. Serve immediately over hot cooked brown rice, if desired.

Buttermilk Paprika Chicken

Prep time: 7 minutes | Cook time: 17 to 23 minutes | Serves 4

4 (5-ounce / 142-g) low-sodium boneless, skinless chicken breasts, pounded to about ½ inch thick	2 tablespoons cornstarch
½ cup buttermilk	1 teaspoon dried thyme
½ cup all-purpose flour	1 teaspoon ground paprika
	1 egg white
	1 tablespoon olive oil

1. In a shallow bowl, mix the chicken and buttermilk. Let stand for 10 minutes.
2. Meanwhile, in another shallow bowl, mix the flour, cornstarch, thyme, and paprika.
3. In a small bowl, whisk the egg white and olive oil. Quickly stir this egg mixture into the flour mixture so the dry ingredients are evenly moistened.
4. Remove the chicken from the buttermilk and shake off any excess liquid. Dip each piece of chicken into the flour mixture to coat. Transfer to the air fryer basket.
5. Select the AIR FRY function and cook at 390ºF (199ºC) for 17 to 23 minutes minutes, or until the chicken reaches an internal temperature of 165ºF (74ºC) on a meat thermometer. Serve immediately.

Coconut Chicken Meatballs

Prep time: 10 minutes | Cook time: 14 minutes | Serves 4

1 pound (454 g) ground chicken	1 tablespoon soy sauce
2 scallions, finely chopped	2 teaspoons sriracha or other hot sauce
1 cup chopped fresh cilantro leaves	1 teaspoon toasted sesame oil
¼ cup unsweetened shredded coconut	½ teaspoon kosher salt
1 tablespoon hoisin sauce	1 teaspoon black pepper

1. In a large bowl, gently mix the chicken, scallions, cilantro, coconut, hoisin, soy sauce, sriracha, sesame oil, salt, and pepper until thoroughly combined (the mixture will be wet and sticky).

2. Place a sheet of parchment paper in the air fryer basket. Using a small scoop or teaspoon, drop rounds of the mixture in a single layer onto the parchment paper.
3. Select the AIR FRY function and cook at 350ºF (177ºC) for 10 minutes, turning the meatballs halfway through the cooking time. Increase the temperature to 400ºF (204ºC) and air fry for 4 minutes more to brown the outsides of the meatballs. Use a meat thermometer to ensure the meatballs have reached an internal temperature of 165ºF (74ºC).
4. Transfer the meatballs to a serving platter. Repeat with any remaining chicken mixture. Serve.

Easy Tandoori Chicken

Prep time: 5 minutes | Cook time: 18 to 23 minutes | Serves 4

⅔ cup plain low-fat yogurt	cinnamon
2 tablespoons freshly squeezed lemon juice	2 garlic cloves, minced
2 teaspoons curry powder	2 teaspoons olive oil
½ teaspoon ground	4 (5-ounce / 142-g) low-sodium boneless, skinless chicken breasts

1. In a medium bowl, whisk the yogurt, lemon juice, curry powder, cinnamon, garlic, and olive oil.
2. With a sharp knife, cut thin slashes into the chicken. Add it to the yogurt mixture and turn to coat. Let stand for 10 minutes at room temperature. You can also prepare this ahead of time and marinate the chicken in the refrigerator for up to 24 hours.
3. Select the ROAST function and preheat MAXX to 360ºF (182ºC).
4. Remove the chicken from the marinade and shake off any excess liquid. Discard any remaining marinade.
5. Roast the chicken for 10 minutes. With tongs, carefully turn each piece. Roast for 8 to 13 minutes more, or until the chicken reaches an internal temperature of 165ºF (74ºC) on a meat thermometer. Serve immediately.

Jerk Chicken Leg Quarters

Prep time: 8 minutes | Cook time: 27 minutes | Serves 2

1 tablespoon packed brown sugar
1 teaspoon ground allspice
1 teaspoon pepper
1 teaspoon garlic powder
¾ teaspoon dry mustard
¾ teaspoon dried thyme
½ teaspoon salt
¼ teaspoon cayenne pepper
2 (10-ounce / 284-g) chicken leg quarters, trimmed
1 teaspoon vegetable oil
1 scallion, green part only, sliced thin
Lime wedges

1. Combine sugar, allspice, pepper, garlic powder, mustard, thyme, salt, and cayenne in a bowl. Pat chicken dry with paper towels. Using metal skewer, poke 10 to 15 holes in skin of each chicken leg. Rub with oil and sprinkle evenly with spice mixture.
2. Arrange chicken skin-side up in the air fryer basket, spaced evenly apart. Select the AIR FRY function and cook at 400ºF (204ºC) for 27 to 30 minutes, or until chicken is well browned and crisp, rotating chicken halfway through cooking (do not flip).
3. Transfer chicken to plate, tent loosely with aluminum foil, and let rest for 5 minutes. Sprinkle with scallion. Serve with lime wedges.

Tex-Mex Chicken Breasts

Prep time: 10 minutes | Cook time: 17 to 20 minutes | Serves 4

1 pound (454 g) low-sodium boneless, skinless chicken breasts, cut into 1-inch cubes
1 medium onion, chopped
1 red bell pepper, chopped
1 jalapeño pepper, minced
2 teaspoons olive oil
²/₃ cup canned low-sodium black beans, rinsed and drained
½ cup low-sodium salsa
2 teaspoons chili powder

1. Select the ROAST function and preheat MAXX to 400ºF (204ºC).
2. In a medium metal bowl, mix the chicken, onion, bell pepper, jalapeño, and olive oil. Roast for 10 minutes, stirring once during cooking.
3. Add the black beans, salsa, and chili powder. Roast for 7 to 10 minutes more, stirring once, until the chicken reaches an internal temperature of 165ºF (74ºC) on a meat thermometer. Serve immediately.

Herbed Turkey Breast

Prep time: 20 minutes | Cook time: 45 minutes | Serves 6

1 tablespoon olive oil
Cooking spray
2 garlic cloves, minced
2 teaspoons Dijon mustard
1½ teaspoons rosemary
1½ teaspoons sage
1½ teaspoons thyme
1 teaspoon salt
½ teaspoon freshly ground black pepper
3 pounds (1.4 kg) turkey breast, thawed if frozen

1. Spray the air fryer basket lightly with cooking spray.
2. In a small bowl, mix together the garlic, olive oil, Dijon mustard, rosemary, sage, thyme, salt, and pepper to make a paste. Smear the paste all over the turkey breast.
3. Place the turkey breast in the air fryer basket. Select the AIR FRY function and cook at 370ºF (188ºC) for 20 minutes. Flip turkey breast over and baste it with any drippings that have collected in the bottom drawer of the air fryer oven. Air fry until the internal temperature of the meat reaches at least 170ºF (77ºC), 20 more minutes.
4. If desired, increase the temperature to 400ºF (204ºC), flip the turkey breast over one last time, and air fry for 5 minutes to get a crispy exterior.
5. Let the turkey rest for 10 minutes before slicing and serving.

air fryer oven Chicken Fajitas

Prep time: 15 minutes | Cook time: 10 to 15 minutes | Serves 4

4 (5-ounce / 142-g) low-sodium boneless, skinless chicken breasts, cut into 4-by-½-inch strips	2 teaspoons chili powder
1 tablespoon freshly squeezed lemon juice	2 red bell peppers, sliced
2 teaspoons olive oil	4 low-sodium whole-wheat tortillas
	⅓ cup nonfat sour cream
	1 cup grape tomatoes, sliced

1. Select the ROAST function and preheat MAXX to 380ºF (193ºC).
2. In a large bowl, mix the chicken, lemon juice, olive oil, and chili powder. Toss to coat. Transfer the chicken to the air fryer basket. Add the red bell peppers. Roast for 10 to 15 minutes, or until the chicken reaches an internal temperature of 165ºF (74ºC) on a meat thermometer.
3. Assemble the fajitas with the tortillas, chicken, bell peppers, sour cream, and tomatoes. Serve immediately.

Roasted Chicken with Garlic

Prep time: 5 minutes | Cook time: 25 minutes | Serves 4

4 (5-ounce / 142-g) low-sodium bone-in skinless chicken breasts	3 tablespoons cornstarch
1 tablespoon olive oil	1 teaspoon dried basil leaves
1 tablespoon freshly squeezed lemon juice	⅛ teaspoon freshly ground black pepper
	20 garlic cloves, unpeeled

1. Select the ROAST function and preheat MAXX to 370ºF (188ºC).
2. Rub the chicken with the olive oil and lemon juice on both sides and sprinkle with the cornstarch, basil, and pepper.
3. Place the seasoned chicken in the air fryer basket and top with the garlic cloves. Roast for about 25 minutes, or until the garlic is soft and the chicken reaches an internal temperature of 165ºF (74ºC) on a meat thermometer. Serve immediately.

Orange and Honey Glazed Duck with Apples

Prep time: 5 minutes | Cook time: 15 minutes | Serves 2 to 3

1 pound (454 g) duck breasts (2 to 3 breasts)	orange
Kosher salt and pepper, to taste	¼ cup honey
Juice and zest of 1	2 sprigs thyme, plus more for garnish
	2 firm tart apples, such as Fuji

1. Select the ROAST function and preheat MAXX to 400ºF (204ºC).
2. Pat the duck breasts dry and, using a sharp knife, make 3 to 4 shallow, diagonal slashes in the skin. Turn the breasts and score the skin on the diagonal in the opposite direction to create a cross-hatch pattern. Season well with salt and pepper.
3. Place the duck breasts skin-side up in the air fryer basket. Roast for 8 minutes, then flip and roast for 4 more minutes on the second side.
4. While the duck is cooking, prepare the sauce. Combine the orange juice and zest, honey, and thyme in a small saucepan. Bring to a boil, stirring to dissolve the honey, then reduce the heat and simmer until thickened. Core the apples and cut into quarters. Cut each quarter into 3 or 4 slices depending on the size.
5. After the duck has cooked on both sides, turn it and brush the skin with the orange-honey glaze. Roast for 1 more minute. Remove the duck breasts to a cutting board and allow to rest.
6. Toss the apple slices with the remaining orange-honey sauce in a medium bowl. Arrange the apples in a single layer in the air fryer basket. Switch from ROAST to AIR FRY. Air fry for 10 minutes while the duck breast rests. Slice the duck breasts on the bias and divide them and the apples among 2 or 3 plates.
7. Serve warm, garnished with additional thyme.

Roasted Chicken and Vegetable Salad

Prep time: 10 minutes | Cook time: 10 to 13 minutes | Serves 4

3 (4-ounce / 113-g) low-sodium boneless, skinless chicken breasts, cut into 1-inch cubes
1 small red onion, sliced
1 red bell pepper, sliced
1 cup green beans, cut into 1-inch pieces
2 tablespoons low-fat ranch salad dressing
2 tablespoons freshly squeezed lemon juice
½ teaspoon dried basil
4 cups mixed lettuce

1. Select the ROAST function and preheat MAXX to 400°F (204°C).
2. In the air fryer basket, roast the chicken, red onion, red bell pepper, and green beans for 10 to 13 minutes, or until the chicken reaches an internal temperature of 165°F (74°C) on a meat thermometer, tossing the food in the basket once during cooking.
3. While the chicken cooks, in a serving bowl, mix the ranch dressing, lemon juice, and basil.
4. Transfer the chicken and vegetables to a serving bowl and toss with the dressing to coat. Serve immediately on lettuce leaves.

Chicken Manchurian

Prep time: 10 minutes | Cook time: 20 minutes | Serves 2

1 pound (454 g) boneless, skinless chicken breasts, cut into 1-inch pieces
¼ cup ketchup
1 tablespoon tomato-based chili sauce, such as Heinz
1 tablespoon soy sauce
1 tablespoon rice vinegar
2 teaspoons vegetable oil
1 teaspoon hot sauce, such as Tabasco
½ teaspoon garlic powder
¼ teaspoon cayenne pepper
2 scallions, thinly sliced
Cooked white rice, for serving

1. Select the BAKE function and preheat MAXX to 350°F (177°C).
2. In a bowl, combine the chicken, ketchup, chili sauce, soy sauce, vinegar, oil, hot sauce, garlic powder, cayenne, and three-quarters of the scallions and toss until evenly coated.
3. Scrape the chicken and sauce into a metal cake pan and place the pan in the air fryer oven. Bake until the chicken is cooked through and the sauce is reduced to a thick glaze, about 20 minutes, flipping the chicken pieces halfway through.
4. Remove the pan from the air fryer oven. Spoon the chicken and sauce over rice and top with the remaining scallions. Serve immediately.

Merguez Meatballs

Prep time: 10 minutes | Cook time: 10 minutes | Serves 4

1 pound (454 g) ground chicken
2 garlic cloves, finely minced
1 tablespoon sweet Hungarian paprika
1 teaspoon kosher salt
1 teaspoon sugar
1 teaspoon ground cumin
½ teaspoon black pepper
½ teaspoon ground fennel
½ teaspoon ground coriander
½ teaspoon cayenne pepper
¼ teaspoon ground allspice

1. In a large bowl, gently mix the chicken, garlic, paprika, salt, sugar, cumin, black pepper, fennel, coriander, cayenne, and allspice until all the ingredients are incorporated. Let stand for 30 minutes at room temperature, or cover and refrigerate for up to 24 hours.
2. Form the mixture into 16 meatballs. Arrange them in a single layer in the air fryer basket.
3. Select the AIR FRY function and cook at 400°F (204°C) for 10 minutes, turning the meatballs halfway through the cooking time. Use a meat thermometer to ensure the meatballs have reached an internal temperature of 165°F (74°C).
4. Serve warm.

Mayonnaise-Mustard Chicken

Prep time: 10 minutes | Cook time: 15 minutes | Serves 4

6 tablespoons mayonnaise
2 tablespoons coarse-ground mustard
2 teaspoons honey (optional)
2 teaspoons curry powder
1 teaspoon kosher salt
1 teaspoon cayenne pepper
1 pound (454 g) chicken tenders

1. Select the BAKE function and preheat MAXX to 350ºF (177ºC).
2. In a large bowl, whisk together the mayonnaise, mustard, honey (if using), curry powder, salt, and cayenne. Transfer half of the mixture to a serving bowl to serve as a dipping sauce. Add the chicken tenders to the large bowl and toss until well coated.
3. Place the tenders in the air fryer basket and bake for 15 minutes. Use a meat thermometer to ensure the chicken has reached an internal temperature of 165ºF (74ºC).
4. Serve the chicken with the dipping sauce.

Hawaiian Tropical Chicken

Prep time: 10 minutes | Cook time: 15 minutes | Serves 4

4 boneless, skinless chicken thighs (about 1½ pounds / 680 g)
1 (8-ounce / 227-g) can pineapple chunks in juice, drained, ¼ cup juice reserved
¼ cup soy sauce
¼ cup sugar
2 tablespoons ketchup
1 tablespoon minced fresh ginger
1 tablespoon minced garlic
¼ cup chopped scallions

1. Use a fork to pierce the chicken all over to allow the marinade to penetrate better. Place the chicken in a large bowl or large resealable plastic bag.
2. Set the drained pineapple chunks aside. In a small microwave-safe bowl, combine the pineapple juice, soy sauce, sugar, ketchup, ginger, and garlic. Pour half the sauce over the chicken; toss to coat. Reserve the remaining sauce. Marinate the chicken at room temperature for 30 minutes, or cover and refrigerate for up to 24 hours.
3. Select the BAKE function and preheat MAXX to 350ºF (177ºC).
4. Place the chicken in the air fryer basket, discarding marinade. Bake for 15 minutes, turning halfway through the cooking time.
5. Meanwhile, microwave the reserved sauce on high for 45 to 60 seconds, stirring every 15 seconds, until the sauce has the consistency of a thick glaze.
6. At the end of the cooking time, use a meat thermometer to ensure the chicken has reached an internal temperature of 165ºF (74ºC).
7. Transfer the chicken to a serving platter. Pour the sauce over the chicken. Garnish with the pineapple chunks and scallions before serving.

Crisp Paprika Chicken Drumsticks

Prep time: 5 minutes | Cook time: 22 minutes | Serves 2

2 teaspoons paprika
1 teaspoon packed brown sugar
1 teaspoon garlic powder
½ teaspoon dry mustard
½ teaspoon salt
Pinch pepper
4 (5-ounce / 142-g) chicken drumsticks, trimmed
1 teaspoon vegetable oil
1 scallion, green part only, sliced thin on bias

1. Combine paprika, sugar, garlic powder, mustard, salt, and pepper in a bowl. Pat drumsticks dry with paper towels. Using metal skewer, poke 10 to 15 holes in skin of each drumstick. Rub with oil and sprinkle evenly with spice mixture.
2. Arrange drumsticks in air fryer basket, spaced evenly apart, alternating ends. Select the AIR FRY function and cook at 400ºF (204ºC) for 22 to 25 minutes, or until chicken is crisp and registers 195ºF (91ºC), flipping chicken halfway through cooking.
3. Transfer chicken to serving platter, tent loosely with aluminum foil, and let rest for 5 minutes. Sprinkle with scallion and serve.

Thai Curry Meatballs

Prep time: 10 minutes | Cook time: 10 minutes | Serves 4

1 pound (454 g) ground chicken
¼ cup chopped fresh cilantro
1 teaspoon chopped fresh mint
1 tablespoon fresh lime juice
1 tablespoon Thai red, green, or yellow curry paste
1 tablespoon fish sauce
2 garlic cloves, minced
2 teaspoons minced fresh ginger
½ teaspoon kosher salt
½ teaspoon black pepper
¼ teaspoon red pepper flakes

1. In a large bowl, gently mix the ground chicken, cilantro, mint, lime juice, curry paste, fish sauce, garlic, ginger, salt, black pepper, and red pepper flakes until thoroughly combined.
2. Form the mixture into 16 meatballs. Place the meatballs in a single layer in the air fryer basket.
3. Select the AIR FRY function and cook at 400ºF (204ºC) for 10 minutes, turning the meatballs halfway through the cooking time. Use a meat thermometer to ensure the meatballs have reached an internal temperature of 165ºF (74ºC).
4. Serve immediately.

Cranberry Curry Chicken

Prep time: 12 minutes | Cook time: 18 minutes | Serves 4

3 (5-ounce / 142-g) low-sodium boneless, skinless chicken breasts, cut into 1½-inch cubes
2 teaspoons olive oil
2 tablespoons cornstarch
1 tablespoon curry powder
1 tart apple, chopped
½ cup low-sodium chicken broth
⅓ cup dried cranberries
2 tablespoons freshly squeezed orange juice
Brown rice, cooked (optional)

1. Select the BAKE function and preheat MAXX to 380ºF (193ºC).

2. In a medium bowl, mix the chicken and olive oil. Sprinkle with the cornstarch and curry powder. Toss to coat. Stir in the apple and transfer to a metal pan. Bake in the air fryer oven for 8 minutes, stirring once during cooking.
3. Add the chicken broth, cranberries, and orange juice. Bake for about 10 minutes more, or until the sauce is slightly thickened and the chicken reaches an internal temperature of 165ºF (74ºC) on a meat thermometer. Serve over hot cooked brown rice, if desired.

Simple Chicken Shawarma

Prep time: 10 minutes | Cook time: 15 minutes | Serves 4

Shawarma Spice:

2 teaspoons dried oregano
1 teaspoon ground cinnamon
1 teaspoon ground cumin
1 teaspoon ground coriander
1 teaspoon kosher salt
½ teaspoon ground allspice
½ teaspoon cayenne pepper

Chicken:

1 pound (454 g) boneless, skinless chicken thighs, cut into large bite-size chunks
2 tablespoons vegetable oil

For Serving:

Tzatziki
Pita bread

1. For the shawarma spice: In a small bowl, combine the oregano, cayenne, cumin, coriander, salt, cinnamon, and allspice.
2. For the chicken: In a large bowl, toss together the chicken, vegetable oil, and shawarma spice to coat. Marinate at room temperature for 30 minutes or cover and refrigerate for up to 24 hours.
3. Place the chicken in the air fryer basket. Select the AIR FRY function and cook at 350ºF (177ºC) for 15 minutes, or until the chicken reaches an internal temperature of 165ºF (74ºC).
4. Transfer the chicken to a serving platter. Serve with tzatziki and pita bread.

Lemon Garlic Chicken

Prep time: 10 minutes | Cook time: 16 to 19 minutes | Serves 4

4 (5-ounce / 142-g) low-sodium boneless, skinless chicken breasts, cut into 4-by-½-inch strips
2 teaspoons olive oil
2 tablespoons cornstarch
3 garlic cloves, minced
½ cup low-sodium chicken broth
¼ cup freshly squeezed lemon juice
1 tablespoon honey
½ teaspoon dried thyme
Brown rice, cooked (optional)

1. Select the BAKE function and preheat MAXX to 400ºF (204ºC).
2. In a large bowl, mix the chicken and olive oil. Sprinkle with the cornstarch. Toss to coat.
3. Add the garlic and transfer to a metal pan. Bake in the air fryer oven for 10 minutes, stirring once during cooking.
4. Add the chicken broth, lemon juice, honey, and thyme to the chicken mixture. Bake for 6 to 9 minutes more, or until the sauce is slightly thickened and the chicken reaches an internal temperature of 165ºF (74ºC) on a meat thermometer. Serve over hot cooked brown rice, if desired.

Curried Orange Honey Chicken

Prep time: 10 minutes | Cook time: 16 to 19 minutes | Serves 4

¾ pound (340 g) boneless, skinless chicken thighs, cut into 1-inch pieces
1 yellow bell pepper, cut into 1½-inch pieces
1 small red onion, sliced
Olive oil for misting
¼ cup chicken stock
2 tablespoons honey
¼ cup orange juice
1 tablespoon cornstarch
2 to 3 teaspoons curry powder

1. Select the ROAST function and preheat MAXX to 370ºF (188ºC).
2. Put the chicken thighs, pepper, and red onion in the air fryer basket and mist with olive oil.

3. Roast for 12 to 14 minutes or until the chicken is cooked to 165ºF (74ºC), shaking the basket halfway through cooking time.
4. Remove the chicken and vegetables from the air fryer basket and set aside.
5. In a metal bowl, combine the stock, honey, orange juice, cornstarch, and curry powder, and mix well. Add the chicken and vegetables, stir, and put the bowl in the basket.
6. Return the basket to the air fryer oven and roast for 2 minutes. Remove and stir, then roast for 2 to 3 minutes or until the sauce is thickened and bubbly.
7. Serve warm.

Garlic Soy Chicken Thighs

Prep time: 10 minutes | Cook time: 30 minutes | Serves 1 to 2

2 tablespoons chicken stock
2 tablespoons reduced-sodium soy sauce
1½ tablespoons sugar
4 garlic cloves, smashed and peeled
2 large scallions, cut into 2- to 3-inch batons, plus more, thinly sliced, for garnish
2 bone-in, skin-on chicken thighs (7 to 8 ounces / 198 to 227 g each)

1. Select the BAKE function and preheat MAXX to 375ºF (191ºC).
2. In a metal cake pan, combine the chicken stock, soy sauce, and sugar and stir until the sugar dissolves. Add the garlic cloves, scallions, and chicken thighs, turning the thighs to coat them in the marinade, then resting them skin-side up. Place the pan in the air fryer oven and bake, flipping the thighs every 5 minutes after the first 10 minutes, until the chicken is cooked through and the marinade is reduced to a sticky glaze over the chicken, about 30 minutes.
3. Remove the pan from the air fryer oven and serve the chicken thighs warm, with any remaining glaze spooned over top and sprinkled with more sliced scallions.

Barbecue Chicken

Prep time: 10 minutes | Cook time: 18 to 20 minutes | Serves 4

⅓ cup no-salt-added tomato sauce
2 tablespoons low-sodium grainy mustard
2 tablespoons apple cider vinegar
1 tablespoon honey
2 garlic cloves, minced
1 jalapeño pepper, minced
3 tablespoons minced onion
4 (5-ounce / 142-g) low-sodium boneless, skinless chicken breasts

1. In a small bowl, stir together the tomato sauce, mustard, cider vinegar, honey, garlic, jalapeño, and onion.
2. Brush the chicken breasts with some sauce and transfer to the air fryer basket. Select the AIR FRY function and cook at 370ºF (188ºC) for 10 minutes.
3. Remove the air fryer basket and turn the chicken; brush with more sauce. Air fry for 5 minutes more.
4. Remove the air fryer basket and turn the chicken again; brush with more sauce. Air fry for 3 to 5 minutes more, or until the chicken reaches an internal temperature of 165ºF (74ºC) on a meat thermometer. Discard any remaining sauce.
5. Serve immediately.

Cheesy Chicken Tacos

Prep time: 10 minutes | Cook time: 12 to 16 minutes | Serves 2 to 4

1 teaspoon chili powder
½ teaspoon ground cumin
½ teaspoon garlic powder
Salt and pepper, to taste
Pinch cayenne pepper
1 pound (454 g) boneless, skinless chicken thighs, trimmed
1 teaspoon vegetable oil
1 tomato, cored and chopped
2 tablespoons finely chopped red onion
2 teaspoons minced jalapeño chile
1½ teaspoons lime juice
6 to 12 (6-inch) corn tortillas, warmed
1 cup shredded iceberg lettuce
3 ounces (85 g) cheddar cheese, shredded (¾ cup)

1. Combine chili powder, cumin, garlic powder, ½ teaspoon salt, ¼ teaspoon pepper, and cayenne in bowl. Pat chicken dry with paper towels, rub with oil, and sprinkle evenly with spice mixture. Place chicken in air fryer basket.
2. Select the AIR FRY function and cook at 400ºF (204ºC) for 12 to 16 minutes, or until chicken registers 165ºF (74ºC), flipping chicken halfway through cooking.
3. Meanwhile, combine tomato, onion, jalapeño, and lime juice in a bowl; season with salt and pepper to taste and set aside until ready to serve.
4. Transfer chicken to a cutting board, let cool slightly, then shred into bite-size pieces using 2 forks. Serve chicken on warm tortillas, topped with salsa, lettuce, and cheddar.

Apricot-Glazed Chicken

Prep time: 5 minutes | Cook time: 12 minutes | Serves 2

2 tablespoons apricot preserves
½ teaspoon minced fresh thyme or ⅛ teaspoon dried
2 (8-ounce / 227-g) boneless, skinless chicken breasts, trimmed
1 teaspoon vegetable oil
Salt and pepper, to taste

1. Microwave apricot preserves and thyme in bowl until fluid, about 30 seconds; set aside. Pound chicken to uniform thickness as needed. Pat dry with paper towels, rub with oil, and season with salt and pepper.
2. Arrange breasts skin-side down in air fryer basket, spaced evenly apart, alternating ends.
3. Select the AIR FRY function and cook at 400ºF (204ºC) for 4 minutes. Flip chicken and brush skin side with apricot-thyme mixture. Air fry until chicken registers 160ºF (71ºC), 8 to 12 minutes more.
4. Transfer chicken to serving platter, tent loosely with aluminum foil, and let rest for 5 minutes. Serve.

Thai Cornish Game Hens

Prep time: 15 minutes | Cook time: 20 minutes | Serves 4

1 cup chopped fresh cilantro leaves and stems	2 teaspoons black pepper
¼ cup fish sauce	2 teaspoons ground coriander
1 tablespoon soy sauce	1 teaspoon kosher salt
1 serrano chile, seeded and chopped	1 teaspoon ground turmeric
8 garlic cloves, smashed	2 Cornish game hens, giblets removed, split in half lengthwise
2 tablespoons sugar	
2 tablespoons lemongrass paste	

1. In a blender, combine the cilantro, fish sauce, soy sauce, serrano, garlic, sugar, lemongrass, black pepper, coriander, salt, and turmeric. Blend until smooth.
2. Place the game hen halves in a large bowl. Pour the cilantro mixture over the hen halves and toss to coat. Marinate at room temperature for 30 minutes, or cover and refrigerate for up to 24 hours.
3. Select the ROAST function and preheat MAXX to 400ºF (204ºC).
4. Arrange the hen halves in a single layer in the air fryer basket. Roast for 20 minutes. Use a meat thermometer to ensure the game hens have reached an internal temperature of 165ºF (74ºC). Serve warm.

Barbecued Chicken with Creamy Coleslaw

Prep time: 10 minutes | Cook time: 20 minutes | Serves 2

3 cups shredded coleslaw mix	barbecue sauce, plus extra for serving
Salt and pepper	2 tablespoons mayonnaise
2 (12-ounce / 340-g) bone-in split chicken breasts, trimmed	2 tablespoons sour cream
1 teaspoon vegetable oil	1 teaspoon distilled white vinegar, plus extra for seasoning
2 tablespoons	¼ teaspoon sugar

1. Select the BAKE function and preheat MAXX to 350ºF (177ºC).
2. Toss coleslaw mix and ¼ teaspoon salt in a colander set over bowl. Let sit until wilted slightly, about 30 minutes. Rinse, drain, and dry well with a dish towel.
3. Meanwhile, pat chicken dry with paper towels, rub with oil, and season with salt and pepper. Arrange breasts skin-side down in air fryer basket, spaced evenly apart, alternating ends. Bake for 10 minutes. Flip breasts and brush skin side with barbecue sauce. Return basket to air fryer oven and bake until well browned and chicken registers 160ºF (71ºC), 10 to 15 minutes.
4. Transfer chicken to serving platter, tent loosely with aluminum foil, and let rest for 5 minutes. While chicken rests, whisk mayonnaise, sour cream, vinegar, sugar, and pinch pepper together in a large bowl. Stir in coleslaw mix and season with salt, pepper, and additional vinegar to taste. Serve chicken with coleslaw, passing extra barbecue sauce separately.

Turkey and Cranberry Quesadillas

Prep time: 7 minutes | Cook time: 4 to 8 minutes | Serves 4

6 low-sodium whole-wheat tortillas	2 tablespoons cranberry sauce
⅓ cup shredded low-sodium low-fat Swiss cheese	2 tablespoons dried cranberries
¾ cup shredded cooked low-sodium turkey breast	½ teaspoon dried basil
	Olive oil spray, for spraying the tortillas

1. Put 3 tortillas on a work surface.
2. Evenly divide the Swiss cheese, turkey, cranberry sauce, and dried cranberries among the tortillas. Sprinkle with the basil and top with the remaining tortillas.
3. Spray the outsides of the tortillas with olive oil spray. Transfer to the air fryer basket. You may need to work in batches.
4. Select the AIR FRY function and cook at 400ºF (204ºC) for 4 to 8 minutes, or until crisp and the cheese is melted. Cut into quarters and serve.

Fajita Chicken Strips

Prep time: 10 minutes | Cook time: 15 minutes | Serves 4

1 pound (454 g) boneless, skinless chicken tenderloins, cut into strips
3 bell peppers, any color, cut into chunks
1 onion, cut into chunks
1 tablespoon olive oil
1 tablespoon fajita seasoning mix
Cooking spray

1. In a large bowl, mix together the chicken, bell peppers, onion, olive oil, and fajita seasoning mix until completely coated.
2. Spray the air fryer basket lightly with cooking spray.
3. Place the chicken and vegetables in the air fryer basket and lightly spray with cooking spray.
4. Select the AIR FRY function and cook at 370ºF (188ºC) for 7 minutes. Shake the basket and air fry for an additional 5 to 8 minutes, until the chicken is cooked through and the veggies are starting to char.
5. Serve warm.

Crisp Chicken Wings

Prep time: 15 minutes | Cook time: 20 minutes | Serves 4

1 pound (454 g) chicken wings
3 tablespoons vegetable oil
½ cup all-purpose flour
½ teaspoon smoked paprika
½ teaspoon garlic powder
½ teaspoon kosher salt
1½ teaspoons freshly cracked black pepper

1. Place the chicken wings in a large bowl. Drizzle the vegetable oil over wings and toss to coat.
2. In a separate bowl, whisk together the flour, paprika, garlic powder, salt, and pepper until combined.
3. Dredge the wings in the flour mixture one at a time, coating them well, and place in the air fryer basket.
4. Select the AIR FRY function and cook at 400ºF (204ºC) for 20 minutes, turning the wings halfway through the cooking time, until the breading is browned and crunchy.
5. Serve hot.

Israeli Chicken Schnitzel

Prep time: 5 minutes | Cook time: 10 minutes | Serves 4

2 large boneless, skinless chicken breasts, each weighing about 1 pound (454 g)
1 cup all-purpose flour
2 teaspoons garlic powder
2 teaspoons kosher salt
1 teaspoon black pepper
1 teaspoon paprika
2 eggs beaten with 2 tablespoons water
2 cups panko bread crumbs
Vegetable oil spray
Lemon juice, for serving

1. Place 1 chicken breast between 2 pieces of plastic wrap. Use a mallet or a rolling pin to pound the chicken until it is ¼ inch thick. Set aside. Repeat with the second breast. Whisk together the flour, garlic powder, salt, pepper, and paprika on a large plate. Place the panko in a separate shallow bowl or pie plate.
2. Dredge 1 chicken breast in the flour, shaking off any excess, then dip it in the egg mixture. Dredge the chicken breast in the panko, making sure to coat it completely. Shake off any excess panko. Place the battered chicken breast on a plate. Repeat with the second chicken breast.
3. Spray the air fryer basket with oil spray. Place 1 of the battered chicken breasts in the basket and spray the top with oil spray. Select the AIR FRY function and cook at 375ºF (191ºC) for 5 minutes, or until the top is browned. Flip the chicken and spray the second side with oil spray. Air fry until the second side is browned and crispy and the internal temperature reaches 165ºF (74ºC). Remove the first chicken breast from the air fryer oven and repeat with the second chicken breast.
4. Serve hot with lemon juice.

Parmesan Chicken Wings

Prep time: 15 minutes | Cook time: 16 to 18 minutes | Serves 4

1¼ cups grated Parmesan cheese
1 tablespoon garlic powder
1 teaspoon salt
½ teaspoon freshly ground black pepper
¾ cup all-purpose flour
1 large egg, beaten
12 chicken wings (about 1 pound / 454 g)
Cooking spray

1. Line the air fryer basket with parchment paper.
2. In a shallow bowl, whisk the Parmesan cheese, garlic powder, salt, and pepper until blended. Place the flour in a second shallow bowl and the beaten egg in a third shallow bowl.
3. One at a time, dip the chicken wings into the flour, the beaten egg, and the Parmesan cheese mixture, coating thoroughly.
4. Place the chicken wings on the parchment and spritz with cooking spray.
5. Select the AIR FRY function and cook at 390°F (199°C) for 8 minutes. Flip the chicken, spritz it with cooking spray, and air fry for 8 to 10 minutes more until the internal temperature reaches 165°F (74°C) and the insides are no longer pink. Let sit for 5 minutes before serving.

Nutty Chicken Tenders

Prep time: 5 minutes | Cook time: 12 minutes | Serves 4

1 pound (454 g) chicken tenders
1 teaspoon kosher salt
1 teaspoon black pepper
½ teaspoon smoked
paprika
¼ cup coarse mustard
2 tablespoons honey
1 cup finely crushed pecans

1. Select the BAKE function and preheat MAXX to 350°F (177°C).
2. Place the chicken in a large bowl. Sprinkle with the salt, pepper, and paprika. Toss until the chicken is coated with the spices. Add the mustard and honey and toss until the chicken is coated.
3. Place the pecans on a plate. Working with one piece of chicken at a time, roll the chicken in the pecans until both sides are coated. Lightly brush off any loose pecans. Place the chicken in the air fryer basket.
4. Bake for 12 minutes, or until the chicken is cooked through and the pecans are golden brown.
5. Serve warm.

Chicken and Vegetable Fajitas

Prep time: 15 minutes | Cook time: 23 minutes | Serves 6

Chicken:
1 pound (454 g) boneless, skinless chicken thighs, cut crosswise into thirds
1 tablespoon vegetable oil
4½ teaspoons taco seasoning
Vegetables
1 cup sliced onion
1 cup sliced bell
pepper
1 or 2 jalapeños, quartered lengthwise
1 tablespoon vegetable oil
½ teaspoon kosher salt
½ teaspoon ground cumin

For Serving:
Tortillas
Sour cream
Shredded cheese
Guacamole
Salsa

1. For the chicken: In a medium bowl, toss together the chicken, vegetable oil, and taco seasoning to coat.
2. For the vegetables: In a separate bowl, toss together the onion, bell pepper, jalapeño (s), vegetable oil, salt, and cumin to coat.
3. Place the chicken in the air fryer basket.
4. Select the AIR FRY function and cook at 375°F (191°C) for 10 minutes. Add the vegetables to the basket, toss everything together to blend the seasonings, and air fry for 13 minutes more. Use a meat thermometer to ensure the chicken has reached an internal temperature of 165°F (74°C).
5. Transfer the chicken and vegetables to a serving platter. Serve with tortillas and the desired fajita fixings.

Chicken Burgers with Ham and Cheese

Prep time: 12 minutes | Cook time: 13 to 16 minutes | Serves 4

1/3 cup soft bread crumbs
3 tablespoons milk
1 egg, beaten
½ teaspoon dried thyme
Pinch salt
Freshly ground black

pepper, to taste
1¼ pounds (567 g) ground chicken
¼ cup finely chopped ham
1/3 cup grated Havarti cheese
Olive oil for misting

1. Select the BAKE function and preheat MAXX to 350ºF (177ºC).
2. In a medium bowl, combine the bread crumbs, milk, egg, thyme, salt, and pepper. Add the chicken and mix gently but thoroughly with clean hands.
3. Form the chicken into eight thin patties and place on waxed paper.
4. Top four of the patties with the ham and cheese. Top with remaining four patties and gently press the edges together to seal, so the ham and cheese mixture is in the middle of the burger.
5. Place the burgers in the basket and mist with olive oil. Bake for 13 to 16 minutes or until the chicken is thoroughly cooked to 165ºF (74ºC) as measured with a meat thermometer. Serve immediately.

Crispy Chicken Cordon Bleu

Prep time: 15 minutes | Cook time: 13 to 15 minutes | Serves 4

4 chicken breast fillets
¼ cup chopped ham
1/3 cup grated Swiss or Gruyère cheese
¼ cup flour
Pinch salt
Freshly ground black

pepper, to taste
½ teaspoon dried marjoram
1 egg
1 cup panko bread crumbs
Olive oil for misting

1. Select the BAKE function and preheat MAXX to 380ºF (193ºC).
2. Put the chicken breast fillets on a work surface and gently press them with the palm of your hand to make them a bit thinner. Don't tear the meat.

3. In a small bowl, combine the ham and cheese. Divide this mixture among the chicken fillets. Wrap the chicken around the filling to enclose it, using toothpicks to hold the chicken together.
4. In a shallow bowl, mix the flour, salt, pepper, and marjoram. In another bowl, beat the egg. Spread the bread crumbs out on a plate.
5. Dip the chicken into the flour mixture, then into the egg, then into the bread crumbs to coat thoroughly.
6. Put the chicken in the air fryer basket and mist with olive oil.
7. Bake for 13 to 15 minutes or until the chicken is thoroughly cooked to 165ºF (74ºC). Carefully remove the toothpicks and serve.

Crispy Chicken Strips

Prep time: 15 minutes | Cook time: 20 minutes | Serves 4

1 tablespoon olive oil
1 pound (454 g) boneless, skinless chicken tenderloins
1 teaspoon salt
½ teaspoon freshly ground black pepper
½ teaspoon paprika

½ teaspoon garlic powder
½ cup whole-wheat seasoned bread crumbs
1 teaspoon dried parsley
Cooking spray

1. Spray the air fryer basket lightly with cooking spray.
2. In a medium bowl, toss the chicken with the salt, pepper, paprika, and garlic powder until evenly coated.
3. Add the olive oil and toss to coat the chicken evenly.
4. In a separate, shallow bowl, mix together the bread crumbs and parsley.
5. Coat each piece of chicken evenly in the bread crumb mixture.
6. Place the chicken in the air fryer basket in a single layer and spray it lightly with cooking spray. You may need to cook them in batches.
7. Select the AIR FRY function and cook at 370ºF (188ºC) for 10 minutes. Flip the chicken over, lightly spray it with cooking spray, and air fry for an additional 8 to 10 minutes, until golden brown. Serve.

Turkish Chicken Kebabs

Prep time: 15 minutes | Cook time: 15 minutes | Serves 4

¼ cup plain Greek yogurt
1 tablespoon minced garlic
1 tablespoon tomato paste
1 tablespoon fresh lemon juice
1 tablespoon vegetable oil
1 teaspoon kosher salt
1 teaspoon ground cumin
1 teaspoon sweet Hungarian paprika
½ teaspoon ground cinnamon
½ teaspoon black pepper
½ teaspoon cayenne pepper
1 pound (454 g) boneless, skinless chicken thighs, quartered crosswise

1. In a large bowl, combine the yogurt, garlic, tomato paste, lemon juice, vegetable oil, salt, cumin, paprika, cinnamon, black pepper, and cayenne. Stir until the spices are blended into the yogurt.
2. Add the chicken to the bowl and toss until well coated. Marinate at room temperature for 30 minutes, or cover and refrigerate for up to 24 hours.
3. Arrange the chicken in a single layer in the air fryer basket.
4. Select the AIR FRY function and cook at 375ºF (191ºC) for 10 minutes. Turn the chicken and air fry for 5 minutes more. Use a meat thermometer to ensure the chicken has reached an internal temperature of 165ºF (74ºC).
5. Serve warm.

Yellow Curry Chicken Thighs with Peanuts

Prep time: 10 minutes | Cook time: 20 minutes | Serves 6

½ cup unsweetened full-fat coconut milk
2 tablespoons yellow curry paste
1 tablespoon minced fresh ginger
1 tablespoon minced garlic
1 teaspoon kosher salt
1 pound (454 g) boneless, skinless chicken thighs, halved crosswise
2 tablespoons chopped peanuts

1. In a large bowl, stir together the coconut milk, curry paste, ginger, garlic, and salt until well blended. Add the chicken; toss well to coat. Marinate at room temperature for 30 minutes, or cover and refrigerate for up to 24 hours.
2. Select the BAKE function and preheat MAXX to 375ºF (191ºC).
3. Place the chicken (along with marinade) in a baking pan. Place the pan in the air fryer basket. Bake for 20 minutes, turning the chicken halfway through the cooking time. Use a meat thermometer to ensure the chicken has reached an internal temperature of 165ºF (74ºC).
4. Sprinkle the chicken with the chopped peanuts and serve.

Lemon Parmesan Chicken

Prep time: 10 minutes | Cook time: 20 minutes | Serves 4

1 egg
2 tablespoons lemon juice
2 teaspoons minced garlic
½ teaspoon salt
½ teaspoon freshly ground black pepper
4 boneless, skinless chicken breasts, thin cut
Olive oil spray
½ cup whole-wheat bread crumbs
¼ cup grated Parmesan cheese

1. In a medium bowl, whisk together the egg, lemon juice, garlic, salt, and pepper. Add the chicken breasts, cover, and refrigerate for up to 1 hour.
2. In a shallow bowl, combine the bread crumbs and Parmesan cheese.
3. Spray the air fryer basket lightly with olive oil spray.
4. Remove the chicken breasts from the egg mixture, then dredge them in the bread crumb mixture, and place in the air fryer basket in a single layer. Lightly spray the chicken breasts with olive oil spray. You may need to cook the chicken in batches.
5. Select the AIR FRY function and cook at 360ºF (182ºC) for 8 minutes. Flip the chicken over, lightly spray with olive oil spray, and air fry until the chicken reaches an internal temperature of 165ºF (74ºC), for an additional 7 to 12 minutes.
6. Serve warm.

Chicken Satay with Peanut Sauce

Prep time: 12 minutes | Cook time: 12 to 18 minutes | Serves 4

½ cup crunchy peanut butter
⅓ cup chicken broth
3 tablespoons low-sodium soy sauce
2 tablespoons lemon juice
2 cloves garlic, minced
2 tablespoons olive oil
1 teaspoon curry powder
1 pound (454 g) chicken tenders

1. In a medium bowl, combine the peanut butter, chicken broth, soy sauce, lemon juice, garlic, olive oil, and curry powder, and mix well with a wire whisk until smooth. Remove 2 tablespoons of this mixture to a small bowl. Put remaining sauce into a serving bowl and set aside.
2. Add the chicken tenders to the bowl with the 2 tablespoons sauce and stir to coat. Let stand for a few minutes to marinate, then run a bamboo skewer through each chicken tender lengthwise.
3. Put the chicken in the air fryer basket. You may need to work in batches.
4. Select the AIR FRY function and cook at 390ºF (199ºC) for 6 to 9 minutes, or until the chicken reaches 165ºF (74ºC) on a meat thermometer. Serve the chicken with the reserved sauce.

Celery Chicken

Prep time: 10 minutes | Cook time: 15 minutes | Serves 4

½ cup soy sauce
2 tablespoons hoisin sauce
4 teaspoons minced garlic
1 teaspoon freshly ground black pepper
8 boneless, skinless chicken tenderloins
1 cup chopped celery
1 medium red bell pepper, diced
Olive oil spray

1. Spray the air fryer basket lightly with olive oil spray.
2. In a large bowl, mix together the soy sauce, hoisin sauce, garlic, and black pepper to make a marinade. Add the chicken, celery, and bell pepper and toss to coat.

3. Shake the excess marinade off the chicken, place it and the vegetables in the air fryer basket, and lightly spray with olive oil spray. You may need to cook them in batches. Reserve the remaining marinade.
4. Select the AIR FRY function and cook at 375ºF (191ºC) for 8 minutes. Turn the chicken over and brush with some of the remaining marinade. Air fry for an additional 5 to 7 minutes, or until the chicken reaches an internal temperature of at least 165ºF (74ºC). Serve.

Ginger Chicken Thighs

Prep time: 10 minutes | Cook time: 10 minutes | Serves 4

¼ cup julienned peeled fresh ginger
2 tablespoons vegetable oil
1 tablespoon honey
1 tablespoon soy sauce
1 tablespoon ketchup
1 teaspoon garam masala
1 teaspoon ground turmeric
¼ teaspoon kosher salt
½ teaspoon cayenne pepper
Vegetable oil spray
1 pound (454 g) boneless, skinless chicken thighs, cut crosswise into thirds
¼ cup chopped fresh cilantro, for garnish

1. In a small bowl, combine the ginger, oil, honey, soy sauce, ketchup, garam masala, turmeric, salt, and cayenne. Whisk until well combined. Place the chicken in a resealable plastic bag and pour the marinade over. Seal the bag and massage to cover all of the chicken with the marinade. Marinate at room temperature for 30 minutes or in the refrigerator for up to 24 hours.
2. Select the BAKE function and preheat MAXX to 350ºF (177ºC).
3. Spray the air fryer basket with vegetable oil spray and add the chicken and as much of the marinade and julienned ginger as possible. Bake for 10 minutes. Use a meat thermometer to ensure the chicken has reached an internal temperature of 165ºF (74ºC).
4. To serve, garnish with cilantro.

Tempero Baiano Brazilian Chicken

Prep time: 5 minutes | Cook time: 20 minutes | Serves 4

1 teaspoon cumin seeds
1 teaspoon dried oregano
1 teaspoon dried parsley
1 teaspoon ground turmeric
½ teaspoon coriander seeds
1 teaspoon kosher salt
½ teaspoon black peppercorns
½ teaspoon cayenne pepper
¼ cup fresh lime juice
2 tablespoons olive oil
1½ pounds (680 g) chicken drumsticks

1. In a clean coffee grinder or spice mill, combine the cumin, oregano, parsley, turmeric, coriander seeds, salt, peppercorns, and cayenne. Process until finely ground.
2. In a small bowl, combine the ground spices with the lime juice and oil. Place the chicken in a resealable plastic bag. Add the marinade, seal, and massage until the chicken is well coated. Marinate at room temperature for 30 minutes or in the refrigerator for up to 24 hours.
3. Place the drumsticks skin-side up in the air fryer basket. Select the AIR FRY function and cook at 400ºF (204ºC) for 20 to 25 minutes, turning the drumsticks halfway through the cooking time. Use a meat thermometer to ensure that the chicken has reached an internal temperature of 165ºF (74ºC). Serve immediately.

Glazed Chicken Drumsticks

Prep time: 5 minutes | Cook time: 20 minutes | Serves 2

4 chicken drumsticks
3 tablespoons soy sauce
2 tablespoons brown sugar
1 teaspoon minced garlic
1 teaspoon minced fresh ginger
1 teaspoon toasted sesame oil
½ teaspoon red pepper flakes
½ teaspoon kosher salt
½ teaspoon black pepper

1. Line a round baking pan with aluminum foil. (If you don't do this, you'll either end up scrubbing forever or throwing out the pan.) Arrange the drumsticks in the prepared pan.
2. In a medium bowl, stir together the soy sauce, brown sugar, garlic, ginger, sesame oil, red pepper flakes, salt, and black pepper. Pour the sauce over the drumsticks and toss to coat.
3. Place the pan in the air fryer basket.
4. Select the AIR FRY function and cook at 400ºF (204ºC) for 20 minutes, turning the drumsticks halfway through the cooking time. Use a meat thermometer to ensure the chicken has reached an internal temperature of 165ºF (74ºC). Serve immediately.

Sweet-and-Sour Drumsticks

Prep time: 5 minutes | Cook time: 23 to 25 minutes | Serves 4

6 chicken drumsticks
3 tablespoons lemon juice, divided
3 tablespoons low-sodium soy sauce, divided
1 tablespoon peanut oil
3 tablespoons honey
3 tablespoons brown sugar
2 tablespoons ketchup
¼ cup pineapple juice

1. Select the BAKE function and preheat MAXX to 350ºF (177ºC).
2. Sprinkle the drumsticks with 1 tablespoon of lemon juice and 1 tablespoon of soy sauce. Place in the air fryer basket and drizzle with the peanut oil. Toss to coat. Bake for 18 minutes or until the chicken is almost done.
3. Meanwhile, in a metal bowl, combine the remaining 2 tablespoons of lemon juice, the remaining 2 tablespoons of soy sauce, honey, brown sugar, ketchup, and pineapple juice.
4. Add the cooked chicken to the bowl and stir to coat the chicken well with the sauce.
5. Place the metal bowl in the basket. Bake for 5 to 7 minutes or until the chicken is glazed and registers 165ºF (74ºC) on a meat thermometer. Serve warm.

Roasted Chicken Tenders with Veggies

Prep time: 10 minutes | Cook time: 18 to 20 minutes | Serves 4

1 pound (454 g) chicken tenders
1 tablespoon honey
Pinch salt
Freshly ground black pepper, to taste
½ cup soft fresh bread crumbs
½ teaspoon dried thyme
1 tablespoon olive oil
2 carrots, sliced
12 small red potatoes

1. Select the ROAST function and preheat MAXX to 380ºF (193ºC).
2. In a medium bowl, toss the chicken tenders with the honey, salt, and pepper.
3. In a shallow bowl, combine the bread crumbs, thyme, and olive oil, and mix.
4. Coat the tenders in the bread crumbs, pressing firmly onto the meat.
5. Place the carrots and potatoes in the air fryer basket and top with the chicken tenders.
6. Roast for 18 to 20 minutes or until the chicken is cooked to 165ºF (74ºC) and the vegetables are tender, shaking the basket halfway during the cooking time.
7. Serve warm.

Fried Buffalo Chicken Taquitos

Prep time: 15 minutes | Cook time: 5 to 10 minutes | Serves 6

8 ounces (227 g) fat-free cream cheese, softened
⅛ cup Buffalo sauce
2 cups shredded
cooked chicken
12 (7-inch) low-carb flour tortillas
Olive oil spray

1. Spray the air fryer basket lightly with olive oil spray.
2. In a large bowl, mix together the cream cheese and Buffalo sauce until well combined. Add the chicken and stir until combined.
3. Place the tortillas on a clean workspace. Spoon 2 to 3 tablespoons of the chicken mixture in a thin line down the center of each tortilla. Roll up the tortillas.
4. Place the tortillas in the air fryer basket, seam-side down. Spray each tortilla lightly with olive oil spray. You may need to cook the taquitos in batches.
5. Select the AIR FRY function and cook at 360ºF (182ºC) for 5 to 10 minutes, or until golden brown. Serve hot.

Piri-Piri Chicken Thighs

Prep time: 5 minutes | Cook time: 25 minutes | Serves 4

¼ cup piri-piri sauce
1 tablespoon freshly squeezed lemon juice
2 tablespoons brown sugar, divided
2 cloves garlic, minced
1 tablespoon extra-
virgin olive oil
4 bone-in, skin-on chicken thighs, each weighing approximately 7 to 8 ounces (198 to 227 g)
½ teaspoon cornstarch

1. To make the marinade, whisk together the piri-piri sauce, lemon juice, 1 tablespoon of brown sugar, and the garlic in a small bowl. While whisking, slowly pour in the oil in a steady stream and continue to whisk until emulsified. Using a skewer, poke holes in the chicken thighs and place them in a small glass dish. Pour the marinade over the chicken and turn the thighs to coat them with the sauce. Cover the dish and refrigerate for at least 15 minutes and up to 1 hour.
2. Remove the chicken thighs from the dish, reserving the marinade, and place them skin-side down in the air fryer basket. Select the AIR FRY function and cook at 375ºF (191ºC) for 15 to 20 minutes, or until the internal temperature reaches 165ºF (74ºC).
3. Meanwhile, whisk the remaining brown sugar and the cornstarch into the marinade and microwave it on high power for 1 minute until it is bubbling and thickened to a glaze.
4. Once the chicken is cooked, turn the thighs over and brush them with the glaze. Air fry for a few additional minutes until the glaze browns and begins to char in spots.
5. Remove the chicken to a platter and serve with additional piri-piri sauce, if desired.

Turkey Stuffed Bell Peppers

Prep time: 20 minutes | Cook time: 15 minutes | Serves 4

½ pound (227 g) lean ground turkey
4 medium bell peppers
1 (15-ounce / 425-g) can black beans, drained and rinsed
1 cup shredded reduced-fat Cheddar cheese
1 cup cooked long-grain brown rice
1 cup mild salsa
1¼ teaspoons chili powder
1 teaspoon salt
½ teaspoon ground cumin
½ teaspoon freshly ground black pepper
Olive oil spray
Chopped fresh cilantro, for garnish

1. In a large skillet over medium-high heat, cook the turkey, breaking it up with a spoon, until browned, about 5 minutes. Drain off any excess fat.
2. Cut about ½ inch off the tops of the peppers and then cut in half lengthwise. Remove and discard the seeds and set the peppers aside.
3. In a large bowl, combine the browned turkey, black beans, Cheddar cheese, rice, salsa, chili powder, salt, cumin, and black pepper. Spoon the mixture into the bell peppers.
4. Lightly spray the air fryer basket with olive oil spray.
5. Place the stuffed peppers in the air fryer basket. Select the AIR FRY function and cook at 360°F (182°C) for 10 to 15 minutes, or until heated through. Garnish with cilantro and serve.

Blackened Chicken Breasts

Prep time: 10 minutes | Cook time: 20 minutes | Serves 4

1 large egg, beaten
¾ cup Blackened seasoning
2 whole boneless, skinless chicken
breasts (about 1 pound / 454 g each), halved
Cooking spray

1. Line the air fryer basket with parchment paper.
2. Place the beaten egg in one shallow bowl and the Blackened seasoning in another shallow bowl.
3. One at a time, dip the chicken pieces in the beaten egg and the Blackened seasoning, coating thoroughly.
4. Place the chicken pieces on the parchment and spritz with cooking spray.
5. Select the AIR FRY function and cook at 360°F (182°C) for 10 minutes. Flip the chicken, spritz it with cooking spray, and air fry for 10 minutes more until the internal temperature reaches 165°F (74°C) and the chicken is no longer pink inside. Let sit for 5 minutes before serving.

Dill Chicken Strips

Prep time: 15 minutes | Cook time: 10 minutes | Serves 4

2 whole boneless, skinless chicken breasts, halved lengthwise
1 cup Italian dressing
3 cups finely
crushed potato chips
1 tablespoon dried dill weed
1 tablespoon garlic powder
1 large egg, beaten
Cooking spray

1. In a large resealable bag, combine the chicken and Italian dressing. Seal the bag and refrigerate to marinate at least 1 hour.
2. In a shallow dish, stir together the potato chips, dill, and garlic powder. Place the beaten egg in a second shallow dish.
3. Remove the chicken from the marinade. Roll the chicken pieces in the egg and the potato chip mixture, coating thoroughly.
4. Select the BAKE function and preheat MAXX to 325°F (163°C). Line the air fryer basket with parchment paper.
5. Place the coated chicken on the parchment and spritz with cooking spray.
6. Bake for 5 minutes. Flip the chicken, spritz it with cooking spray, and bake for 5 minutes more until the outsides are crispy and the insides are no longer pink. Serve immediately.

Pecan-Crusted Turkey Cutlets

Prep time: 10 minutes | Cook time: 10 to 12 minutes | Serves 4

¾ cup panko bread crumbs
¼ teaspoon salt
¼ teaspoon pepper
¼ teaspoon dry mustard
¼ teaspoon poultry seasoning
½ cup pecans

¼ cup cornstarch
1 egg, beaten
1 pound (454 g) turkey cutlets, ½-inch thick
Salt and pepper, to taste
Cooking spray

1. Place the panko crumbs, salt, pepper, mustard, and poultry seasoning in a food processor. Process until crumbs are finely crushed. Add pecans and process just until nuts are finely chopped.
2. Place cornstarch in a shallow dish and beaten egg in another. Transfer coating mixture from food processor into a third shallow dish.
3. Sprinkle turkey cutlets with salt and pepper to taste.
4. Dip cutlets in cornstarch and shake off excess, then dip in beaten egg and finally roll in crumbs, pressing to coat well. Spray both sides with cooking spray.
5. Place 2 cutlets in air fryer basket in a single layer. Select the AIR FRY function and cook at 360ºF (182ºC) for 10 to 12 minutes. Repeat with the remaining cutlets.
6. Serve warm.

Honey Rosemary Chicken

Prep time: 10 minutes | Cook time: 20 minutes | Serves 4

¼ cup balsamic vinegar
¼ cup honey
2 tablespoons olive oil
1 tablespoon dried rosemary leaves
1 teaspoon salt

½ teaspoon freshly ground black pepper
2 whole boneless, skinless chicken breasts (about 1 pound / 454 g each), halved
Cooking spray

1. In a large resealable bag, combine the vinegar, honey, olive oil, rosemary, salt, and pepper. Add the chicken pieces, seal the bag, and refrigerate to marinate for at least 2 hours.

2. Select the BAKE function and preheat MAXX to 325ºF (163ºC). Line the air fryer basket with parchment paper.
3. Remove the chicken from the marinade and place it on the parchment. Spritz with cooking spray.
4. Bake for 10 minutes. Flip the chicken, spritz it with cooking spray, and bake for 10 minutes more until the internal temperature reaches 165ºF (74ºC) and the chicken is no longer pink inside. Let sit for 5 minutes before serving.

Sweet and Spicy Turkey Meatballs

Prep time: 15 minutes | Cook time: 15 minutes | Serves 6

1 pound (454 g) lean ground turkey
½ cup whole-wheat panko bread crumbs
1 egg, beaten
1 tablespoon soy sauce
¼ cup plus 1 tablespoon hoisin

sauce, divided
2 teaspoons minced garlic
⅛ teaspoon salt
⅛ teaspoon freshly ground black pepper
1 teaspoon sriracha
Olive oil spray

1. Spray the air fryer basket lightly with olive oil spray.
2. In a large bowl, mix together the turkey, panko bread crumbs, egg, soy sauce, 1 tablespoon of hoisin sauce, garlic, salt, and black pepper.
3. Using a tablespoon, form the mixture into 24 meatballs.
4. In a small bowl, combine the remaining ¼ cup of hoisin sauce and sriracha to make a glaze and set aside.
5. Place the meatballs in the air fryer basket in a single layer. You may need to cook them in batches.
6. Select the AIR FRY function and cook at 350ºF (177ºC) for 8 minutes. Brush the meatballs generously with the glaze and air fry until cooked through, an additional 4 to 7 minutes. Serve warm.

Roasted Cajun Turkey

Prep time: 10 minutes | Cook time: 30 minutes | Serves 4

2 pounds (907 g) turkey thighs, skinless and boneless
1 red onion, sliced
2 bell peppers, sliced
1 habanero pepper, minced

1 carrot, sliced
1 tablespoon Cajun seasoning mix
1 tablespoon fish sauce
2 cups chicken broth
Nonstick cooking spray

1. Select the ROAST function and preheat MAXX to 360ºF (182ºC).
2. Spritz the bottom and sides of a baking dish with nonstick cooking spray.
3. Arrange the turkey thighs in the baking dish. Add the onion, peppers, and carrot. Sprinkle with Cajun seasoning. Add the fish sauce and chicken broth.
4. Roast in the preheated air fryer oven for 30 minutes until cooked through. Serve warm.

Apricot Glazed Turkey Tenderloin

Prep time: 20 minutes | Cook time: 30 minutes | Serves 4

¼ cup sugar-free apricot preserves
½ tablespoon spicy brown mustard
1½ pounds (680 g) turkey breast

tenderloin
Salt and freshly ground black pepper, to taste
Olive oil spray

1. Spray the air fryer basket lightly with olive oil spray.
2. In a small bowl, combine the apricot preserves and mustard to make a paste.
3. Season the turkey with salt and pepper. Spread the apricot paste all over the turkey.
4. Place the turkey in the air fryer basket and lightly spray with olive oil spray.
5. Select the AIR FRY function and cook at 370ºF (188ºC) for 15 minutes. Flip the turkey over and lightly spray with olive oil spray. Air fry until the internal temperature reaches at least 170ºF (77ºC), an additional 10 to 15 minutes.
6. Let the turkey rest for 10 minutes before slicing and serving.

Turkey, Hummus, and Cheese Wraps

Prep time: 10 minutes | Cook time: 3 to 4 minutes | Serves 4

4 large whole wheat wraps
½ cup hummus
16 thin slices deli turkey

8 slices provolone cheese
1 cup fresh baby spinach, or more to taste

1. To assemble, place 2 tablespoons of hummus on each wrap and spread to within about a half inch from edges. Top with 4 slices of turkey and 2 slices of provolone. Finish with ¼ cup of baby spinach, or pile on as much as you like.
2. Roll up each wrap. You don't need to fold or seal the ends.
3. Place 2 wraps in air fryer basket, seam-side down.
4. Select the AIR FRY function and cook at 360ºF (182ºC) for 3 to 4 minutes to warm filling and melt cheese.
5. Repeat with the remaining wraps. Serve immediately.

Spiced Turkey Tenderloin

Prep time: 20 minutes | Cook time: 30 minutes | Serves 4

½ teaspoon paprika
½ teaspoon garlic powder
½ teaspoon salt
½ teaspoon freshly ground black pepper

Pinch cayenne pepper
1½ pounds (680 g) turkey breast tenderloin
Olive oil spray

1. Spray the air fryer basket lightly with olive oil spray.
2. In a small bowl, combine the paprika, garlic powder, salt, black pepper, and cayenne pepper. Rub the mixture all over the turkey.
3. Place the turkey in the air fryer basket and lightly spray with olive oil spray.
4. Select the AIR FRY function and cook at 370ºF (188ºC) for 15 minutes. Flip the turkey over and lightly spray with olive oil spray. Air fry until the internal temperature reaches at least 170ºF (77ºC) for an additional 10 to 15 minutes.
5. Let the turkey rest for 10 minutes before slicing and serving.

Potato Cheese Crusted Chicken

Prep time: 15 minutes | Cook time: 22 to 25 minutes | Serves 4

¼ cup buttermilk
1 large egg, beaten
1 cup instant potato flakes
¼ cup grated Parmesan cheese
1 teaspoon salt
½ teaspoon freshly

ground black pepper
2 whole boneless, skinless chicken breasts (about 1 pound / 454 g each), halved
Cooking spray

1. Select the BAKE function and preheat MAXX to 325ºF (163ºC). Line the air fryer basket with parchment paper.
2. In a shallow bowl, whisk the buttermilk and egg until blended. In another shallow bowl, stir together the potato flakes, cheese, salt, and pepper.
3. One at a time, dip the chicken pieces in the buttermilk mixture and the potato flake mixture, coating thoroughly.
4. Place the coated chicken on the parchment and spritz with cooking spray.
5. Bake for 15 minutes. Flip the chicken, spritz it with cooking spray, and bake for 7 to 10 minutes more until the outside is crispy and the inside is no longer pink. Serve immediately.

Turkey Hoisin Burgers

Prep time: 10 minutes | Cook time: 20 minutes | Serves 4

1 pound (454 g) lean ground turkey
¼ cup whole-wheat bread crumbs
¼ cup hoisin sauce

2 tablespoons soy sauce
4 whole-wheat buns
Olive oil spray

1. In a large bowl, mix together the turkey, bread crumbs, hoisin sauce, and soy sauce.
2. Form the mixture into 4 equal patties. Cover with plastic wrap and refrigerate the patties for 30 minutes.
3. Spray the air fryer basket lightly with olive oil spray.
4. Place the patties in the air fryer basket in a single layer. Spray the patties lightly with olive oil spray.

5. Select the AIR FRY function and cook at 370ºF (188ºC) for 10 minutes. Flip the patties over, lightly spray with olive oil spray, and air fry for an additional 5 to 10 minutes, until golden brown.
6. Place the patties on buns and top with your choice of low-calorie burger toppings like sliced tomatoes, onions, and cabbage slaw. Serve immediately.

Easy Asian Turkey Meatballs

Prep time: 10 minutes | Cook time: 11 to 14 minutes | Serves 4

2 tablespoons peanut oil, divided
1 small onion, minced
¼ cup water chestnuts, finely chopped
½ teaspoon ground

ginger
2 tablespoons low-sodium soy sauce
¼ cup panko bread crumbs
1 egg, beaten
1 pound (454 g) ground turkey

1. Select the BAKE function and preheat MAXX to 400ºF (204ºC).
2. In a round metal pan, combine 1 tablespoon of peanut oil and onion. Bake for 1 to 2 minutes or until crisp and tender. Transfer the onion to a medium bowl.
3. Add the water chestnuts, ground ginger, soy sauce, and bread crumbs to the onion and mix well. Add egg and stir well. Mix in the ground turkey until combined.
4. Form the mixture into 1-inch meatballs. Drizzle the remaining 1 tablespoon of oil over the meatballs.
5. Bake the meatballs in the pan in batches for 10 to 12 minutes or until they are 165ºF (74ºC) on a meat thermometer. Rest for 5 minutes before serving.

Tex-Mex Turkey Burgers

Prep time: 10 minutes | Cook time: 14 to 16 minutes | Serves 4

⅓ cup finely crushed corn tortilla chips
1 egg, beaten
¼ cup salsa
⅓ cup shredded pepper Jack cheese
Pinch salt

Freshly ground black pepper, to taste
1 pound (454 g) ground turkey
1 tablespoon olive oil
1 teaspoon paprika

1. In a medium bowl, combine the tortilla chips, egg, salsa, cheese, salt, and pepper, and mix well.
2. Add the turkey and mix gently but thoroughly with clean hands.
3. Form the meat mixture into patties about ½ inch thick. Make an indentation in the center of each patty with your thumb so the burgers don't puff up while cooking.
4. Brush the patties on both sides with the olive oil and sprinkle with paprika.
5. Put in the air fryer basket. Select the AIR FRY function and cook at 330°F (166°C) for 14 to 16 minutes, or until the meat registers at least 165°F (74°C).
6. Let sit for 5 minutes before serving.

Mini Turkey Meatloaves with Carrot

Prep time: 6 minutes | Cook time: 20 to 24 minutes | Serves 4

⅓ cup minced onion
¼ cup grated carrot
2 garlic cloves, minced
2 tablespoons ground almonds
2 teaspoons olive oil

1 teaspoon dried marjoram
1 egg white
¾ pound (340 g) ground turkey breast

1. Select the BAKE function and preheat MAXX to 400°F (204°C).
2. In a medium bowl, stir together the onion, carrot, garlic, almonds, olive oil, marjoram, and egg white.
3. Add the ground turkey. With your hands, gently but thoroughly mix until combined.

4. Double 16 foil muffin cup liners to make 8 cups. Divide the turkey mixture evenly among the liners.
5. Bake for 20 to 24 minutes, or until the meatloaves reach an internal temperature of 165°F (74°C) on a meat thermometer. Serve immediately.

air fryer oven Naked Chicken Tenders

Prep time: 5 minutes | Cook time: 7 minutes | Serves 4

Seasoning:
1 teaspoon kosher salt
½ teaspoon garlic powder
½ teaspoon onion powder

½ teaspoon chili powder
¼ teaspoon sweet paprika
¼ teaspoon freshly ground black pepper

Chicken:
8 chicken breast tenders (1 pound / 454 g total)

2 tablespoons mayonnaise

1. For the seasoning: In a small bowl, combine the salt, garlic powder, onion powder, chili powder, paprika, and pepper.
2. For the chicken: Place the chicken in a medium bowl and add the mayonnaise. Mix well to coat all over, then sprinkle with the seasoning mix.
3. Working in batches, arrange a single layer of the chicken in the air fryer basket. Select the AIR FRY function and cook at 375°F (191°C) for 6 to 7 minutes, flipping halfway, until cooked through in the center. Serve immediately.

Chapter 6 Rotisserie Recipes

Marinated Medium Rare Rotisserie Beef

Prep time: 15 minutes | Cook time: 1 hour 40 minutes | Serves 6 to 8

5 pounds (2.3 kg) eye round beef roast
2 onions, sliced
3 cups white wine
3 cloves garlic, minced
1 teaspoon chopped fresh rosemary
1 teaspoon celery seeds
1 teaspoon fresh

thyme leaves
¾ cup olive oil
1 tablespoon coarse sea salt
1 tablespoon ground black pepper
1 teaspoon dried sage
2 tablespoons unsalted butter

1. Place beef roast and onions in a large resealable bag.
2. In a small bowl, combine the wine, garlic, rosemary, celery seeds, thyme leaves, oil, salt, pepper, and sage.
3. Pour the marinade mixture over the beef roast and seal the bag. Refrigerate the roast for up to one day.
4. Remove the beef roast from the marinade. Using the rotisserie spit, push through the beef roast and attach the rotisserie forks.
5. If desired, place aluminum foil onto the drip pan. (It makes for easier clean-up!)
6. Select the ROAST function and preheat MAXX to 400ºF (205ºC). Press ROTATE button and set time to 1 hour 40 minutes.
7. Once preheated, place the prepared lamb leg with rotisserie spit into the oven. Baste the beef roast with marinade for every 30 minutes.
8. When cooking is complete, remove the lamb leg using the rotisserie handle and, using hot pads or gloves, carefully remove the lamb leg from the spit.
9. Remove the roast to a platter and allow the roast to rest for 10 minutes.
10. Slice thin and serve.

Rotisserie Chicken with Lemon

Prep time: 10 minutes | Cook time: 40 minutes | Serves 6

1 (4 pounds / 1.8 kg) whole chicken
2 teaspoons paprika
1½ teaspoons thyme
1 teaspoon onion powder
1 teaspoon garlic

powder
Salt and pepper, to taste
¼ cup butter, melted
2 tablespoons olive oil
1 lemon, sliced
2 sprigs rosemary

1. Remove the giblets from the chicken cavity and carefully loosen the skin starting at the neck.
2. In a bowl, mix together the paprika, thyme, onion powder, garlic powder, salt, and pepper. Set aside.
3. Rub the melted butter under the skin and pat the skin back into place.
4. Truss the chicken, ensuring the wings and legs are tied closely together and the cavity is closed up.
5. Drizzle the olive oil all over the chicken and rub it into the chicken.
6. Rub the spice mixture onto the chicken's skin.
7. Place the lemon slices and sprigs of rosemary into the cavity.
8. Using the rotisserie spit, push through the chicken and attach the rotisserie forks.
9. If desired, place aluminum foil onto the drip pan. (It makes for easier clean-up!)
10. Select the ROAST function and preheat MAXX to 380ºF (193ºC). Press ROTATE button and set time to 40 minutes.
11. Once the unit has preheated, place the prepared chicken with the rotisserie spit into the oven.
12. When cooking is complete, remove the chicken using the rotisserie handle and, using hot pads or gloves, carefully remove the chicken from the spit.
13. Let sit for 10 minutes before slicing and serving.

Red Wine Rotisserie Lamb Leg

Prep time: 25 minutes | Cook time: 1 hour 30 hours | Serves 6 to 8

1 (5-pound / 2.3-kg) leg of lamb, bone-in, fat trimmed, rinsed and drained

For the Marinade:

¼ cup dry red wine
1 large shallot, roughly chopped
4 garlic cloves, peeled and roughly chopped
5 large sage leaves
Juice of 1 lemon
2 teaspoons Worcestershire sauce
½ teaspoon allspice
¾ cup fresh mint leaves
3 tablespoons fresh rosemary
⅓ cup beef stock
½ teaspoon coriander powder
2 teaspoons brown sugar
½ teaspoon cayenne pepper
½ cup olive oil
2 teaspoons salt
1 teaspoon black pepper

For the Baste:

1 cup beef stock
¼ cup marinade mixture
Garnish: salt and black pepper

1. Combine the marinade ingredients in a large bowl. Stir to mix well. Remove ¼ cup of the marinade and set aside.
2. Apply remaining marinade onto lamb leg. Place the lamb leg into a baking dish, cover and refrigerate for 1 to 2 hours.
3. Combine the ingredients for the baste in a small bowl. Stir to mix well. Set aside until ready to use.
4. Using the rotisserie spit, push through the lamb leg and attach the rotisserie forks.
5. If desired, place aluminum foil onto the drip pan. (It makes for easier clean-up!)
6. Select the ROAST function and preheat MAXX to 350ºF (180ºC). Press ROTATE button and set time to 1 hour 30 minutes.
7. Once preheated, place the prepared lamb leg with rotisserie spit into the oven.
8. After the first 30 minutes of cooking, apply the baste over the lamb leg for every 20 minutes.
9. When cooking is complete, remove the lamb leg using the rotisserie handle and, using hot pads or gloves, carefully remove the lamb leg from the spit.
10. Carve and serve.

Bourbon Rotisserie Pork Shoulder

Prep time: 30 minutes | Cook time: 4 hours 30 minutes | Serves 6 to 8

1 (5-pound / 2.3-kg) boneless pork shoulder
1 tablespoon kosher salt

For the Rub:

2 teaspoons ground black peppercorns
2 teaspoons ground mustard seed
2 tablespoons light brown sugar
1 teaspoon onion powder
1 teaspoon garlic powder
1 teaspoon paprika

For the Mop:

1 cup bourbon
1 small onion, granulated
¼ cup corn syrup
¼ cup ketchup
2 tablespoons brown mustard
½ cup light brown sugar

1. Combine the ingredients for the rub in a small bowl. Stir to mix well.
2. Season pork shoulder all over with rub, wrap in plastic, and place in refrigerator for 12 to 15 hours.
3. Remove roast from the fridge and let meat stand at room temperature for 30 to 45 minutes. Season with kosher salt.
4. Whisk ingredients for mop in a medium bowl. Set aside until ready to use.
5. Using the rotisserie spit, push through the pork should and attach the rotisserie forks.
6. If desired, place aluminum foil onto the drip pan. (It makes for easier clean-up!)
7. Select the ROAST function and preheat MAXX to 450ºF (235ºC). Press ROTATE button and set time to 30 minutes.
8. Once preheated, place the prepared pork with rotisserie spit into the oven.
9. After 30 minutes, reduce the temperature to 250ºF (121ºC) and roast for 4 more hours or until an meat thermometer inserted in the center of the pork reads at least 145ºF (63ºC).
10. After the first hour of cooking, apply mop over the pork for every 20 minutes.
11. When cooking is complete, remove the pork using the rotisserie handle and, using hot pads or gloves, carefully remove the pork tenderloin from the spit.
12. Let stand for 10 minutes before slicing and serving.

Air Fried Beef Roast

Prep time: 5 minutes | Cook time: 38 minutes | Serves 6

2.5 pound (1.1 kg) beef roast
1 tablespoon olive oil
1 tablespoon Poultry seasoning

1. Tie the beef roast and rub the olive oil all over the roast. Sprinkle with the seasoning.
2. Using the rotisserie spit, push through the beef roast and attach the rotisserie forks.
3. If desired, place aluminum foil onto the drip pan. (It makes for easier clean-up!)
4. Select the AIR FRY function and set the temperature to 360°F (182°C). Press ROTATE button and set time to 38 minutes for medium rare beef.
5. Place the prepared chicken with rotisserie spit into the oven.
6. When cooking is complete, remove the beef roast using the rotisserie handle and, using hot pads or gloves, carefully remove the beef roast from the spit.
7. Let cool for 5 minutes before serving.

Easy Rotisserie Chicken

Prep time: 10 minutes | Cook time: 50 minutes | Serves 4

2 cups buttermilk
¼ cup olive oil
1 teaspoon garlic powder
1 tablespoon sea
salt
1 whole chicken
Salt and pepper, to taste

1. In a large bag, place the buttermilk, oil, garlic powder, and sea salt and mix to combine.
2. Add the whole chicken and let marinate for 24 hours up to two days.
3. Remove the chicken and sprinkle with the salt and pepper.
4. Truss the chicken, removing the wings and ensuring the legs are tied closely together and the thighs are held in place.
5. Using the rotisserie spit, push through the chicken and attach the rotisserie forks.

6. If desired, place aluminum foil onto the drip pan. (It makes for easier clean-up!)
7. Select the AIR FRY function and set the temperature to 380°F (193°C). Press ROTATE button and set time to 50 minutes.
8. Once the unit has preheated, place the prepared chicken with the rotisserie spit into the oven.
9. When cooking is complete, the chicken should be dark brown and internal temperature should measure 165 degrees (measure at the meatiest part of the thigh).
10. Remove the chicken using the rotisserie handle and, using hot pads or gloves, carefully remove the chicken from the spit.
11. Let sit for 10 minutes before slicing and serving.

Sriracha Honey Pork Tenderloin

Prep time: 20 minutes | Cook time: 25 minutes | Serves 2 to 3

1 pound (454 g) pork tenderloin
2 tablespoons Sriracha hot sauce
2 tablespoons honey
1½ teaspoons kosher salt

1. Stir together the Sriracha hot sauce, honey and salt in a bowl. Rub the sauce all over the pork tenderloin.
2. Using the rotisserie spit, push through the pork tenderloin and attach the rotisserie forks.
3. If desired, place aluminum foil onto the drip pan. (It makes for easier clean-up!)
4. Select the AIR FRY function and set the temperature to 350°F (180°C). Press ROTATE button and set time to 20 minutes.
5. Place the prepared pork tenderloin with rotisserie spit into the oven.
6. When cooking is complete, remove the pork tenderloin using the rotisserie handle and, using hot pads or gloves, carefully remove the chicken from the spit.
7. Let rest for 5 minutes and serve.

Honey Glazed Rotisserie Ham

Prep time: 20 minutes | Cook time: 3 hours | Serves 6

1 (5-pound/2.3-kg) cooked boneless ham, pat dry

For the Glaze:

½ cup honey	cloves
2 teaspoons lemon juice	1 teaspoon cinnamon
1 teaspoon ground	½ cup brown sugar

1. Using the rotisserie spit, push through the ham and attach the rotisserie forks.
2. If desired, place aluminum foil onto the drip pan. (It makes for easier clean-up!)
3. Select the ROAST function and preheat MAXX to 250ºF (121ºC). Press ROTATE button and set time to 3 hours.
4. Once preheated, place the prepared ham with rotisserie spit into the oven.
5. Meanwhile, combine the ingredients for the glaze in a small bowl. Stir to mix well.
6. When the ham has reached 145ºF (63ºC), brush the glaze mixture over all surfaces of the ham.
7. When cooking is complete, remove the ham using the rotisserie handle and, using hot pads or gloves, carefully remove the ham from the spit.
8. Let it rest for 10 minutes covered loosely with foil and then carve and serve.

Greek Rotisserie Lamb Leg

Prep time: 25 minutes | Cook time: 1 hour 30 minutes | Serves 4 to 6

3 pounds (1.4 kg) leg of lamb, boned in

For the Marinade:

1 tablespoon lemon zest (about 1 lemon)	powder
3 tablespoons lemon juice (about 1½ lemons)	1 teaspoon fresh thyme
	¼ cup fresh oregano
3 cloves garlic, minced	¼ cup olive oil
1 teaspoon onion	1 teaspoon ground black pepper

For the Herb Dressing:

1 tablespoon lemon juice (about ½ lemon)	thyme
	1 tablespoon olive oil
¼ cup chopped fresh oregano	1 teaspoon sea salt
1 teaspoon fresh	Ground black pepper, to taste

1. Place lamb leg into a large resealable plastic bag. Combine the ingredients for the marinade in a small bowl. Stir to mix well.
2. Pour the marinade over the lamb, making sure the meat is completely coated. Seal the bag and place in the refrigerator. Marinate for 4 to 6 hours before grilling.
3. Remove the lamb leg from the marinade. Using the rotisserie spit, push through the lamb leg and attach the rotisserie forks.
4. If desired, place aluminum foil onto the drip pan. (It makes for easier clean-up!)
5. Select the ROAST function and preheat MAXX to 350ºF (180ºC). Press ROTATE button and set time to 1 hour 30 minutes.
6. Once preheated, place the prepared lamb leg with rotisserie spit into the oven. Baste with marinade for every 30 minutes.
7. Meanwhile, combine the ingredients for the herb dressing in a bowl. Stir to mix well.
8. When cooking is complete, remove the lamb leg using the rotisserie handle and, using hot pads or gloves, carefully remove the lamb leg from the spit.
9. Cover lightly with aluminum foil for 8 to 10 minutes.
10. Carve the leg and arrange on a platter,. Drizzle with herb dressing. Serve immediately.

Apple and Carrot Stuffed Rotisserie Turkey

Prep time: 30 minutes | Cook time: 3 hours | Serves 12 to 14

1 (12-pound/5.4-kg) turkey, giblet removed, rinsed and pat dry

For the Seasoning:

¼ cup lemon pepper
2 tablespoons chopped fresh parsley
1 tablespoon celery salt
2 cloves garlic, minced
2 teaspoons ground black pepper
1 teaspoon sage

For the Stuffing:

1 medium onion, cut into 8 equal parts
1 carrot, sliced
1 apple, cored and cut into 8 thick slices

1. Mix together the seasoning in a small bowl. Rub over the surface and inside of the turkey.
2. Stuff the turkey with the onions, carrots, and apples. Using the rotisserie spit, push through the turkey and attach the rotisserie forks.
3. If desired, place aluminum foil onto the drip pan. (It makes for easier clean-up!)
4. Select the ROAST function and preheat MAXX to 350ºF (180ºC). Press ROTATE button and set time to 3 hours.
5. Once preheated, place the prepared turkey with rotisserie spit into the oven.
6. When cooking is complete, the internal temperature should read at least 180ºF (82ºC). Remove the lamb leg using the rotisserie handle and, using hot pads or gloves, carefully remove the turkey from the spit.
7. Server hot.

Whole Rotisserie Chicken

Prep time: 10 minutes | Cook time: 45 minutes | Serves 4

3 pounds (1.4 kg) tied whole chicken
3 cloves garlic, halved
1 whole lemon, quartered
2 sprigs fresh rosemary whole
2 tablespoons olive oil

Chicken Rub:

½ teaspoon fresh ground pepper
½ teaspoon salt
1 teaspoon garlic powder
1 teaspoon dried oregano
1 teaspoon paprika
1 sprig rosemary (leaves only)

1. Mix together the rub ingredients in a small bowl. Set aside.
2. Place the chicken on a clean cutting board. Ensure the cavity of the chicken is clean. Stuff the chicken cavity with the garlic, lemon, and rosemary.
3. Tie your chicken with twine if needed. Pat the chicken dry.
4. Drizzle the olive oil all over and coat the entire chicken with a brush.
5. Shake the rub on the chicken and rub in until the chicken is covered.
6. Using the rotisserie spit, push through the chicken and attach the rotisserie forks.
7. If desired, place aluminum foil onto the drip pan. (It makes for easier clean-up!)
8. Select the AIR FRY function and set the temperature to 375ºF (190ºC). Press ROTATE button and set time to 40 minutes.
9. Once the unit has preheated, place the prepared chicken with the rotisserie spit into the oven.
10. At 40 minutes, check the temperature every 5 minutes until the chicken reaches 165ºF (74ºC) in the breast, or 165ºF (85ºC) in the thigh.
11. Once cooking is complete, remove the chicken using the rotisserie handle and, using hot pads or gloves, carefully remove the chicken from the spit.
12. Let the chicken sit, covered, for 5 to 10 minutes.
13. Slice and serve.

Chapter 7 Meats

BBQ Pork Steaks

Prep time: 5 minutes | Cook time: 15 minutes | Serves 4

4 pork steaks
1 tablespoon Cajun seasoning
2 tablespoons BBQ sauce
1 tablespoon vinegar
1 teaspoon soy sauce
½ cup brown sugar
½ cup ketchup

1. Sprinkle pork steaks with Cajun seasoning.
2. Combine remaining ingredients and brush onto steaks.
3. Add coated steaks to air fryer oven. Select the AIR FRY function and cook at 290ºF (143ºC) for 15 minutes, or until just browned.
4. Serve immediately.

Cheddar Bacon Burst with Spinach

Prep time: 5 minutes | Cook time: 60 minutes | Serves 8

30 slices bacon
1 tablespoon Chipotle seasoning
2 teaspoons Italian
seasoning
2½ cups Cheddar cheese
4 cups raw spinach

1. Select the BAKE function and preheat MAXX to 375ºF (191ºC).
2. Weave the bacon into 15 vertical pieces and 12 horizontal pieces. Cut the extra 3 in half to fill in the rest, horizontally.
3. Season the bacon with Chipotle seasoning and Italian seasoning.
4. Add the cheese to the bacon.
5. Add the spinach and press down to compress.
6. Tightly roll up the woven bacon.
7. Line a baking sheet with kitchen foil and add plenty of salt to it.
8. Put the bacon on top of a cooling rack and put that on top of the baking sheet.
9. Bake for 60 minutes.
10. Let cool for 15 minutes before slicing and serving.

Herbed Beef

Prep time: 5 minutes | Cook time: 22 minutes | Serves 6

1 teaspoon dried dill
1 teaspoon dried thyme
1 teaspoon garlic
powder
2 pounds (907 g) beef steak
3 tablespoons butter

1. Combine the dill, thyme, and garlic powder in a small bowl, and massage into the steak. Transfer the steak to the air fryer basket.
2. Select the AIR FRY function and cook at 360ºF (182ºC) for 20 minutes. Then remove, shred, and return to the air fryer oven.
3. Add the butter and air fry the shredded steak for a further 2 minutes at 365ºF (185ºC). Make sure the beef is coated in the butter before serving.

Peppercorn Crusted Beef Tenderloin

Prep time: 5 minutes | Cook time: 25 minutes | Serves 6

2 pounds (907 g) beef tenderloin
2 teaspoons roasted garlic, minced
2 tablespoons salted
butter, melted
3 tablespoons ground 4 peppercorn blend

1. Remove any surplus fat from the beef tenderloin.
2. Combine the roasted garlic and melted butter to apply to the tenderloin with a brush.
3. On a plate, spread out the peppercorns and roll the tenderloin in them, making sure they are covering and clinging to the meat. Transfer the tenderloin to the air fryer basket.
4. Select the AIR FRY function and cook at 400ºF (204ºC) for 25 minutes, turning halfway through cooking.
5. Let the tenderloin rest for ten minutes before slicing and serving.

Beef Loin with Thyme and Parsley

Prep time: 5 minutes | Cook time: 15 minutes | Serves 4

1 tablespoon butter, melted
¼ dried thyme
1 teaspoon garlic salt
¼ teaspoon dried parsley
1 pound (454 g) beef loin

1. In a bowl, combine the melted butter, thyme, garlic salt, and parsley.
2. Cut the beef loin into slices and generously apply the seasoned butter using a brush. Transfer to the air fryer basket.
3. Select the AIR FRY function and cook at 400ºF (204ºC) for 15 minutes.
4. Take care when removing it and serve hot.

Lamb Meatballs

Prep time: 20 minutes | Cook time: 8 minutes | Serves 4

Meatballs:

½ small onion, finely diced
1 clove garlic, minced
1 pound (454 g) ground lamb
2 tablespoons fresh parsley, finely chopped (plus more for garnish)
2 teaspoons fresh oregano, finely chopped
2 tablespoons milk
1 egg yolk
Salt and freshly ground black pepper, to taste
½ cup crumbled feta cheese, for garnish

Tomato Sauce:

2 tablespoons butter
1 clove garlic, smashed
Pinch crushed red pepper flakes
¼ teaspoon ground cinnamon
1 (28-ounce / 794-g) can crushed tomatoes
Salt, to taste
Olive oil, for greasing

1. Combine all ingredients for the meatballs in a large bowl and mix just until everything is combined. Shape the mixture into 1½-inch balls or shape the meat between two spoons to make quenelles.
2. While the air fryer oven is preheating, start the quick tomato sauce. Put the butter, garlic and red pepper flakes in a sauté pan and heat over medium heat on the stovetop. Let the garlic sizzle a little, but before the butter browns, add the cinnamon and tomatoes. Bring to a simmer and simmer for 15 minutes. Season with salt.
3. Grease the bottom of the air fryer basket with olive oil and transfer the meatballs to the air fryer basket in one layer, air frying in batches if necessary.
4. Select the AIR FRY function and cook at 400ºF (204ºC) for 8 minutes, giving the basket a shake once during the cooking process to turn the meatballs over.
5. To serve, spoon a pool of the tomato sauce onto plates and add the meatballs. Sprinkle the feta cheese on top and garnish with more fresh parsley.

Super Bacon with Meat

Prep time: 5 minutes | Cook time: 1 hour | Serves 4

30 slices thick-cut bacon
4 ounces (113 g) Cheddar cheese, shredded
12 ounces (340 g) steak
10 ounces (283 g) pork sausage
Salt and ground black pepper, to taste

1. Select the BAKE function and preheat MAXX to 400ºF (204ºC).
2. Lay out 30 slices of bacon in a woven pattern and bake for 20 minutes until crisp. Put the cheese in the center of the bacon.
3. Combine the steak and sausage to form a meaty mixture.
4. Lay out the meat in a rectangle of similar size to the bacon strips. Season with salt and pepper.
5. Roll the meat into a tight roll and refrigerate.
6. Bake for 60 minutes or until the internal temperature reaches at least 165ºF (74ºC).
7. Let rest for 5 minutes before serving.

Spinach and Beef Braciole

Prep time: 25 minutes | Cook time: 1 hour 32 minutes | Serves 4

½ onion, finely chopped
1 teaspoon olive oil
⅓ cup red wine
2 cups crushed tomatoes
1 teaspoon Italian seasoning
½ teaspoon garlic powder
¼ teaspoon crushed red pepper flakes
2 tablespoons chopped fresh parsley
2 top round steaks (about 1½ pounds /

680 g)
salt and freshly ground black pepper
2 cups fresh spinach, chopped
1 clove minced garlic
½ cup roasted red peppers, julienned
½ cup grated pecorino cheese
¼ cup pine nuts, toasted and roughly chopped
2 tablespoons olive oil

1. Toss the onions and olive oil together in a baking pan or casserole dish. Select the AIR FRY function and cook at 400ºF (204ºC) for 5 minutes, stirring a couple times during the cooking process. Add the red wine, crushed tomatoes, Italian seasoning, garlic powder, red pepper flakes and parsley and stir. Cover the pan tightly with aluminum foil, lower the air fryer oven temperature to 350ºF (177ºC) and continue to air fry for 15 minutes.
2. While the sauce is simmering, prepare the beef. Using a meat mallet, pound the beef until it is ¼-inch thick. Season both sides of the beef with salt and pepper. Combine the spinach, garlic, red peppers, pecorino cheese, pine nuts and olive oil in a medium bowl. Season with salt and freshly ground black pepper. Disperse the mixture over the steaks. Starting at one of the short ends, roll the beef around the filling, tucking in the sides as you roll to ensure the filling is completely enclosed. Secure the beef rolls with toothpicks.
3. Remove the baking pan with the sauce from the air fryer oven and set it aside. Increase the air fryer oven temperature to 400ºF (204ºC).
4. Brush or spray the beef rolls with a little olive oil and air fry for 12 minutes, rotating the beef during the cooking process for even browning. When the beef is browned, submerge the rolls into the sauce in the baking pan, cover the pan with foil and return it to the air fryer oven. Reduce the temperature of the air fryer oven to 250ºF (121ºC) and air fry for 60 minutes.
5. Remove the beef rolls from the sauce. Cut each roll into slices and serve, ladling some sauce on top.

Sun-dried Tomato Crusted Chops

Prep time: 15 minutes | Cook time: 10 minutes | Serves 4

½ cup oil-packed sun-dried tomatoes
½ cup toasted almonds
¼ cup grated Parmesan cheese
½ cup olive oil, plus more for brushing the air fryer basket

2 tablespoons water
½ teaspoon salt
Freshly ground black pepper, to taste
4 center-cut boneless pork chops (about 1¼ pounds / 567 g)

1. Put the sun-dried tomatoes into a food processor and pulse them until they are coarsely chopped. Add the almonds, Parmesan cheese, olive oil, water, salt and pepper. Process into a smooth paste. Spread most of the paste (leave a little in reserve) onto both sides of the pork chops and then pierce the meat several times with a needle-style meat tenderizer or a fork. Let the pork chops sit and marinate for at least 1 hour (refrigerate if marinating for longer than 1 hour).
2. Brush more olive oil on the bottom of the air fryer basket. Transfer the pork chops into the air fryer basket, spooning a little more of the sun-dried tomato paste onto the pork chops if there are any gaps where the paste may have been rubbed off.
3. Select the AIR FRY function and cook at 370ºF (188ºC) for 10 minutes, turning the chops over halfway through.
4. When the pork chops have finished cooking, transfer them to a serving plate and serve.

Air Fried Baby Back Ribs

Prep time: 5 minutes | Cook time: 30 minutes | Serves 2

2 teaspoons red pepper flakes	Salt and ground black pepper, to taste
¾ ground ginger	
3 cloves minced garlic	2 baby back ribs

1. Combine the red pepper flakes, ginger, garlic, salt and pepper in a bowl, making sure to mix well. Massage the mixture into the baby back ribs. Transfer to the air fryer basket.
2. Select the AIR FRY function and cook at 350ºF (177ºC) for 30 minutes.
3. Take care when taking the rubs out of the air fryer oven. Put them on a serving dish and serve.

Bacon Wrapped Pork with Apple Gravy

Prep time: 10 minutes | Cook time: 25 minutes | Serves 4

Pork:

1 tablespoons Dijon mustard	1 pork tenderloin
	3 strips bacon

Apple Gravy:

3 tablespoons ghee, divided	flour
1 small shallot, chopped	1 cup vegetable broth
2 apples	½ teaspoon Dijon mustard
1 tablespoon almond	

1. Spread Dijon mustard all over tenderloin and wrap with strips of bacon.
2. Put into air fryer oven. Select the AIR FRY function and cook at 360ºF (182ºC) for 12 minutes. Use a meat thermometer to check for doneness.
3. To make sauce, heat 1 tablespoons of ghee in a pan and add shallots. Cook for 1 minute.
4. Then add apples, cooking for 4 minutes until softened.
5. Add flour and 2 tablespoons of ghee to make a roux. Add broth and mustard, stirring well to combine.
6. When sauce starts to bubble, add 1 cup of sautéed apples, cooking until sauce thickens.
7. Once pork tenderloin is cooked, allow to sit 8 minutes to rest before slicing.
8. Serve topped with apple gravy.

Pork Chop Stir Fry

Prep time: 10 minutes | Cook time: 20 minutes | Serves 4

1 tablespoon olive oil	2 sliced jalapeño peppers
¼ teaspoon ground black pepper	2 sliced scallions
½ teaspoon salt	2 tablespoons olive oil
1 egg white	¼ teaspoon ground white pepper
4 (4-ounce / 113-g) pork chops	1 teaspoon sea salt
¾ cup almond flour	

1. Coat the air fryer basket with olive oil.
2. Whisk black pepper, salt, and egg white together until foamy.
3. Cut pork chops into pieces, leaving just a bit on bones. Pat dry.
4. Add pieces of pork to egg white mixture, coating well. Let sit for marinade 20 minutes.
5. Put marinated chops into a large bowl and add almond flour. Dredge and shake off excess and place into air fryer oven.
6. Select the AIR FRY function and cook at 360ºF (182ºC) for 12 minutes.
7. Turn up the heat to 400ºF (205ºC) and air fry for another 6 minutes until pork chops are nice and crisp.
8. Meanwhile, remove jalapeño seeds and chop up. Chop scallions and mix with jalapeño pieces.
9. Heat a skillet with olive oil. Stir-fry the white pepper, salt, scallions, and jalapeños for 60 seconds. Then add fried pork pieces to skills and toss with scallion mixture. Stir-fry for 1 to 2 minutes until well coated and hot.
10. Serve immediately.

Bacon and Pear Stuffed Pork Chops

Prep time: 20 minutes | Cook time: 24 minutes | Serves 3

4 slices bacon, chopped
1 tablespoon butter
½ cup finely diced onion
⅓ cup chicken stock
1½ cups seasoned stuffing cubes
1 egg, beaten
½ teaspoon dried thyme
½ teaspoon salt
⅛ teaspoon freshly
ground black pepper
1 pear, finely diced
⅓ cup crumbled blue cheese
3 boneless center-cut pork chops (2-inch thick)
Olive oil, for greasing
Salt and freshly ground black pepper, to taste

1. Put the bacon into the air fryer basket. Select the AIR FRY function and cook at 400°F (204°C) for 6 minutes, stirring halfway through the cooking time. Remove the bacon and set it aside on a paper towel. Pour out the grease from the bottom of the air fryer oven.
2. To make the stuffing, melt the butter in a medium saucepan over medium heat on the stovetop. Add the onion and sauté for a few minutes until it starts to soften. Add the chicken stock and simmer for 1 minute. Remove the pan from the heat and add the stuffing cubes. Stir until the stock has been absorbed. Add the egg, dried thyme, salt and freshly ground black pepper, and stir until combined. Fold in the diced pear and crumbled blue cheese.
3. Put the pork chops on a cutting board. Using the palm of the hand to hold the chop flat and steady, slice into the side of the pork chop to make a pocket in the center of the chop. Leave about an inch of chop uncut and make sure you don't cut all the way through the pork chop. Brush both sides of the pork chops with olive oil and season with salt and freshly ground black pepper. Stuff each pork chop with a third of the stuffing, packing the stuffing tightly inside the pocket.
4. Adjust the temperature to 360°F (182°C).
5. Spray or brush the sides of the air fryer basket with oil. Put the pork chops in the air fryer basket with the open, stuffed edge of the pork chop facing the outside edges of the basket.
6. Air fry the pork chops for 18 minutes, turning the pork chops over halfway through the cooking time. When the chops are done, let them rest for 5 minutes and then transfer to a serving platter.

Orange Pork Tenderloin

Prep time: 15 minutes | Cook time: 23 minutes | Serves 3 to 4

2 tablespoons brown sugar
2 teaspoons cornstarch
2 teaspoons Dijon mustard
½ cup orange juice
½ teaspoon soy sauce
2 teaspoons grated fresh ginger
¼ cup white wine
Zest of 1 orange
1 pound (454 g) pork tenderloin
Salt and freshly ground black pepper, to taste
Oranges, halved, for garnish
Fresh parsley, for garnish

1. Combine the brown sugar, cornstarch, Dijon mustard, orange juice, soy sauce, ginger, white wine and orange zest in a small saucepan and bring the mixture to a boil on the stovetop. Lower the heat and simmer while you air fry the pork tenderloin or until the sauce has thickened.
2. Season all sides of the pork tenderloin with salt and freshly ground black pepper. Transfer the tenderloin to the air fryer basket.
3. Select the AIR FRY function and cook at 370°F (188°C) for 20 to 23 minutes, or until the internal temperature reaches 145°F (63°C). Flip the tenderloin over halfway through the cooking process and baste with the sauce.
4. Transfer the tenderloin to a cutting board and let it rest for 5 minutes. Slice the pork at a slight angle and serve immediately with orange halves and fresh parsley.

Carne Asada Tacos

Prep time: 5 minutes | Cook time: 14 minutes | Serves 4

1/3 cup olive oil
1½ pounds (680 g) flank steak
Salt and freshly ground black pepper, to taste
1/3 cup freshly squeezed lime juice
½ cup chopped fresh cilantro
4 teaspoons minced garlic
1 teaspoon ground cumin
1 teaspoon chili powder

1. Brush the air fryer basket with olive oil.
2. Put the flank steak in a large mixing bowl. Season with salt and pepper.
3. Add the lime juice, cilantro, garlic, cumin, and chili powder and toss to coat the steak.
4. For the best flavor, let the steak marinate in the refrigerator for about 1 hour.
5. Put the steak in the air fryer basket. Select the AIR FRY function and cook at 400ºF (204ºC) for 7 minutes. Flip the steak. Air fry for 7 minutes more or until an internal temperature reaches at least 145ºF (63ºC).
6. Let the steak rest for about 5 minutes, then cut into strips to serve.

Beef Egg Rolls

Prep time: 15 minutes | Cook time: 12 minutes | Makes 8 egg rolls

½ chopped onion
2 garlic cloves, chopped
½ packet taco seasoning
Salt and ground black pepper, to taste
1 pound (454 g)
lean ground beef
½ can cilantro lime rotel
16 egg roll wrappers
1 cup shredded Mexican cheese
1 tablespoon olive oil
1 teaspoon cilantro

1. Add onions and garlic to a skillet, cooking until fragrant. Then add taco seasoning, pepper, salt, and beef, cooking until beef is broke up into tiny pieces and cooked thoroughly.
2. Add rotel and stir well.
3. Lay out egg wrappers and brush with a touch of water to soften a bit.
4. Load wrappers with beef filling and add cheese to each.
5. Fold diagonally to close and use water to secure edges.
6. Brush filled egg wrappers with olive oil and add to the air fryer oven.
7. Select the AIR FRY function and cook at 400ºF (205ºC) for 8 minutes. Flip, and air fry for another 4 minutes.
8. Serve sprinkled with cilantro.

Beef Chuck with Brussels Sprouts

Prep time: 20 minutes | Cook time: 15 minutes | Serves 4

1 pound (454 g) beef chuck shoulder steak
2 tablespoons vegetable oil
1 tablespoon red wine vinegar
1 teaspoon fine sea salt
½ teaspoon ground black pepper
1 teaspoon smoked paprika
1 teaspoon onion powder
½ teaspoon garlic powder
½ pound (227 g) Brussels sprouts, cleaned and halved
½ teaspoon fennel seeds
1 teaspoon dried basil
1 teaspoon dried sage

1. Massage the beef with the vegetable oil, wine vinegar, salt, black pepper, paprika, onion powder, and garlic powder, coating it well.
2. Allow to marinate for a minimum of 3 hours.
3. Remove the beef from the marinade and put in the air fryer oven. Select the AIR FRY function and cook at 390ºF (199ºC) for 10 minutes. Flip the beef halfway through.
4. Put the prepared Brussels sprouts in the air fryer oven along with the fennel seeds, basil, and sage.
5. Lower the heat to 380ºF (193ºC) and air fry everything for another 5 minutes.
6. Give them a good stir. Air fry for an additional 10 minutes.
7. Serve immediately.

Italian Lamb Chops with Avocado Mayo

Prep time: 5 minutes | Cook time: 12 minutes | Serves 2

2 lamp chops
2 teaspoons Italian herbs
2 avocados

½ cup mayonnaise
1 tablespoon lemon juice

1. Season the lamb chops with the Italian herbs, then set aside for 5 minutes.
2. Place the rack in the air fryer basket. Select the AIR FRY function and cook at 400ºF (204ºC) for 12 minutes.
3. In the meantime, halve the avocados and open to remove the pits. Spoon the flesh into a blender.
4. Add the mayonnaise and lemon juice and pulse until a smooth consistency is achieved.
5. Take care when removing the chops from the air fryer oven, then plate up and serve with the avocado mayo.

Chicken Fried Steak

Prep time: 15 minutes | Cook time: 10 minutes | Serves 4

½ cup flour
2 teaspoons salt, divided
Freshly ground black pepper, to taste
¼ teaspoon garlic powder
1 cup buttermilk

1 cup fine bread crumbs
4 (6-ounce / 170-g) tenderized top round steaks, ½-inch thick
Vegetable or canola oil

For the Gravy:

2 tablespoons butter or bacon drippings
¼ onion, minced
1 clove garlic, smashed
¼ teaspoon dried thyme
3 tablespoons flour

1 cup milk
Salt and freshly ground black pepper, to taste
Dashes of Worcestershire sauce

1. Set up a dredging station. Combine the flour, 1 teaspoon of salt, black pepper and garlic powder in a shallow bowl. Pour the buttermilk into a second shallow bowl. Finally, put the bread crumbs and 1 teaspoon of salt in a third shallow bowl.
2. Dip the tenderized steaks into the flour, then the buttermilk, and then the bread crumb mixture, pressing the crumbs onto the steak. Put them on a baking sheet and spray both sides generously with vegetable or canola oil.
3. Transfer the steaks to the air fryer basket, two at a time. Select the AIR FRY function and cook at 400ºF (204ºC) for 10 minutes, flipping the steaks over halfway through the cooking time. Hold the first batch of steaks warm in a 170ºF (77ºC) oven while you air fry the second batch.
4. While the steaks are cooking, make the gravy. Melt the butter in a small saucepan over medium heat on the stovetop. Add the onion, garlic and thyme and cook for five minutes, until the onion is soft and just starting to brown. Stir in the flour and cook for another five minutes, stirring regularly, until the mixture starts to brown. Whisk in the milk and bring the mixture to a boil to thicken. Season to taste with salt, lots of freshly ground black pepper, and a few dashes of Worcestershire sauce.
5. Pour the gravy over the chicken fried steaks and serve.

Kale and Beef Omelet

Prep time: 15 minutes | Cook time: 16 minutes | Serves 4

½ pound (227 g) leftover beef, coarsely chopped
2 garlic cloves, pressed
1 cup kale, torn into pieces and wilted
1 tomato, chopped
¼ teaspoon sugar
4 eggs, beaten

4 tablespoons heavy cream
½ teaspoon turmeric powder
Salt and ground black pepper, to taste
⅛ teaspoon ground allspice
Cooking spray

1. Spritz four ramekins with cooking spray.
2. Put equal amounts of each of the ingredients into each ramekin and mix well. Transfer to the air fryer oven.
3. Select the AIR FRY function and cook at 360ºF (182ºC) for 16 minutes.
4. Serve immediately.

Beef and Pork Sausage Meatloaf

Prep time: 20 minutes | Cook time: 25 minutes | Serves 4

¾ pound (340 g) ground chuck
4 ounces (113 g) ground pork sausage
1 cup shallots, finely chopped
2 eggs, well beaten
3 tablespoons plain milk
1 tablespoon oyster sauce
1 teaspoon porcini mushrooms
½ teaspoon cumin powder
1 teaspoon garlic paste
1 tablespoon fresh parsley
Salt and crushed red pepper flakes, to taste
1 cup crushed saltines
Cooking spray

1. Select the BAKE function and preheat MAXX to 360ºF (182ºC). Spritz a baking dish with cooking spray.
2. Mix all the ingredients in a large bowl, combining everything well.
3. Transfer to the baking dish and bake in the air fryer oven for 25 minutes.
4. Serve hot.

Pork Chops with Rinds

Prep time: 5 minutes | Cook time: 15 minutes | Serves 4

1 teaspoon chili powder
½ teaspoon garlic powder
1½ ounces (43 g) pork rinds, finely
ground
4 (4-ounce / 113-g) pork chops
1 tablespoon coconut oil, melted

1. Combine the chili powder, garlic powder, and ground pork rinds.
2. Coat the pork chops with the coconut oil, followed by the pork rind mixture, taking care to cover them completely. Then place the chops in the air fryer basket.
3. Select the AIR FRY function and cook at 400ºF (204ºC) for 15 minutes, or until the internal temperature of the chops reaches at least 145ºF (63ºC), turning halfway through.
4. Serve immediately.

Pepperoni and Bell Pepper Pockets

Prep time: 5 minutes | Cook time: 8 minutes | Serves 4

4 bread slices, 1-inch thick
Olive oil, for misting
24 slices pepperoni
1 ounce (28 g) roasted red peppers,
drained and patted dry
1 ounce (28 g) Pepper Jack cheese, cut into 4 slices

1. Spray both sides of bread slices with olive oil.
2. Stand slices upright and cut a deep slit in the top to create a pocket (almost to the bottom crust, but not all the way through).
3. Stuff each bread pocket with 6 slices of pepperoni, a large strip of roasted red pepper, and a slice of cheese.
4. Put bread pockets in air fryer basket, standing up. Select the AIR FRY function and cook at 360ºF (182ºC) for 8 minutes, until filling is heated through and bread is lightly browned.
5. Serve hot.

Miso Marinated Steak

Prep time: 5 minutes | Cook time: 12 minutes | Serves 4

¾ pound (340 g) flank steak
1½ tablespoons sake
1 tablespoon brown miso paste
1 teaspoon honey
2 cloves garlic, pressed
1 tablespoon olive oil

1. Put all the ingredients in a Ziploc bag. Shake to cover the steak well with the seasonings and refrigerate for at least 1 hour.
2. Coat all sides of the steak with cooking spray. Put the steak in the baking pan.
3. Select the AIR FRY function and cook at 400ºF (204ºC) for 12 minutes, turning the steak twice during the cooking time, then serve immediately.

Potato and Prosciutto Salad

Prep time: 10 minutes | Cook time: 7 minutes | Serves 8

Salad:

4 pounds (1.8 kg) potatoes, boiled and cubed	diced
	2 cups shredded Cheddar cheese
15 slices prosciutto,	

Dressing:

15 ounces (425 g) sour cream	1 teaspoon black pepper
2 tablespoons mayonnaise	1 teaspoon dried basil
1 teaspoon salt	

1. Put the potatoes, prosciutto, and Cheddar in a baking dish. Put it in the air fryer oven.
2. Select the AIR FRY function and cook at 350ºF (177ºC) for 7 minutes.
3. In a separate bowl, mix the sour cream, mayonnaise, salt, pepper, and basil using a whisk.
4. Coat the salad with the dressing and serve.

Beef Cheeseburger Egg Rolls

Prep time: 15 minutes | Cook time: 8 minutes | Makes 6 egg rolls

8 ounces (227 g) raw lean ground beef	3 tablespoons cream cheese
½ cup chopped onion	1 tablespoon yellow mustard
½ cup chopped bell pepper	3 tablespoons shredded Cheddar cheese
¼ teaspoon onion powder	6 chopped dill pickle chips
¼ teaspoon garlic powder	6 egg roll wrappers

1. In a skillet, add the beef, onion, bell pepper, onion powder, and garlic powder. Stir and crumble beef until fully cooked, and vegetables are soft.
2. Take skillet off the heat and add cream cheese, mustard, and Cheddar cheese, stirring until melted.
3. Pour beef mixture into a bowl and fold in pickles.

4. Lay out egg wrappers and divide the beef mixture into each one. Moisten egg roll wrapper edges with water. Fold sides to the middle and seal with water.
5. Repeat with all other egg rolls.
6. Put rolls into air fryer oven, one batch at a time. Select the AIR FRY function and cook at 392ºF (200ºC) for 8 minutes.
7. Serve immediately.

Lollipop Lamb Chops

Prep time: 15 minutes | Cook time: 7 minutes | Serves 4

½ small clove garlic	½ cup olive oil
¼ cup packed fresh parsley	8 lamb chops (1 rack)
¾ cup packed fresh mint	2 tablespoons vegetable oil
½ teaspoon lemon juice	Salt and freshly ground black pepper, to taste
¼ cup grated Parmesan cheese	1 tablespoon dried rosemary, chopped
⅓ cup shelled pistachios	1 tablespoon dried thyme
¼ teaspoon salt	

1. Make the pesto by combining the garlic, parsley and mint in a food processor and process until finely chopped. Add the lemon juice, Parmesan cheese, pistachios and salt. Process until all the ingredients have turned into a paste. With the processor running, slowly pour the olive oil in. Scrape the sides of the processor with a spatula and process for another 30 seconds.
2. Rub both sides of the lamb chops with vegetable oil and season with salt, pepper, rosemary and thyme, pressing the herbs into the meat gently with the fingers. Transfer the lamb chops to the air fryer basket.
3. Select the AIR FRY function and cook at 400ºF (204ºC) for 5 minutes. Flip the chops over and air fry for an additional 2 minutes.
4. Serve the lamb chops with mint pesto drizzled on top.

Marinated Pork Tenderloin

Prep time: 10 minutes | Cook time: 30 minutes | Serves 4 to 6

¼ cup olive oil
¼ cup soy sauce
¼ cup freshly squeezed lemon juice
1 garlic clove, minced

1 tablespoon Dijon mustard
1 teaspoon salt
½ teaspoon freshly ground black pepper
2 pounds (907 g) pork tenderloin

1. In a large mixing bowl, make the marinade: Mix the olive oil, soy sauce, lemon juice, minced garlic, Dijon mustard, salt, and pepper. Reserve ¼ cup of the marinade.
2. Put the tenderloin in a large bowl and pour the remaining marinade over the meat. Cover and marinate in the refrigerator for about 1 hour.
3. Select the ROAST function and preheat MAXX to 400ºF (204ºC).
4. Put the marinated pork tenderloin into the air fryer basket. Roast for 10 minutes. Flip the pork and baste it with half of the reserved marinade. Roast for 10 minutes more.
5. Flip the pork, then baste with the remaining marinade. Roast for another 10 minutes, for a total cooking time of 30 minutes.
6. Serve immediately.

Kielbasa Sausage with Pierogies

Prep time: 15 minutes | Cook time: 30 minutes | Serves 3 to 4

1 sweet onion, sliced
1 teaspoon olive oil
Salt and freshly ground black pepper, to taste
2 tablespoons butter, cut into small cubes
1 teaspoon sugar
1 pound (454 g)

light Polish kielbasa sausage, cut into 2-inch chunks
1 (13-ounce / 369-g) package frozen mini pierogies
2 teaspoons vegetable or olive oil
Chopped scallions, for garnish

1. Toss the sliced onions with olive oil, salt and pepper and transfer them to the air fryer basket. Dot the onions with pieces of butter. Select the AIR FRY function and cook at 400ºF (204ºC) for 2 minutes. Then sprinkle the sugar over the onions and stir. Pour any melted butter from the bottom of the air fryer oven drawer over the onions. Continue to air fry for another 13 minutes, stirring or shaking the basket every few minutes to air fry the onions evenly.
2. Add the kielbasa chunks to the onions and toss. Air fry for another 5 minutes, shaking the basket halfway through the cooking time. Transfer the kielbasa and onions to a bowl and cover with aluminum foil to keep warm.
3. Toss the frozen pierogies with the vegetable or olive oil and transfer them to the air fryer basket. Air fry for 8 minutes, shaking the basket twice during the cooking time.
4. When the pierogies have finished cooking, return the kielbasa and onions to the air fryer oven and gently toss with the pierogies. Air fry for 2 more minutes and then transfer everything to a serving platter. Garnish with the chopped scallions and serve hot.

Beef Steak Fingers

Prep time: 5 minutes | Cook time: 8 minutes | Serves 4

4 small beef cube steaks
Salt and ground black pepper, to

taste
½ cup flour
Cooking spray

1. Cut cube steaks into 1-inch-wide strips.
2. Sprinkle lightly with salt and pepper to taste.
3. Roll in flour to coat all sides.
4. Spritz air fryer basket with cooking spray.
5. Put steak strips in air fryer basket in a single layer. Spritz top of steak strips with cooking spray.
6. Select the AIR FRY function and cook at 390ºF (199ºC) for 4 minutes. Turn strips over, and spritz with cooking spray.
7. Air fry 4 more minutes and test with fork for doneness. Steak fingers should be crispy outside with no red juices inside.
8. Repeat with the remaining strips.
9. Serve immediately.

Greek Lamb Rack

Prep time: 5 minutes | Cook time: 10 minutes | Serves 4

¼ cup freshly squeezed lemon juice
1 teaspoon oregano
2 teaspoons minced fresh rosemary
1 teaspoon minced fresh thyme
2 tablespoons

minced garlic
Salt and freshly ground black pepper, to taste
2 to 4 tablespoons olive oil
1 lamb rib rack (7 to 8 ribs)

1. Select the ROAST function and preheat MAXX to 360ºF (182ºC).
2. In a small mixing bowl, combine the lemon juice, oregano, rosemary, thyme, garlic, salt, pepper, and olive oil and mix well.
3. Rub the mixture over the lamb, covering all the meat. Put the rack of lamb in the air fryer oven. Roast for 10 minutes. Flip the rack halfway through.
4. After 10 minutes, measure the internal temperature of the rack of lamb reaches at least 145ºF (63ºC).
5. Serve immediately.

Pork Medallions with Radicchio and Endive Salad

Prep time: 25 minutes | Cook time: 7 minutes | Serves 4

1 (8-ounce / 227-g) pork tenderloin
Salt and freshly ground black pepper, to taste
¼ cup flour
2 eggs, lightly beaten
¾ cup cracker meal
1 teaspoon paprika

1 teaspoon dry mustard
1 teaspoon garlic powder
1 teaspoon dried thyme
1 teaspoon salt
vegetable or canola oil, in spray bottle

Vinaigrette:

¼ cup white balsamic vinegar
2 tablespoons agave syrup (or honey or maple syrup)
1 tablespoon Dijon

mustard
juice of ½ lemon
2 tablespoons chopped chervil or flat-leaf parsley
salt and freshly

ground black pepper
½ cup extra-virgin olive oil
Radicchio and Endive Salad:
1 heart romaine lettuce, torn into large pieces
½ head radicchio, coarsely chopped

2 heads endive, sliced
½ cup cherry tomatoes, halved
3 ounces (85 g) fresh Mozzarella, diced
Salt and freshly ground black pepper, to taste

1. Slice the pork tenderloin into 1-inch slices. Using a meat pounder, pound the pork slices into thin ½-inch medallions. Generously season the pork with salt and freshly ground black pepper on both sides.
2. Set up a dredging station using three shallow dishes. Put the flour in one dish and the beaten eggs in a second dish. Combine the cracker meal, paprika, dry mustard, garlic powder, thyme and salt in a third dish.
3. Dredge the pork medallions in flour first and then into the beaten egg. Let the excess egg drip off and coat both sides of the medallions with the cracker meal crumb mixture. Spray both sides of the coated medallions with vegetable or canola oil.
4. Select the AIR FRY function and cook the medallions in two batches at 400ºF (204ºC) for 5 minutes. Once you have air-fried all the medallions, flip them all over and return the first batch of medallions back into the air fryer oven on top of the second batch. Air fry for an additional 2 minutes.
5. While the medallions are cooking, make the salad and dressing. Whisk the white balsamic vinegar, agave syrup, Dijon mustard, lemon juice, chervil, salt and pepper together in a small bowl. Whisk in the olive oil slowly until combined and thickened.
6. Combine the romaine lettuce, radicchio, endive, cherry tomatoes, and Mozzarella cheese in a large salad bowl. Drizzle the dressing over the vegetables and toss to combine. Season with salt and freshly ground black pepper.
7. Serve the pork medallions warm on or beside the salad.

Beef and Spinach Rolls

Prep time: 10 minutes | Cook time: 14 minutes | Serves 2

3 teaspoons pesto
2 pounds (907 g) beef flank steak
6 slices provolone cheese
3 ounces (85 g)

roasted red bell peppers
¾ cup baby spinach
1 teaspoon sea salt
1 teaspoon black pepper

1. Spoon equal amounts of the pesto onto each flank steak and spread it across evenly.
2. Put the cheese, roasted red peppers and spinach on top of the meat, about three-quarters of the way down.
3. Roll the steak up, holding it in place with toothpicks. Sprinkle with the sea salt and pepper.
4. Put inside the air fryer oven. Select the AIR FRY function and cook at 400ºF (204ºC) for 14 minutes, turning halfway through the cooking time.
5. Allow the beef to rest for 10 minutes before slicing up and serving.

Beef Chuck Cheeseburgers

Prep time: 10 minutes | Cook time: 15 minutes | Serves 4

¾ pound (340 g) ground beef chuck
1 envelope onion soup mix
Kosher salt and freshly ground black

pepper, to taste
1 teaspoon paprika
4 slices Monterey Jack cheese
4 ciabatta rolls

1. In a bowl, stir together the ground chuck, onion soup mix, salt, black pepper, and paprika to combine well.
2. Take four equal portions of the mixture and mold each one into a patty. Transfer to the air fryer oven. Select the AIR FRY function and cook at 385ºF (196ºC) for 10 minutes.
3. Put the slices of cheese on the top of the burgers.
4. Air fry for another minute before serving on ciabatta rolls.

Air Fried Beef Ribs

Prep time: 20 minutes | Cook time: 8 minutes | Serves 4

1 pound (454 g) meaty beef ribs, rinsed and drained
3 tablespoons apple cider vinegar
1 cup coriander, finely chopped
1 tablespoon fresh basil leaves, chopped
2 garlic cloves,

finely chopped
1 chipotle powder
1 teaspoon fennel seeds
1 teaspoon hot paprika
Kosher salt and black pepper, to taste
½ cup vegetable oil

1. Coat the ribs with the remaining ingredients and refrigerate for at least 3 hours.
2. Separate the ribs from the marinade and put them in the air fryer basket.
3. Select the AIR FRY function and cook at 360ºF (182ºC) for 8 minutes.
4. Pour the remaining marinade over the ribs before serving.

Mexican Pork Chops

Prep time: 5 minutes | Cook time: 15 minutes | Serves 2

¼ teaspoon dried oregano
1½ teaspoons taco seasoning mix
2 (4-ounce / 113-g)

boneless pork chops
2 tablespoons unsalted butter, divided

1. Combine the dried oregano and taco seasoning in a small bowl and rub the mixture into the pork chops. Brush the chops with 1 tablespoon butter. Transfer to the air fryer basket.
2. Select the AIR FRY function and cook at 400ºF (204ºC) for 15 minutes, turning them over halfway through to air fry on the other side.
3. When the chops are a brown color, check the internal temperature has reached 145ºF (63ºC) and remove from the air fryer oven. Serve with a garnish of remaining butter.

Cheese Crusted Chops

Prep time: 10 minutes | Cook time: 12 minutes | Serves 4 to 6

¼ teaspoon pepper
½ teaspoons salt
4 to 6 thick boneless pork chops
1 cup pork rind crumbs
¼ teaspoon chili powder
½ teaspoons onion powder
1 teaspoon smoked paprika
2 beaten eggs
3 tablespoons grated Parmesan cheese
Cooking spray

1. Rub the pepper and salt on both sides of pork chops.
2. In a food processor, pulse pork rinds into crumbs. Mix crumbs with chili powder, onion powder, and paprika in a bowl.
3. Beat eggs in another bowl.
4. Dip pork chops into eggs then into pork rind crumb mixture.
5. Spritz the air fryer basket with cooking spray and add pork chops to the basket.
6. Select the AIR FRY function and cook at 400ºF (205ºC) for 12 minutes.
7. Serve garnished with the Parmesan cheese.

Avocado Buttered Flank Steak

Prep time: 5 minutes | Cook time: 12 minutes | Serves 1

1 flank steak
Salt and ground black pepper, to taste
2 avocados
2 tablespoons butter, melted
½ cup chimichurri sauce

1. Rub the flank steak with salt and pepper to taste and leave to sit for 20 minutes.
2. Halve the avocados and take out the pits. Spoon the flesh into a bowl and mash with a fork. Mix in the melted butter and chimichurri sauce, making sure everything is well combined.
3. Put the steak in the air fryer basket. Select the AIR FRY function and cook at 400ºF (204ºC) for 6 minutes. Flip over and allow to air fry for another 6 minutes.
4. Serve the steak with the avocado butter.

Crumbed Golden Filet Mignon

Prep time: 15 minutes | Cook time: 12 minutes | Serves 4

½ pound (227 g) filet mignon
Sea salt and ground black pepper, to taste
½ teaspoon cayenne pepper
1 teaspoon dried basil
1 teaspoon dried rosemary
1 teaspoon dried thyme
1 tablespoon sesame oil
1 small egg, whisked
½ cup bread crumbs

1. Cover the filet mignon with the salt, black pepper, cayenne pepper, basil, rosemary, and thyme. Coat with sesame oil.
2. Put the egg in a shallow plate.
3. Pour the bread crumbs in another plate.
4. Dip the filet mignon into the egg. Roll it into the crumbs.
5. Transfer the steak to the air fryer oven. Select the AIR FRY function and cook at 360ºF (182ºC) for 12 minutes, or until it turns golden.
6. Serve immediately.

Air Fried London Broil

Prep time: 15 minutes | Cook time: 25 minutes | Serves 8

2 pounds (907 g) London broil
3 large garlic cloves, minced
3 tablespoons balsamic vinegar
3 tablespoons whole-grain mustard
2 tablespoons olive oil
Sea salt and ground black pepper, to taste
½ teaspoons dried hot red pepper flakes

1. Wash and dry the London broil. Score its sides with a knife.
2. Mix the remaining ingredients. Rub this mixture into the broil, coating it well. Allow to marinate for a minimum of 3 hours.
3. Transfer the broil to the air fryer basket.
4. Select the AIR FRY function and cook at 400ºF (204ºC) for 15 minutes. Turn it over and air fry for an additional 10 minutes before serving.

Cheesy Beef Meatballs

Prep time: 5 minutes | Cook time: 18 minutes | Serves 6

1 pound (454 g) ground beef
½ cup grated Parmesan cheese
1 tablespoon minced garlic
½ cup Mozzarella cheese
1 teaspoon freshly ground pepper

1. In a bowl, mix all the ingredients together.
2. Roll the meat mixture into 5 generous meatballs. Arrange in the air fryer basket.
3. Select the AIR FRY function and cook at 400ºF (204ºC) for 18 minutes.
4. Serve immediately.

Lamb Burger

Prep time: 15 minutes | Cook time: 16 minutes | Serves 3 to 4

2 teaspoons olive oil
⅓ onion, finely chopped
1 clove garlic, minced
1 pound (454 g) ground lamb
2 tablespoons fresh parsley, finely chopped
1½ teaspoons fresh
oregano, finely chopped
½ cup black olives, finely chopped
⅓ cup crumbled feta cheese
½ teaspoon salt
Freshly ground black pepper, to taste
4 thick pita breads

1. Preheat a medium skillet over medium-high heat on the stovetop. Add the olive oil and cook the onion until tender, but not browned about 4 to 5 minutes. Add the garlic and cook for another minute. Transfer the onion and garlic to a mixing bowl and add the ground lamb, parsley, oregano, olives, feta cheese, salt and pepper. Gently mix the ingredients together.
2. Divide the mixture into 3 or 4 equal portions and then form the hamburgers, being careful not to over-handle the meat. One good way to do this is to throw the meat back and forth between the hands like a baseball, packing the meat each time you catch it. Flatten the balls into patties, making an indentation in the center of each patty. Flatten the sides of the patties as well to make it easier to fit them into the air fryer basket.
3. Select the AIR FRY function and cook at 370ºF (188ºC) for 8 minutes. Flip the burgers over and air fry for another 8 minutes. If you cooked the burgers in batches, return the first batch of burgers to the air fryer oven for the last two minutes of cooking to re-heat. This should give you a medium-well burger. If you'd prefer a medium-rare burger, shorten the cooking time to about 13 minutes. Remove the burgers to a resting plate and let the burgers rest for a few minutes before dressing and serving.
4. While the burgers are resting, switch from AIR FRY to BAKE and bake the pita breads in the air fryer oven for 2 minutes. Tuck the burgers into the toasted pita breads, or wrap the pitas around the burgers and serve with a tzatziki sauce or some mayonnaise.

Smoked Beef

Prep time: 10 minutes | Cook time: 45 minutes | Serves 8

2 pounds (907 g) roast beef, at room temperature
2 tablespoons extra-virgin olive oil
1 teaspoon sea salt flakes
1 teaspoon ground
black pepper
1 teaspoon smoked paprika
Few dashes of liquid smoke
2 jalapeño peppers, thinly sliced

1. Select the ROAST function and preheat MAXX to 330ºF (166ºC).
2. With kitchen towels, pat the beef dry.
3. Massage the extra-virgin olive oil, salt, black pepper, and paprika into the meat. Cover with liquid smoke.
4. Put the beef in the air fryer oven and roast for 30 minutes. Flip the roast over and allow to roast for another 15 minutes.
5. When cooked through, serve topped with sliced jalapeños.

Mushroom and Beef Meatloaf

Prep time: 10 minutes | Cook time: 25 minutes | Serves 4

1 pound (454 g) ground beef	chopped
1 egg, beaten	3 tablespoons bread crumbs
1 mushrooms, sliced	Ground black pepper, to taste
1 tablespoon thyme	
1 small onion,	

1. Select the BAKE function and preheat MAXX to 400°F (204°C).
2. Put all the ingredients into a large bowl and combine entirely.
3. Transfer the meatloaf mixture into the loaf pan and move it to the air fryer basket.
4. Bake for 25 minutes. Slice up before serving.

Char Siew

Prep time: 10 minutes | Cook time: 20 minutes | Serves 4 to 6

1 strip of pork shoulder butt with a good amount of fat	marbling
	Olive oil, for brushing the pan

Marinade:

1 teaspoon sesame oil	1 teaspoon light soy sauce
4 tablespoons raw honey	1 tablespoon rose wine
1 teaspoon low-sodium dark soy sauce	2 tablespoons Hoisin sauce

1. Combine all the marinade ingredients together in a Ziploc bag. Put pork in bag, making sure all sections of pork strip are engulfed in the marinade. Chill for 3 to 24 hours.
2. Take out the strip 30 minutes before planning to roast.
3. Select the ROAST function and preheat MAXX to 350°F (177°C).
4. Put foil on small pan and brush with olive oil. Put marinated pork strip onto prepared pan.
5. Roast in the preheated air fryer oven for 20 minutes.
6. Glaze with marinade every 5 to 10 minutes.
7. Remove strip and leave to cool a few minutes before slicing.
8. Serve immediately.

Greek Lamb Pita Pockets

Prep time: 15 minutes | Cook time: 6 minutes | Serves 4

Dressing:

1 cup plain yogurt	weed, crushed
1 tablespoon lemon juice	1 teaspoon ground oregano
1 teaspoon dried dill	½ teaspoon salt

Meatballs:

½ pound (227 g) ground lamb	¼ teaspoon oregano
1 tablespoon diced onion	¼ teaspoon coriander
1 teaspoon dried parsley	¼ teaspoon ground cumin
1 teaspoon dried dill weed, crushed	¼ teaspoon salt
	4 pita halves

Suggested Toppings:

1 red onion, slivered	cheese
1 medium cucumber, deseeded, thinly sliced	Sliced black olives
Crumbled feta	Chopped fresh peppers

1. Stir the dressing ingredients together in a small bowl and refrigerate while preparing lamb.
2. Combine all meatball ingredients in a large bowl and stir to distribute seasonings.
3. Shape meat mixture into 12 small meatballs, rounded or slightly flattened if you prefer.
4. Transfer the meatballs to the air fryer oven. Select the AIR FRY function and cook at 390°F (199°C) for 6 minutes, until well done. Remove and drain on paper towels.
5. To serve, pile meatballs and the choice of toppings in pita pockets and drizzle with dressing.

Mongolian Flank Steak

Prep time: 20 minutes | Cook time: 15 minutes | Serves 4

1½ pounds (680 g) flank steak, thinly sliced on the bias into ¼-inch strips

Marinade:

2 tablespoons soy sauce
1 clove garlic,
smashed
Pinch crushed red pepper flakes

Sauce:

1 tablespoon vegetable oil
2 cloves garlic, minced
1 tablespoon finely grated fresh ginger
3 dried red chili peppers
¾ cup soy sauce
¾ cup chicken stock
5 to 6 tablespoons brown sugar
½ cup cornstarch, divided
1 bunch scallions, sliced into 2-inch pieces

1. Marinate the beef in the soy sauce, garlic and red pepper flakes for one hour.
2. In the meantime, make the sauce. Preheat a small saucepan over medium heat on the stovetop. Add the oil, garlic, ginger and dried chili peppers and sauté for just a minute or two. Add the soy sauce, chicken stock and brown sugar and continue to simmer for a few minutes. Dissolve 3 tablespoons of cornstarch in 3 tablespoons of water and stir this into the saucepan. Stir the sauce over medium heat until it thickens. Set this aside.
3. Remove the beef from the marinade and transfer it to a zipper sealable plastic bag with the remaining cornstarch. Shake it around to completely coat the beef and transfer the coated strips of beef to a baking sheet or plate, shaking off any excess cornstarch. Spray the strips with vegetable oil on all sides and transfer them to the air fryer basket.
4. Select the AIR FRY function and cook at 400ºF (204ºC) for 15 minutes, shaking the basket to toss and rotate the beef strips throughout the cooking process. Add the scallions for the last 4 minutes of the cooking. Transfer the hot beef strips and scallions to a bowl and toss with the sauce, coating all the beef strips with the sauce. Serve warm.

Fast Lamb Satay

Prep time: 5 minutes | Cook time: 8 minutes | Serves 2

¼ teaspoon cumin
1 teaspoon ginger
½ teaspoons nutmeg
Salt and ground
black pepper, to taste
2 boneless lamb steaks
Cooking spray

1. Combine the cumin, ginger, nutmeg, salt and pepper in a bowl.
2. Cube the lamb steaks and massage the spice mixture into each one.
3. Leave to marinate for 10 minutes, then transfer onto metal skewers.
4. Spritz the skewers with the cooking spray and place in the air fryer basket.
5. Select the AIR FRY function and cook at 400ºF (204ºC) for 8 minutes.
6. Take care when removing them from the air fryer oven and serve.

Spaghetti Squash Lasagna

Prep time: 5 minutes | Cook time: 1 hour 15 minutes | Serves 6

2 large spaghetti squash, cooked (about 2¾ pounds / 1.2 kg)
4 pounds (1.8 kg) ground beef
1 (2½-pound /
1.1-kg) large jar Marinara sauce
25 slices Mozzarella cheese
30 ounces whole-milk ricotta cheese

1. Select the BAKE function and preheat MAXX to 375ºF (191ºC).
2. Slice the spaghetti squash and place it face down inside a baking dish. Fill with water until covered.
3. Bake in the preheated air fryer oven for 45 minutes until skin is soft.
4. Sear the ground beef in a skillet over medium-high heat for 5 minutes or until browned, then add the marinara sauce and heat until warm. Set aside.
5. Scrape the flesh off the cooked squash to resemble strands of spaghetti.
6. Layer the lasagna in a large greased pan in alternating layers of spaghetti squash, beef sauce, Mozzarella, ricotta. Repeat until all the ingredients have been used.
7. Bake for 30 minutes and serve!

Classic Spring Rolls

Prep time: 10 minutes | Cook time: 8 minutes | Serves 20

1/3 cup noodles
1 cup ground beef
1 teaspoon soy sauce
1 cup fresh mix vegetables
3 garlic cloves, minced

1 small onion, diced
1 tablespoon sesame oil
1 packet spring roll sheets
2 tablespoons cold water

1. Cook the noodle in enough hot water to soften them up, drain them and snip them to make them shorter.
2. In a frying pan over medium heat, cook the beef, soy sauce, mixed vegetables, garlic, and onion in sesame oil until the beef is cooked through. Take the pan off the heat and throw in the noodles. Mix well to incorporate everything.
3. Unroll a spring roll sheet and lay it flat. Scatter the filling diagonally across it and roll it up, brushing the edges lightly with water to act as an adhesive. Repeat until you have used up all the sheets and the filling.
4. Coat each spring roll with a light brushing of oil and transfer to the air fryer oven.
5. Select the AIR FRY function and cook at 350ºF (177ºC) for 8 minutes.
6. Serve hot.

Pork and Pinto Bean Gorditas

Prep time: 20 minutes | Cook time: 21 minutes | Serves 4

1 pound (454 g) lean ground pork
2 tablespoons chili powder
2 tablespoons ground cumin
1 teaspoon dried oregano
2 teaspoons paprika
1 teaspoon garlic powder
1/2 cup water
1 (15-ounce / 425-g) can pinto beans,

drained and rinsed
1/2 cup taco sauce
Salt and freshly ground black pepper, to taste
2 cups grated Cheddar cheese
5 (12-inch) flour tortillas
4 (8-inch) crispy corn tortilla shells
4 cups shredded lettuce
1 tomato, diced

1/3 cup sliced black olives
Sour cream, for serving

Tomato salsa, for serving
Cooking spray

1. Spritz the air fryer basket with cooking spray.
2. Put the ground pork in the air fryer basket. Select the AIR FRY function and cook at 400ºF (204ºC) for 10 minutes, stirring a few times to gently break up the meat. Combine the chili powder, cumin, oregano, paprika, garlic powder and water in a small bowl. Stir the spice mixture into the browned pork. Stir in the beans and taco sauce and air fry for an additional minute. Transfer the pork mixture to a bowl. Season with salt and freshly ground black pepper.
3. Sprinkle 1/2 cup of the grated cheese in the center of the flour tortillas, leaving a 2-inch border around the edge free of cheese and filling. Divide the pork mixture among the four tortillas, placing it on top of the cheese. Put a crunchy corn tortilla on top of the pork and top with shredded lettuce, diced tomatoes, and black olives. Cut the remaining flour tortilla into 4 quarters. These quarters of tortilla will serve as the bottom of the gordita. Put one quarter tortilla on top of each gordita and fold the edges of the bottom flour tortilla up over the sides, enclosing the filling. While holding the seams down, brush the bottom of the gordita with olive oil and place the seam side down on the countertop while you finish the remaining three gorditas.
4. Adjust the temperature to 380ºF (193ºC).
5. Air fry one gordita at a time. Transfer the gordita carefully to the air fryer basket, seam side down. Brush or spray the top tortilla with oil and air fry for 5 minutes. Carefully turn the gordita over and air fry for an additional 4 to 5 minutes until both sides are browned. When finished air frying all four gorditas, layer them back into the air fryer oven for an additional minute to make sure they are all warm before serving with sour cream and salsa.

Sumptuous Pizza Tortilla Rolls

Prep time: 10 minutes | Cook time: 6 minutes | Serves 4

1 teaspoon butter
½ medium onion, slivered
½ red or green bell pepper, julienned
4 ounces (113 g) fresh white mushrooms, chopped

½ cup pizza sauce
8 flour tortillas
8 thin slices deli ham
24 pepperoni slices
1 cup shredded Mozzarella cheese
Cooking spray

1. Select the BAKE function and preheat MAXX to 390ºF (199ºC).
2. Put butter, onions, bell pepper, and mushrooms in a baking pan. Bake in the preheated air fryer oven for 3 minutes. Stir and cook 3 to 4 minutes longer until just crisp and tender. Remove pan and set aside.
3. To assemble rolls, spread about 2 teaspoons of pizza sauce on one half of each tortilla. Top with a slice of ham and 3 slices of pepperoni. Divide sautéed vegetables among tortillas and top with cheese.
4. Roll up tortillas, secure with toothpicks if needed, and spray with oil.
5. Put 4 rolls in air fryer basket. Switch from BAKE to AIR FRY and air fry for 4 minutes. Turn and air fry for 4 minutes, until heated through and lightly browned.
6. Repeat with the remaining pizza rolls.
7. Serve immediately.

Citrus Pork Loin Roast

Prep time: 10 minutes | Cook time: 45 minutes | Serves 8

1 tablespoon lime juice
1 tablespoon orange marmalade
1 teaspoon coarse brown mustard
1 teaspoon curry powder
1 teaspoon dried

lemongrass
2 pound (907 g) boneless pork loin roast
Salt and ground black pepper, to taste
Cooking spray

1. Mix the lime juice, marmalade, mustard, curry powder, and lemongrass.
2. Rub mixture all over the surface of the pork loin. Season with salt and pepper.
3. Spray air fryer basket with cooking spray and place pork roast diagonally in the basket.
4. Select the AIR FRY function and cook at 360ºF (182ºC) for 45 minutes, until the internal temperature reaches at least 145ºF (63ºC).
5. Wrap roast in foil and let rest for 10 minutes before slicing.
6. Serve immediately.

Beef and Vegetable Cubes

Prep time: 15 minutes | Cook time: 17 minutes | Serves 4

2 tablespoons olive oil
1 tablespoon apple cider vinegar
1 teaspoon fine sea salt
½ teaspoons ground black pepper
1 teaspoon shallot powder
¾ teaspoon smoked cayenne pepper
½ teaspoons garlic powder

¼ teaspoon ground cumin
1 pound (454 g) top round steak, cut into cubes
4 ounces (113 g) broccoli, cut into florets
4 ounces (113 g) mushrooms, sliced
1 teaspoon dried basil
1 teaspoon celery seeds

1. Massage the olive oil, vinegar, salt, black pepper, shallot powder, cayenne pepper, garlic powder, and cumin into the cubed steak, ensuring to coat each piece evenly.
2. Allow to marinate for a minimum of 3 hours.
3. Put the beef cubes in the air fryer basket.
4. Select the AIR FRY function and cook at 365ºF (185ºC) for 12 minutes.
5. When the steak is cooked through, place it in a bowl.
6. Wipe the grease from the basket and pour in the vegetables. Season them with basil and celery seeds.
7. Increase the temperature of the air fryer oven to 400ºF (204ºC) and air fry for 5 to 6 minutes. When the vegetables are hot, serve them with the steak.

Rosemary Ribeye Steaks

Prep time: 10 minutes | Cook time: 15 minutes | Serves 2

¼ cup butter
1 clove garlic, minced
Salt and ground black pepper, to taste

1½ tablespoons balsamic vinegar
¼ cup rosemary, chopped
2 ribeye steaks

1. Melt the butter in a skillet over medium heat. Add the garlic and fry until fragrant.
2. Remove the skillet from the heat and add the salt, pepper, and vinegar. Allow it to cool.
3. Add the rosemary, then pour the mixture into a Ziploc bag.
4. Put the ribeye steaks in the bag and shake well, coating the meat well. Refrigerate for an hour, then allow to sit for a further twenty minutes.
5. Transfer the steaks to the air fryer basket.
6. Select the AIR FRY function and cook at 400ºF (204ºC) for 15 minutes.
7. Take care when removing the steaks from the air fryer oven and plate up.
8. Serve immediately.

Barbecue Pork Ribs

Prep time: 5 minutes | Cook time: 30 minutes | Serves 4

1 tablespoon barbecue dry rub
1 teaspoon mustard
1 tablespoon apple cider vinegar

1 teaspoon sesame oil
1 pound (454 g) pork ribs, chopped

1. Combine the dry rub, mustard, apple cider vinegar, and sesame oil, then coat the ribs with this mixture. Refrigerate the ribs for 20 minutes.
2. When the ribs are ready, place them in the air fryer oven. Select the AIR FRY function and cook at 360ºF (182ºC) for 15 minutes. Flip them and air fry on the other side for a further 15 minutes.
3. Serve immediately.

Easy Beef Schnitzel

Prep time: 5 minutes | Cook time: 12 minutes | Serves 1

½ cup friendly bread crumbs
2 tablespoons olive oil

Pepper and salt, to taste
1 egg, beaten
1 thin beef schnitzel

1. In a shallow dish, combine the bread crumbs, oil, pepper, and salt.
2. In a second shallow dish, place the beaten egg.
3. Dredge the schnitzel in the egg before rolling it in the bread crumbs.
4. Put the coated schnitzel in the air fryer basket. Select the AIR FRY function and cook at 350ºF (177ºC) for 12 minutes. Flip the schnitzel halfway through.
5. Serve immediately.

Vietnamese Pork Chops

Prep time: 15 minutes | Cook time: 12 minutes | Serves 2

1 tablespoon chopped shallot
1 tablespoon chopped garlic
1 tablespoon fish sauce
3 tablespoons lemongrass
1 teaspoon soy

sauce
1 tablespoon brown sugar
1 tablespoon olive oil
1 teaspoon ground black pepper
2 pork chops

1. Combine shallot, garlic, fish sauce, lemongrass, soy sauce, brown sugar, olive oil, and pepper in a bowl. Stir to mix well.
2. Put the pork chops in the bowl. Toss to coat well. Place the bowl in the refrigerator to marinate for 2 hours.
3. Remove the pork chops from the bowl and discard the marinade. Transfer the chops into the air fryer oven.
4. Select the AIR FRY function and cook at 400ºF (204ºC) for 12 minutes, or until lightly browned. Flip the pork chops halfway through the cooking time.
5. Remove the pork chops from the basket and serve hot.

Swedish Beef Meatballs

Prep time: 10 minutes | Cook time: 12 minutes | Serves 8

1 pound (454 g) ground beef	minced
1 egg, beaten	½ teaspoons garlic salt
2 carrots, shredded	Pepper and salt, to taste
2 bread slices, crumbled	1 cup tomato sauce
1 small onion,	2 cups pasta sauce

1. In a bowl, combine the ground beef, egg, carrots, crumbled bread, onion, garlic salt, pepper and salt.
2. Divide the mixture into equal amounts and shape each one into a small meatball.
3. Put them in the air fryer basket. Select the AIR FRY function and cook at 400°F (204°C). for 7 minutes.
4. Transfer the meatballs to an oven-safe dish and top with the tomato sauce and pasta sauce.
5. Set the dish into the air fryer basket and allow to air fry at 320°F (160°C) for 5 more minutes. Serve hot.

Teriyaki Pork and Mushroom Rolls

Prep time: 10 minutes | Cook time: 8 minutes | Serves 6

4 tablespoons brown sugar	2-inch ginger, chopped
4 tablespoons mirin	6 (4-ounce / 113-g) pork belly slices
4 tablespoons soy sauce	6 ounces (170 g) Enoki mushrooms
1 teaspoon almond flour	

1. Mix the brown sugar, mirin, soy sauce, almond flour, and ginger together until brown sugar dissolves.
2. Take pork belly slices and wrap around a bundle of mushrooms. Brush each roll with teriyaki sauce. Chill for half an hour.
3. Add marinated pork rolls to the air fryer basket.
4. Select the AIR FRY function and cook at 350°F (177°C) for 8 minutes. Flip the rolls halfway through.
5. Serve immediately.

Pork with Aloha Salsa

Prep time: 20 minutes | Cook time: 8 minutes | Serves 4

2 eggs	boneless, thin pork cutlets (⅜- to ½-inch thick)
2 tablespoons milk	
¼ cup flour	
¼ cup panko bread crumbs	Lemon pepper and salt, to taste
4 teaspoons sesame seeds	¼ cup cornstarch
1 pound (454 g)	Cooking spray

Aloha Salsa:

1 cup fresh pineapple, chopped in small pieces	cinnamon
¼ cup red onion, finely chopped	1 teaspoon low-sodium soy sauce
¼ cup green or red bell pepper, chopped	⅛ teaspoon crushed red pepper
½ teaspoon ground	⅛ teaspoon ground black pepper

1. In a medium bowl, stir together all ingredients for salsa. Cover and refrigerate while cooking the pork.
2. Beat the eggs and milk in a shallow dish.
3. In another shallow dish, mix the flour, panko, and sesame seeds.
4. Sprinkle pork cutlets with lemon pepper and salt.
5. Dip pork cutlets in cornstarch, egg mixture, and then panko coating. Spray both sides with cooking spray and transfer to the air fryer basket.
6. Select the AIR FRY function and cook at 390°F (199°C) for 3 minutes. Turn cutlets over, spraying both sides, and continue air frying for 5 minutes or until well done.
7. Serve fried cutlets with salsa on the side.

Ritzy Skirt Steak Fajitas

Prep time: 15 minutes | Cook time: 30 minutes | Serves 4

2 tablespoons olive oil
¼ cup lime juice
1 clove garlic, minced
½ teaspoon ground cumin
½ teaspoon hot sauce
½ teaspoon salt
2 tablespoons chopped fresh cilantro

1 pound (454 g) skirt steak
1 onion, sliced
1 teaspoon chili powder
1 red pepper, sliced
1 green pepper, sliced
Salt and freshly ground black pepper, to taste
8 flour tortillas

Toppings:

Shredded lettuce
Crumbled Queso Fresco (or grated Cheddar cheese)

Sliced black olives
Diced tomatoes
Sour cream
Guacamole

1. Combine the olive oil, lime juice, garlic, cumin, hot sauce, salt and cilantro in a shallow dish. Add the skirt steak and turn it over several times to coat all sides. Pierce the steak with a needle-style meat tenderizer or paring knife. Marinate the steak in the refrigerator for at least 3 hours, or overnight. When you are ready to cook, remove the steak from the refrigerator and let it sit at room temperature for 30 minutes.
2. Toss the onion slices with the chili powder and a little olive oil and transfer them to the air fryer basket. Select the AIR FRY function and cook at 400ºF (204ºC) for 5 minutes. Add the red and green peppers to the air fryer basket with the onions, season with salt and pepper and air fry for 8 more minutes, until the onions and peppers are soft. Transfer the vegetables to a dish and cover with aluminum foil to keep warm.
3. Put the skirt steak in the air fryer basket and pour the marinade over the top. Air fry for 12 minutes. Flip the steak over and air fry for an additional 5 minutes. Transfer the cooked steak to a cutting board and let the steak rest for a few minutes. If the peppers and onions need to be heated, return them to the air fryer oven for just 1 to 2 minutes.
4. Thinly slice the steak at an angle, cutting against the grain of the steak. Serve the steak with the onions and peppers, the warm tortillas and the fajita toppings on the side.

Air Fried Lamb Ribs

Prep time: 5 minutes | Cook time: 18 minutes | Serves 4

2 tablespoons mustard
1 pound (454 g) lamb ribs
1 teaspoon rosemary, chopped

Salt and ground black pepper, to taste
¼ cup mint leaves, chopped
1 cup Greek yogurt

1. Use a brush to apply the mustard to the lamb ribs, and season with rosemary, salt, and pepper. Transfer to the air fryer basket.
2. Select the AIR FRY function and cook at 350ºF (177ºC) for 18 minutes.
3. Meanwhile, combine the mint leaves and yogurt in a bowl.
4. Remove the lamb ribs from the air fryer oven when cooked and serve with the mint yogurt.

Hearty Sweet and Sour Pork

Prep time: 20 minutes | Cook time: 14 minutes | Serves 2 to 4

$1/3$ cup all-purpose flour
$1/3$ cup cornstarch
2 teaspoons Chinese five-spice powder
1 teaspoon salt
Freshly ground black pepper, to taste
1 egg
2 tablespoons milk
¾ pound (340 g) boneless pork, cut into 1-inch cubes
Vegetable or canola oil
1½ cups large chunks of red and green peppers
½ cup ketchup
2 tablespoons rice wine vinegar or apple cider vinegar
2 tablespoons brown sugar
¼ cup orange juice
1 tablespoon soy sauce
1 clove garlic, minced
1 cup cubed pineapple
Chopped scallions, for garnish

1. Set up a dredging station with two bowls. Combine the flour, cornstarch, Chinese five-spice powder, salt and pepper in one large bowl. Whisk the egg and milk together in a second bowl. Dredge the pork cubes in the flour mixture first, then dip them into the egg and then back into the flour to coat on all sides. Spray the coated pork cubes with vegetable or canola oil.
2. Toss the pepper chunks with a little oil and transfer to the air fryer basket. Select the AIR FRY function and cook at 400°F (204°C) for 5 minutes, shaking the basket halfway through the cooking time.
3. While the peppers are cooking, start making the sauce. Combine the ketchup, rice wine vinegar, brown sugar, orange juice, soy sauce, and garlic in a medium saucepan and bring the mixture to a boil on the stovetop. Reduce the heat and simmer for 5 minutes. When the peppers have finished air frying, add them to the saucepan along with the pineapple chunks. Simmer the peppers and pineapple in the sauce for an additional 2 minutes. Set aside and keep warm.
4. Add the dredged pork cubes to the air fryer basket and air fry for 6 minutes, shaking the basket to turn the cubes over for the last minute of the cooking process.
5. When ready to serve, toss the cooked pork with the pineapple, peppers and sauce. Serve garnished with chopped scallions.

Provolone Stuffed Beef and Pork Meatballs

Prep time: 15 minutes | Cook time: 12 minutes | Serves 4 to 6

1 tablespoon olive oil
1 small onion, finely chopped
1 to 2 cloves garlic, minced
¾ pound (340 g) ground beef
¾ pound (340 g) ground pork
¾ cup bread crumbs
¼ cup grated Parmesan cheese
¼ cup finely chopped fresh parsley
½ teaspoon dried oregano
1½ teaspoons salt
Freshly ground black pepper, to taste
2 eggs, lightly beaten
5 ounces (142 g) sharp or aged provolone cheese, cut into 1-inch cubes

1. Preheat a skillet over medium-high heat. Add the oil and cook the onion and garlic until tender, but not browned.
2. Transfer the onion and garlic to a large bowl and add the beef, pork, bread crumbs, Parmesan cheese, parsley, oregano, salt, pepper and eggs. Mix well until all the ingredients are combined. Divide the mixture into 12 evenly sized balls. Make one meatball at a time, by pressing a hole in the meatball mixture with the finger and pushing a piece of provolone cheese into the hole. Mold the meat back into a ball, enclosing the cheese.
3. Working in two batches, transfer six of the meatballs to the air fryer basket. Select the AIR FRY function and cook at 380°F (193°C) for 12 minutes, shaking the basket and turning the meatballs twice during the cooking process. Repeat with the remaining 6 meatballs. Serve warm.

Chapter 8 Wraps and Sandwiches

Tuna and Lettuce Wraps

Prep time: 10 minutes | Cook time: 4 to 7 minutes | Serves 4

1 pound (454 g) fresh tuna steak, cut into 1-inch cubes
1 tablespoon grated fresh ginger
2 garlic cloves, minced
½ teaspoon toasted sesame oil
4 low-sodium whole-wheat tortillas
¼ cup low-fat mayonnaise
2 cups shredded romaine lettuce
1 red bell pepper, thinly sliced

1. In a medium bowl, mix the tuna, ginger, garlic, and sesame oil. Let it stand for 10 minutes.
2. Transfer the tuna to the air fryer basket.
3. Select the AIR FRY function and cook at 390ºF (199ºC) for 4 to 7 minutes, or until lightly browned.
4. Make the wraps with the tuna, tortillas, mayonnaise, lettuce, and bell pepper.
5. Serve immediately.

Lettuce Fajita Meatball Wraps

Prep time: 10 minutes | Cook time: 10 minutes | Serves 4

1 pound (454 g) 85% lean ground beef
½ cup salsa, plus more for serving
¼ cup chopped onions
¼ cup diced green or red bell peppers
1 large egg, beaten
1 teaspoon fine sea salt
½ teaspoon chili powder
½ teaspoon ground cumin
1 clove garlic, minced
Cooking spray

For Serving:
8 leaves Boston lettuce
Pico de gallo or salsa
Lime slices

1. Spray the air fryer basket with cooking spray.
2. In a large bowl, mix together all the ingredients until well combined.
3. Shape the meat mixture into eight 1-inch balls. Place the meatballs in the air fryer basket, leaving a little space between them.
4. Select the AIR FRY function and cook at 350ºF (177ºC) for 10 minutes, or until cooked through and no longer pink inside and the internal temperature reaches 145ºF (63ºC).
5. Serve each meatball on a lettuce leaf, topped with pico de gallo or salsa. Serve with lime slices.

Cheesy Chicken Sandwich

Prep time: 10 minutes | Cook time: 5 to 7 minutes | Serves 1

$1/_3$ cup chicken, cooked and shredded
2 Mozzarella slices
1 hamburger bun
¼ cup shredded cabbage
1 teaspoon mayonnaise
2 teaspoons butter, melted
1 teaspoon olive oil
½ teaspoon balsamic vinegar
¼ teaspoon smoked paprika
¼ teaspoon black pepper
¼ teaspoon garlic powder
Pinch of salt

1. Select the BAKE function and preheat MAXX to 370ºF (188ºC).
2. Brush some butter onto the outside of the hamburger bun.
3. In a bowl, coat the chicken with the garlic powder, salt, pepper, and paprika.
4. In a separate bowl, stir together the mayonnaise, olive oil, cabbage, and balsamic vinegar to make coleslaw.
5. Slice the bun in two. Start building the sandwich, starting with the chicken, followed by the Mozzarella, the coleslaw, and finally the top bun.
6. Transfer the sandwich to the air fryer oven and bake for 5 to 7 minutes.
7. Serve immediately.

Veggie Salsa Wraps

Prep time: 5 minutes | Cook time: 7 minutes | Serves 4

1 cup red onion, sliced
1 zucchini, chopped
1 poblano pepper, deseeded and finely
chopped
1 head lettuce
½ cup salsa
8 ounces (227 g) Mozzarella cheese

1. Place the red onion, zucchini, and poblano pepper in the air fryer basket. Select the AIR FRY function and cook at 390ºF (199ºC) for 7 minutes, or until they are tender and fragrant.
2. Divide the veggie mixture among the lettuce leaves and spoon the salsa over the top. Finish off with Mozzarella cheese. Wrap the lettuce leaves around the filling.
3. Serve immediately.

Chicken-Lettuce Wraps

Prep time: 15 minutes | Cook time: 12 to 16 minutes | Serves 2 to 4

1 pound (454 g) boneless, skinless chicken thighs, trimmed
1 teaspoon vegetable oil
2 tablespoons lime juice
1 shallot, minced
1 tablespoon fish sauce, plus extra for serving
2 teaspoons packed brown sugar
1 garlic clove, minced
⅛ teaspoon red pepper flakes
1 mango, peeled, pitted, and cut into ¼-inch pieces
⅓ cup chopped fresh mint
⅓ cup chopped fresh cilantro
⅓ cup chopped fresh Thai basil
1 head Bibb lettuce, leaves separated (8 ounces / 227 g)
¼ cup chopped dry-roasted peanuts
2 Thai chiles, stemmed and sliced thin

1. Pat the chicken dry with paper towels and rub with oil. Place the chicken in air fryer basket. Select the AIR FRY function and cook at 400ºF (204ºC) for 12 to 16 minutes, or until the chicken registers 175ºF (79ºC), flipping and rotating chicken halfway through cooking.

2. Meanwhile, whisk lime juice, shallot, fish sauce, sugar, garlic, and pepper flakes together in large bowl; set aside.
3. Transfer chicken to cutting board, let cool slightly, then shred into bite-size pieces using 2 forks. Add the shredded chicken, mango, mint, cilantro, and basil to bowl with dressing and toss to coat.
4. Serve the chicken in the lettuce leaves, passing peanuts, Thai chiles, and extra fish sauce separately.

Classic Sloppy Joes

Prep time: 10 minutes | Cook time: 17 to 19 minutes | Makes 4 large sandwiches or 8 sliders

1 pound (454 g) very lean ground beef
1 teaspoon onion powder
⅓ cup ketchup
¼ cup water
½ teaspoon celery seed
1 tablespoon lemon juice
1½ teaspoons brown sugar
1¼ teaspoons low-sodium Worcestershire sauce
½ teaspoon salt (optional)
½ teaspoon vinegar
⅛ teaspoon dry mustard
Hamburger or slider buns, for serving
Cooking spray

1. Select the ROAST function and preheat MAXX to 390ºF (199ºC). Spray the air fryer basket with cooking spray.
2. Break raw ground beef into small chunks and pile into the basket. Roast for 5 minutes. Stir to break apart and roast for 3 minutes. Stir and roast for 2 to 4 minutes longer, or until meat is well done.
3. Remove the meat from the air fryer oven, drain, and use a knife and fork to crumble into small pieces.
4. Give your air fryer basket a quick rinse to remove any bits of meat.
5. Place all the remaining ingredients, except for the buns, in a baking pan and mix together. Add the meat and stir well.
6. Switch from ROAST to BAKE. Bake at 330ºF (166ºC) for 5 minutes. Stir and bake for 2 minutes.
7. Scoop onto buns. Serve hot.

Cheesy Shrimp Sandwich

Prep time: 10 minutes | Cook time: 5 to 7 minutes | Serves 4

1¼ cups shredded Colby, Cheddar, or Havarti cheese
1 (6-ounce / 170-g) can tiny shrimp, drained
3 tablespoons mayonnaise
2 tablespoons minced green onion
4 slices whole grain or whole-wheat bread
2 tablespoons softened butter

1. In a medium bowl, combine the cheese, shrimp, mayonnaise, and green onion, and mix well.
2. Spread this mixture on two of the slices of bread. Top with the other slices of bread to make two sandwiches. Spread the sandwiches lightly with butter.
3. Select the AIR FRY function and cook at 400ºF (204ºC) for 5 to 7 minutes, or until the bread is browned and crisp and the cheese is melted.
4. Cut in half and serve warm.

Cheesy Greens Sandwich

Prep time: 15 minutes | Cook time: 10 to 13 minutes | Serves 4

1½ cups chopped mixed greens
2 garlic cloves, thinly sliced
2 teaspoons olive oil
2 slices low-sodium low-fat Swiss cheese
4 slices low-sodium whole-wheat bread
Cooking spray

1. Select the BAKE function and preheat MAXX to 400ºF (204ºC).
2. In a baking pan, mix the greens, garlic, and olive oil. Bake for 4 to 5 minutes, stirring once, until the vegetables are tender. Drain, if necessary.
3. Make 2 sandwiches, dividing half of the greens and 1 slice of Swiss cheese between 2 slices of bread. Lightly spray the outsides of the sandwiches with cooking spray.
4. Bake the sandwiches in the air fryer oven for 6 to 8 minutes, turning with tongs halfway through, until the bread is toasted and the cheese melts.
5. Cut each sandwich in half and serve.

Chicken Pita Sandwich

Prep time: 10 minutes | Cook time: 9 to 11 minutes | Serves 4

2 boneless, skinless chicken breasts, cut into 1-inch cubes
1 small red onion, sliced
1 red bell pepper, sliced
⅓ cup Italian salad
dressing, divided
½ teaspoon dried thyme
4 pita pockets, split
2 cups torn butter lettuce
1 cup chopped cherry tomatoes

1. Select the BAKE function and preheat MAXX to 380ºF (193ºC).
2. Place the chicken, onion, and bell pepper in the air fryer basket. Drizzle with 1 tablespoon of the Italian salad dressing, add the thyme, and toss.
3. Bake for 9 to 11 minutes, or until the chicken is 165ºF (74ºC) on a food thermometer, stirring once during cooking time.
4. Transfer the chicken and vegetables to a bowl and toss with the remaining salad dressing.
5. Assemble sandwiches with the pita pockets, butter lettuce, and cherry tomatoes. Serve immediately.

Nugget and Veggie Taco Wraps

Prep time: 5 minutes | Cook time: 15 minutes | Serves 4

1 tablespoon water
4 pieces commercial vegan nuggets, chopped
1 small yellow onion, diced
1 small red bell
pepper, chopped
2 cobs grilled corn kernels
4 large corn tortillas
Mixed greens, for garnish

1. Over a medium heat, sauté the nuggets in the water with the onion, corn kernels and bell pepper in a skillet, then remove from the heat.
2. Fill the tortillas with the nuggets and vegetables and fold them up. Transfer to the air fryer basket. Select the AIR FRY function and cook at 400ºF (204ºC) for 15 minutes.
3. Once crispy, serve immediately, garnished with the mixed greens.

Tuna Muffin Sandwich

Prep time: 8 minutes | Cook time: 4 to 8 minutes | Serves 4

1 (6-ounce / 170-g) can chunk light tuna, drained
¼ cup mayonnaise
2 tablespoons mustard
1 tablespoon lemon juice
2 green onions, minced
3 English muffins, split with a fork
3 tablespoons softened butter
6 thin slices Provolone or Muenster cheese

1. Select the BAKE function and preheat MAXX to 390ºF (199ºC).
2. In a small bowl, combine the tuna, mayonnaise, mustard, lemon juice, and green onions. Set aside.
3. Butter the cut side of the English muffins. Bake, butter-side up, in the air fryer oven for 2 to 4 minutes, or until light golden brown. Remove the muffins from the air fryer basket.
4. Top each muffin with one slice of cheese and return to the air fryer oven. Bake for 2 to 4 minutes or until the cheese melts and starts to brown.
5. Remove the muffins from the air fryer oven, top with the tuna mixture, and serve.

Bacon and Bell Pepper Sandwich

Prep time: 10 minutes | Cook time: 6 minutes | Serves 4

⅓ cup spicy barbecue sauce
2 tablespoons honey
8 slices cooked bacon, cut into thirds
1 red bell pepper, sliced
1 yellow bell pepper, sliced
3 pita pockets, cut in half
1¼ cups torn butter lettuce leaves
2 tomatoes, sliced

1. Select the ROAST function and preheat MAXX to 350ºF (177ºC).
2. In a small bowl, combine the barbecue sauce and the honey. Brush this mixture lightly onto the bacon slices and the red and yellow pepper slices.
3. Put the peppers into the air fryer basket and roast for 4 minutes. Then shake the basket, add the bacon, and roast for 2 minutes or until the bacon is browned and the peppers are tender.
4. Fill the pita halves with the bacon, peppers, any remaining barbecue sauce, lettuce, and tomatoes, and serve immediately.

Veggie Pita Sandwich

Prep time: 10 minutes | Cook time: 9 to 12 minutes | Serves 4

1 baby eggplant, peeled and chopped
1 red bell pepper, sliced
½ cup diced red onion
½ cup shredded carrot
1 teaspoon olive oil
⅓ cup low-fat Greek yogurt
½ teaspoon dried tarragon
2 low-sodium whole-wheat pita breads, halved crosswise

1. Select the ROAST function and preheat MAXX to 390ºF (199ºC).
2. In a baking pan, stir together the eggplant, red bell pepper, red onion, carrot, and olive oil. Put the vegetable mixture into the air fryer basket and roast for 7 to 9 minutes, stirring once, until the vegetables are tender. Drain if necessary.
3. In a small bowl, thoroughly mix the yogurt and tarragon until well combined.
4. Stir the yogurt mixture into the vegetables. Stuff one-fourth of this mixture into each pita pocket.
5. Place the sandwiches in the air fryer oven. Switch from ROAST to BAKE and bake for 2 to 3 minutes, or until the bread is toasted.
6. Serve immediately.

Smoky Chicken Sandwich

Prep time: 10 minutes | Cook time: 11 minutes | Serves 2

2 boneless, skinless chicken breasts (8 ounces / 227 g each), sliced horizontally in half and separated into 4 thinner cutlets
Kosher salt and freshly ground black pepper, to taste
½ cup all-purpose flour
3 large eggs, lightly beaten
½ cup dried bread crumbs

1 tablespoon smoked paprika
Cooking spray
½ cup marinara sauce
6 ounces (170 g) smoked Mozzarella cheese, grated
2 store-bought soft, sesame-seed hamburger or Italian buns, split

1. Season the chicken cutlets all over with salt and pepper. Set up three shallow bowls: Place the flour in the first bowl, the eggs in the second, and stir together the bread crumbs and smoked paprika in the third. Coat the chicken pieces in the flour, then dip fully in the egg. Dredge in the paprika bread crumbs, then transfer to a wire rack set over a baking sheet and spray both sides liberally with cooking spray.
2. Transfer 2 of the chicken cutlets to the air fryer oven. Select the AIR FRY function and cook at 350ºF (177ºC) for 6 minutes, or until beginning to brown. Spread each cutlet with 2 tablespoons of the marinara sauce and sprinkle with one-quarter of the smoked Mozzarella.
3. Increase the temperature to 400ºF (204ºC) and air fry for 5 minutes more, or until the chicken is cooked through and crisp and the cheese is melted and golden brown.
4. Transfer the cutlets to a plate, stack on top of each other, and place inside a bun. Repeat with the remaining chicken cutlets, marinara, smoked Mozzarella, and bun.
5. Serve the sandwiches warm.

Chapter 9 Appetizers and Snacks

Fast and Easy Tortilla Chips

Prep time: 5 minutes | Cook time: 3 minutes | Serves 2

8 corn tortillas
1 tablespoon olive oil
Salt, to taste

1. Slice the corn tortillas into triangles. Coat with a light brushing of olive oil.
2. Put the tortilla pieces in the air fryer basket. Select the AIR FRY function and cook at 390ºF (199ºC) for 3 minutes. You may need to do this in batches.
3. Season with salt before serving.

Herbed Pita Chips

Prep time: 5 minutes | Cook time: 5 to 6 minutes | Serves 4

¼ teaspoon dried basil
¼ teaspoon marjoram
¼ teaspoon ground oregano
¼ teaspoon garlic powder
¼ teaspoon ground thyme
¼ teaspoon salt
2 whole 6-inch pitas, whole grain or white
Cooking spray

1. Select the BAKE function and preheat MAXX to 330ºF (166ºC).
2. Mix all the seasonings together.
3. Cut each pita half into 4 wedges. Break apart wedges at the fold.
4. Mist one side of pita wedges with oil. Sprinkle with half of seasoning mix.
5. Turn pita wedges over, mist the other side with oil, and sprinkle with remaining seasonings.
6. Place pita wedges in air fryer basket and bake for 2 minutes.
7. Shake the basket and bake for 2 minutes longer. Shake again, and if needed, bake for 1 or 2 more minutes, or until crisp. Watch carefully because at this point they will cook very quickly.
8. Serve hot.

Crispy Apple Chips

Prep time: 5 minutes | Cook time: 25 to 35 minutes | Serves 1

1 Honeycrisp or Pink Lady apple

1. Core the apple with an apple corer, leaving apple whole. Cut the apple into ⅛-inch-thick slices.
2. Arrange the apple slices in the basket, staggering slices as much as possible.
3. Select the AIR FRY function and cook at 300ºF (149ºC) for 25 to 35 minutes, or until the chips are dry and some are lightly browned, turning 4 times with tongs to separate and rotate them from top to bottom.
4. Place the chips in a single layer on a wire rack to cool. Apples will become crisper as they cool. Serve immediately.

Honey Sriracha Chicken Wings

Prep time: 5 minutes | Cook time: 30 minutes | Serves 4

1 tablespoon Sriracha hot sauce
1 tablespoon honey
1 garlic clove, minced
½ teaspoon kosher salt
16 chicken wings and drumettes
Cooking spray

1. In a large bowl, whisk together the Sriracha hot sauce, honey, minced garlic, and kosher salt, then add the chicken and toss to coat.
2. Spray the air fryer basket with cooking spray, then place 8 wings in the basket.
3. Select the AIR FRY function and cook at 360ºF (182ºC) for 15 minutes, turning halfway through. Repeat with the remaining wings.
4. Remove the wings and allow to cool on a wire rack for 10 minutes before serving.

Lemony Pear Chips

Prep time: 15 minutes | Cook time: 9 to 13 minutes | Serves 4

2 firm Bosc pears, cut crosswise into ⅛-inch-thick slices
1 tablespoon freshly squeezed lemon juice
½ teaspoon ground cinnamon
⅛ teaspoon ground cardamom

1. Separate the smaller stem-end pear rounds from the larger rounds with seeds. Remove the core and seeds from the larger slices. Sprinkle all slices with lemon juice, cinnamon, and cardamom.
2. Put the smaller chips into the air fryer basket. Select the AIR FRY function and cook at 380°F (193°C) for 3 to 5 minutes, or until light golden brown, shaking the basket once during cooking. Remove from the air fryer oven.
3. Repeat with the larger slices, air frying for 6 to 8 minutes, or until light golden brown, shaking the basket once during cooking.
4. Remove the chips from the air fryer oven. Cool and serve or store in an airtight container at room temperature up for to 2 days.

Shishito Peppers with Herb Dressing

Prep time: 10 minutes | Cook time: 6 minutes | Serves 2 to 4

6 ounces (170 g) shishito peppers
1 tablespoon vegetable oil
Kosher salt and freshly ground black pepper, to taste
½ cup mayonnaise
2 tablespoons finely chopped fresh basil leaves
2 tablespoons finely chopped fresh flat-leaf parsley
1 tablespoon finely chopped fresh tarragon
1 tablespoon finely chopped fresh chives
Finely grated zest of ½ lemon
1 tablespoon fresh lemon juice
Flaky sea salt, for serving

1. In a bowl, toss together the shishitos and oil to evenly coat and season with kosher salt and black pepper. Transfer to the air fryer oven. Select the AIR FRY function and cook at 400°F (204°C) for 6 minutes, shaking the basket halfway through, or until the shishitos are blistered and lightly charred.
2. Meanwhile, in a small bowl, whisk together the mayonnaise, basil, parsley, tarragon, chives, lemon zest, and lemon juice.
3. Pile the peppers on a plate, sprinkle with flaky sea salt, and serve hot with the dressing.

Coconut-Crusted Shrimp

Prep time: 10 minutes | Cook time: 4 minutes | Serves 2 to 4

½ pound (227 g) medium shrimp, peeled and deveined (tails intact)
1 cup canned coconut milk
Finely grated zest of 1 lime
Kosher salt, to taste
½ cup panko bread crumbs
½ cup unsweetened shredded coconut
Freshly ground black pepper, to taste
Cooking spray
1 small or ½ medium cucumber, halved and deseeded
1 cup coconut yogurt
1 serrano chile, deseeded and minced

1. In a bowl, combine the shrimp, coconut milk, lime zest, and ½ teaspoon kosher salt. Let the shrimp stand for 10 minutes.
2. Meanwhile, in a separate bowl, stir together the bread crumbs and shredded coconut and season with salt and pepper.
3. A few at a time, add the shrimp to the bread crumb mixture and toss to coat completely. Transfer the shrimp to a wire rack set over a baking sheet. Spray the shrimp all over with cooking spray.
4. Transfer the shrimp to the air fryer oven. Select the AIR FRY function and cook at 400°F (204°C) for 4 minutes, or until golden brown and cooked through. Transfer the shrimp to a serving platter and season with more salt.
5. Grate the cucumber into a small bowl. Stir in the coconut yogurt and chile and season with salt and pepper. Serve alongside the shrimp while they're warm.

BBQ Pork Ribs

Prep time: 5 minutes | Cook time: 35 minutes | Serves 2

1 tablespoon kosher salt
1 tablespoon dark brown sugar
1 tablespoon sweet paprika
1 teaspoon garlic powder
1 teaspoon onion powder

1 teaspoon poultry seasoning
½ teaspoon mustard powder
½ teaspoon freshly ground black pepper
2¼ pounds (1 kg) individually cut St. Louis–style pork spareribs

1. Select the ROAST function and preheat MAXX to 350ºF (177ºC).
2. In a large bowl, whisk together the salt, brown sugar, paprika, garlic powder, onion powder, poultry seasoning, mustard powder, and pepper. Add the ribs and toss. Rub the seasonings into them with your hands until they're fully coated.
3. Arrange the ribs in the air fryer basket, standing up on their ends and leaned up against the wall of the basket and each other. Roast for 35 minutes, or until the ribs are tender inside and golden brown and crisp on the outside. Transfer the ribs to plates and serve hot.

Spiced Sweet Potato Fries

Prep time: 10 minutes | Cook time: 15 minutes | Serves 2

2 tablespoons olive oil
1½ teaspoons smoked paprika
1½ teaspoons kosher salt, plus more as needed
1 teaspoon chili powder
½ teaspoon ground cumin
½ teaspoon ground turmeric
½ teaspoon mustard

powder
¼ teaspoon cayenne pepper
2 medium sweet potatoes (about 10 ounces / 284 g each), cut into wedges, ½ inch thick and 3 inches long
Freshly ground black pepper, to taste
⅔ cup sour cream
1 garlic clove, grated

1. In a large bowl, combine the olive oil, paprika, salt, chili powder, cumin, turmeric, mustard powder, and cayenne. Add the sweet potatoes, season with black pepper, and toss to evenly coat.
2. Transfer the sweet potatoes to the air fryer oven (save the bowl with the leftover oil and spices). Select the AIR FRY function and cook at 400ºF (204ºC) for 15 minutes, shaking the basket halfway through, or until golden brown and crisp. Return the potato wedges to the reserved bowl and toss again while they are hot.
3. Meanwhile, in a small bowl, stir together the sour cream and garlic. Season with salt and black pepper and transfer to a serving dish.
4. Serve the potato wedges hot with the garlic sour cream.

Rosemary-Garlic Shoestring Fries

Prep time: 5 minutes | Cook time: 18 minutes | Serves 2

1 large russet potato (about 12 ounces / 340 g), scrubbed clean, and julienned
1 tablespoon vegetable oil
Leaves from 1 sprig fresh rosemary

Kosher salt and freshly ground black pepper, to taste
1 garlic clove, thinly sliced
Flaky sea salt, for serving

1. Place the julienned potatoes in a large colander and rinse under cold running water until the water runs clear. Spread the potatoes out on a double-thick layer of paper towels and pat dry.
2. In a large bowl, combine the potatoes, oil, and rosemary. Season with kosher salt and pepper and toss to coat evenly. Place the potatoes in the air fryer oven. Select the AIR FRY function and cook at 400ºF (204ºC) for 18 minutes, shaking the basket every 5 minutes and adding the garlic in the last 5 minutes of cooking, or until the fries are golden brown and crisp.
3. Transfer the fries to a plate and sprinkle with flaky sea salt while they're hot. Serve immediately.

Beef and Mango Skewers

Prep time: 10 minutes | Cook time: 4 to 7 minutes | Serves 4

¾ pound (340 g) beef sirloin tip, cut into 1-inch cubes
2 tablespoons balsamic vinegar
1 tablespoon olive oil
1 tablespoon honey
½ teaspoon dried marjoram
Pinch of salt
Freshly ground black pepper, to taste
1 mango

1. Select the ROAST function and preheat MAXX to 390ºF (199ºC).
2. Put the beef cubes in a medium bowl and add the balsamic vinegar, olive oil, honey, marjoram, salt, and pepper. Mix well, then massage the marinade into the beef with your hands. Set aside.
3. To prepare the mango, stand it on end and cut the skin off, using a sharp knife. Then carefully cut around the oval pit to remove the flesh. Cut the mango into 1-inch cubes.
4. Thread metal skewers alternating with three beef cubes and two mango cubes.
5. Roast the skewers in the air fryer basket for 4 to 7 minutes, or until the beef is browned and at least 145ºF (63ºC).
6. Serve hot.

Cheesy Stuffed Mushrooms

Prep time: 10 minutes | Cook time: 8 to 12 minutes | Serves 4

16 medium button mushrooms, rinsed and patted dry
⅓ cup low-sodium salsa
3 garlic cloves, minced
1 medium onion, finely chopped
1 jalapeño pepper, minced
⅛ teaspoon cayenne pepper
3 tablespoons shredded Pepper Jack cheese
2 teaspoons olive oil

1. Remove the stems from the mushrooms and finely chop them, reserving the whole caps.
2. In a medium bowl, mix the salsa, garlic, onion, jalapeño, cayenne, and Pepper Jack cheese. Stir in the chopped mushroom stems.
3. Stuff this mixture into the mushroom caps, mounding the filling. Drizzle the olive oil on the mushrooms. Transfer to the air fryer basket.
4. Select the AIR FRY function and cook at 350ºF (177ºC) for 8 to 12 minutes, or until the filling is hot and the mushrooms are tender.
5. Serve immediately.

Spicy Chicken Wings

Prep time: 5 minutes | Cook time: 20 minutes | Serves 2 to 4

1¼ pounds (567 g) chicken wings, separated into flats and drumettes
1 teaspoon baking powder
1 teaspoon cayenne pepper
¼ teaspoon garlic powder
Kosher salt and freshly ground black pepper, to taste
1 tablespoon unsalted butter, melted

For serving:
Blue cheese dressing
Celery
Carrot sticks

1. Place the chicken wings on a large plate, then sprinkle evenly with the baking powder, cayenne, and garlic powder. Toss the wings with your hands, making sure the baking powder and seasonings fully coat them, until evenly incorporated. Let the wings stand in the refrigerator for 1 hour or up to overnight.
2. Season the wings with salt and black pepper, then transfer to the air fryer oven, standing them up on end against the air fryer basket wall and each other.
3. Select the AIR FRY function and cook at 400ºF (204ºC) for 20 minutes, or until the wings are cooked through and crisp and golden brown. Transfer the wings to a bowl and toss with the butter while they're hot.
4. Arrange the wings on a platter and serve warm with the blue cheese dressing, celery and carrot sticks.

Crispy Phyllo Artichoke Triangles

Prep time: 15 minutes | Cook time: 9 to 12 minutes | Makes 18 triangles

¼ cup Ricotta cheese
1 egg white
⅓ cup minced and drained artichoke hearts
3 tablespoons grated Mozzarella cheese

½ teaspoon dried thyme
6 sheets frozen phyllo dough, thawed
2 tablespoons melted butter

1. Select the BAKE function and preheat MAXX to 400ºF (204ºC).
2. In a small bowl, combine the Ricotta cheese, egg white, artichoke hearts, Mozzarella cheese, and thyme, and mix well.
3. Cover the phyllo dough with a damp kitchen towel while you work so it doesn't dry out. Using one sheet at a time, place on the work surface and cut into thirds lengthwise.
4. Put about 1½ teaspoons of the filling on each strip at the base. Fold the bottom right-hand tip of phyllo over the filling to meet the other side in a triangle, then continue folding in a triangle. Brush each triangle with butter to seal the edges. Repeat with the remaining phyllo dough and filling.
5. Place the triangles in the air fryer basket. Bake, 6 at a time, for about 3 to 4 minutes, or until the phyllo is golden brown and crisp.
6. Serve hot.

Buffalo Cauliflower with Sour Dip

Prep time: 10 minutes | Cook time: 10 to 14 minutes | Serves 6

1 large head cauliflower, separated into small florets
1 tablespoon olive oil
½ teaspoon garlic powder
⅓ cup low-sodium hot wing sauce,

divided
⅔ cup nonfat Greek yogurt
½ teaspoons Tabasco sauce
1 celery stalk, chopped
1 tablespoon crumbled blue cheese

1. In a large bowl, toss the cauliflower florets with the olive oil. Sprinkle with the garlic powder and toss again to coat. Put half of the cauliflower in the air fryer basket.
2. Select the AIR FRY function and cook at 380ºF (193ºC) for 5 to 7 minutes, or until the cauliflower is browned, shaking the basket once during cooking.
3. Transfer to a serving bowl and toss with half of the wing sauce. Repeat with the remaining cauliflower and wing sauce.
4. In a small bowl, stir together the yogurt, Tabasco sauce, celery, and blue cheese. Serve the cauliflower with the dip.

Baked Ricotta

Prep time: 10 minutes | Cook time: 15 minutes | Makes 2 cups

1 (15-ounce / 425-g) container whole milk Ricotta cheese
3 tablespoons grated Parmesan cheese, divided
2 tablespoons extra-virgin olive oil
1 teaspoon chopped fresh thyme leaves

1 teaspoon grated lemon zest
1 clove garlic, crushed with press
¼ teaspoon salt
¼ teaspoon pepper
Toasted baguette slices or crackers, for serving

1. Select the BAKE function and preheat MAXX to 380ºF (193ºC).
2. To get the baking dish in and out of the air fryer oven, create a sling using a 24-inch length of foil, folded lengthwise into thirds.
3. Whisk together the Ricotta, 2 tablespoons of the Parmesan, oil, thyme, lemon zest, garlic, salt, and pepper. Pour into a baking dish. Cover the dish tightly with foil.
4. Place the sling under dish and lift by the ends into the air fryer oven, tucking the ends of the sling around the dish. Bake for 10 minutes. Remove the foil cover and sprinkle with the remaining 1 tablespoon of the Parmesan. Switch from BAKE to AIR FRY and air fry for 5 more minutes, or until bubbly at edges and the top is browned.
5. Serve warm with toasted baguette slices or crackers.

Lemony Chicken Drumsticks

Prep time: 5 minutes | Cook time: 30 minutes | Serves 2

2 teaspoons freshly ground coarse black pepper
1 teaspoon baking powder
½ teaspoon garlic powder
4 chicken drumsticks (4 ounces / 113 g each)
Kosher salt, to taste
1 lemon

1. In a small bowl, stir together the pepper, baking powder, and garlic powder. Place the drumsticks on a plate and sprinkle evenly with the baking powder mixture, turning the drumsticks so they're well coated. Let the drumsticks stand in the refrigerator for at least 1 hour or up to overnight.
2. Sprinkle the drumsticks with salt, then transfer them to the air fryer oven, standing them bone-end up and leaning against the wall of the air fryer basket. Select the AIR FRY function and cook at 375ºF (191ºC) for 30 minutes, or until cooked through and crisp on the outside.
3. Transfer the drumsticks to a serving platter and finely grate the zest of the lemon over them while they're hot. Cut the lemon into wedges and serve with the warm drumsticks.

Peppery Chicken Meatballs

Prep time: 5 minutes | Cook time: 13 to 20 minutes | Makes 16 meatballs

2 teaspoons olive oil
¼ cup minced onion
¼ cup minced red bell pepper
2 vanilla wafers, crushed
1 egg white
½ teaspoon dried thyme
½ pound (227 g) ground chicken breast

1. In a baking pan, mix the olive oil, onion, and red bell pepper. Put the pan in the air fryer oven. Select the AIR FRY function and cook at 370ºF (188ºC) for 3 to 5 minutes, or until the vegetables are tender.
2. In a medium bowl, mix the cooked vegetables, crushed wafers, egg white, and thyme until well combined

3. Mix in the chicken, gently but thoroughly, until everything is combined.
4. Form the mixture into 16 meatballs and place them in the air fryer basket. Air fry for 10 to 15 minutes, or until the meatballs reach an internal temperature of 165ºF (74ºC) on a meat thermometer.
5. Serve immediately.

Crispy Prosciutto-Wrapped Asparagus

Prep time: 5 minutes | Cook time: 16 to 24 minutes | Serves 6

12 asparagus spears, woody ends trimmed
24 pieces thinly sliced prosciutto
Cooking spray

1. Wrap each asparagus spear with 2 slices of prosciutto, then repeat this process with the remaining asparagus and prosciutto.
2. Spray the air fryer basket with cooking spray, then place 2 to 3 bundles in the basket. Select the AIR FRY function and cook at 360ºF (182ºC) for 4 minutes. Repeat with the remaining asparagus bundles.
3. Remove the bundles and allow to cool on a wire rack for 5 minutes before serving.

Spicy Chicken Bites

Prep time: 10 minutes | Cook time: 10 to 12 minutes | Makes 30 bites

8 ounces boneless and skinless chicken thighs, cut into 30 pieces
¼ teaspoon kosher
salt
2 tablespoons hot sauce
Cooking spray

1. Spray the air fryer basket with cooking spray and season the chicken bites with the kosher salt, then place in the basket.
2. Select the AIR FRY function and cook at 390ºF (199ºC) for 10 to 12 minutes, or until crispy.
3. While the chicken bites cook, pour the hot sauce into a large bowl.
4. Remove the bites and add to the sauce bowl, tossing to coat.
5. Serve warm.

Air Fried Olives

Prep time: 5 minutes | Cook time: 8 minutes | Serves 4

1 (5½-ounce / 156-g) jar pitted green olives
½ cup all-purpose flour

Salt and pepper, to taste
½ cup bread crumbs
1 egg
Cooking spray

1. Remove the olives from the jar and dry thoroughly with paper towels.
2. In a small bowl, combine the flour with salt and pepper to taste. Place the bread crumbs in another small bowl. In a third small bowl, beat the egg.
3. Spritz the air fryer basket with cooking spray.
4. Dip the olives in the flour, then the egg, and then the bread crumbs.
5. Place the breaded olives in the air fryer oven. It is okay to stack them. Spray the olives with cooking spray.
6. Select the AIR FRY function and cook at 400ºF (204ºC) for 6 minutes. Flip the olives and air fry for an additional 2 minutes, or until brown and crisp.
7. Cool before serving.

Bacon-Wrapped Shrimp and Jalapeño

Prep time: 20 minutes | Cook time: 26 minutes | Serves 8

24 large shrimp, peeled and deveined, about ¾ pound (340 g)
5 tablespoons barbecue sauce,

divided
12 strips bacon, cut in half
24 small pickled jalapeño slices

1. Toss together the shrimp and 3 tablespoons of the barbecue sauce. Let stand for 15 minutes. Soak 24 wooden toothpicks in water for 10 minutes. Wrap 1 piece bacon around the shrimp and jalapeño slice, then secure with a toothpick.
2. Working in batches, place half of the shrimp in the air fryer basket, spacing them ½ inch apart.

3. Select the AIR FRY function and cook at 350ºF (177ºC) for 10 minutes. Turn shrimp over with tongs and air fry for 3 minutes more, or until bacon is golden brown and shrimp are cooked through.
4. Brush with the remaining barbecue sauce and serve.

Sweet Bacon Tater Tots

Prep time: 5 minutes | Cook time: 7 minutes | Serves 4

24 frozen tater tots
6 slices cooked bacon
2 tablespoons maple

syrup
1 cup shredded Cheddar cheese

1. Put the tater tots in the air fryer basket. Select the AIR FRY function and cook at 400ºF (204ºC) for 10 minutes, shaking the basket halfway through the cooking time.
2. Meanwhile, cut the bacon into 1-inch pieces.
3. Remove the tater tots from the air fryer basket and put into a baking pan. Top with the bacon and drizzle with the maple syrup. Air fry for 5 minutes, or until the tots and bacon are crisp.
4. Top with the cheese and air fry for 2 minutes, or until the cheese is melted.
5. Serve hot.

Bacon-Wrapped Dates

Prep time: 10 minutes | Cook time: 10 to 14 minutes | Serves 6

12 dates, pitted
6 slices high-quality

bacon, cut in half
Cooking spray

1. Select the BAKE function and preheat MAXX to 360ºF (182ºC).
2. Wrap each date with half a bacon slice and secure with a toothpick.
3. Spray the air fryer basket with cooking spray, then place 6 bacon-wrapped dates in the basket and bake for 5 to 7 minutes or until the bacon is crispy. Repeat this process with the remaining dates.
4. Remove the dates and allow to cool on a wire rack for 5 minutes before serving.

Spicy Kale Chips

Prep time: 5 minutes | Cook time: 8 to 12 minutes | Serves 4

5 cups kale, large stems removed and chopped
2 teaspoons canola oil
¼ teaspoon smoked paprika
¼ teaspoon kosher salt
Cooking spray

1. In a large bowl, toss the kale, canola oil, smoked paprika, and kosher salt.
2. Spray the air fryer basket with cooking spray, then place half the kale in the basket.
3. Select the AIR FRY function and cook at 390°F (199°C) for 2 to 3 minutes. Shake the basket and air fry for 2 to 3 more minutes, or until crispy. Repeat this process with the remaining kale.
4. Remove the kale and allow to cool on a wire rack for 3 to 5 minutes before serving.

Crispy Spiced Chickpeas

Prep time: 5 minutes | Cook time: 6 to 12 minutes | Makes 1½ cups

1 can (15-ounce / 425-g) chickpeas, rinsed and dried with paper towels
1 tablespoon olive oil
½ teaspoon dried rosemary
½ teaspoon dried parsley
½ teaspoon dried chives
¼ teaspoon mustard powder
¼ teaspoon sweet paprika
¼ teaspoon cayenne pepper
Kosher salt and freshly ground black pepper, to taste

1. In a large bowl, combine all the ingredients, except for the kosher salt and black pepper, and toss until the chickpeas are evenly coated in the herbs and spices.
2. Scrape the chickpeas and seasonings into the air fryer oven. Select the AIR FRY function and cook at 350°F (177°C) for 6 to 12 minutes, or until browned and crisp, shaking the basket halfway through.
3. Transfer the crispy chickpeas to a bowl, sprinkle with kosher salt and black pepper, and serve warm.

Lemony Endive in Curried Yogurt

Prep time: 5 minutes | Cook time: 10 minutes | Serves 6

6 heads endive
½ cup plain and fat-free yogurt
3 tablespoons lemon juice
1 teaspoon garlic powder
½ teaspoon curry powder
Salt and ground black pepper, to taste

1. Wash the endives, and slice them in half lengthwise.
2. In a bowl, mix together the yogurt, lemon juice, garlic powder, curry powder, salt and pepper.
3. Brush the endive halves with the marinade, coating them completely. Allow to sit for at least 30 minutes or up to 24 hours.
4. Put the endives in the air fryer basket. Select the AIR FRY function and cook at 320°F (160°C) for 10 minutes.
5. Serve hot.

Creamy Spinach-Broccoli Dip

Prep time: 10 minutes | Cook time: 9 to 14 minutes | Serves 4

½ cup low-fat Greek yogurt
¼ cup nonfat cream cheese
½ cup frozen chopped broccoli, thawed and drained
½ cup frozen chopped spinach, thawed and drained
$1/3$ cup chopped red bell pepper
1 garlic clove, minced
½ teaspoon dried oregano
2 tablespoons grated low-sodium Parmesan cheese

1. Select the BAKE function and preheat MAXX to 340°F (171°C).
2. In a medium bowl, blend the yogurt and cream cheese until well combined.
3. Stir in the broccoli, spinach, red bell pepper, garlic, and oregano. Transfer to a baking pan. Sprinkle with the Parmesan cheese.
4. Place the pan in the air fryer basket. Bake for 9 to 14 minutes, or until the dip is bubbly and the top starts to brown.
5. Serve immediately.

Veggie Shrimp Toast

Prep time: 15 minutes | Cook time: 3 to 6 minutes | Serves 4

8 large raw shrimp, peeled and finely chopped
1 egg white
2 garlic cloves, minced
3 tablespoons minced red bell pepper
1 medium celery stalk, minced
2 tablespoons cornstarch
¼ teaspoon Chinese five-spice powder
3 slices firm thin-sliced no-sodium whole-wheat bread

1. In a small bowl, stir together the shrimp, egg white, garlic, red bell pepper, celery, cornstarch, and five-spice powder. Top each slice of bread with one-third of the shrimp mixture, spreading it evenly to the edges. With a sharp knife, cut each slice of bread into 4 strips.
2. Place the shrimp toasts in the air fryer basket in a single layer. You may need to cook them in batches.
3. Select the AIR FRY function and cook at 350ºF (177ºC) for 3 to 6 minutes, until crisp and golden brown.
4. Serve hot.

Veggie Salmon Nachos

Prep time: 10 minutes | Cook time: 9 to 12 minutes | Serves 6

2 ounces (57 g) baked no-salt corn tortilla chips
1 (5-ounce / 142-g) baked salmon fillet, flaked
½ cup canned low-sodium black beans, rinsed and drained
1 red bell pepper, chopped
½ cup grated carrot
1 jalapeño pepper, minced
⅓ cup shredded low-sodium low-fat Swiss cheese
1 tomato, chopped

1. Select the BAKE function and preheat MAXX to 360ºF (182ºC).
2. In a baking pan, layer the tortilla chips. Top with the salmon, black beans, red bell pepper, carrot, jalapeño, and Swiss cheese.
3. Bake in the air fryer oven for 9 to 12 minutes, or until the cheese is melted and starts to brown.
4. Top with the tomato and serve.

Crispy Breaded Beef Cubes

Prep time: 10 minutes | Cook time: 12 to 16 minutes | Serves 4

1 pound (454 g) sirloin tip, cut into 1-inch cubes
1 cup cheese pasta sauce
1½ cups soft bread crumbs
2 tablespoons olive oil
½ teaspoon dried marjoram

1. In a medium bowl, toss the beef with the pasta sauce to coat.
2. In a shallow bowl, combine the bread crumbs, oil, and marjoram, and mix well. Drop the beef cubes, one at a time, into the bread crumb mixture to coat thoroughly. Transfer to the air fryer basket.
3. Select the AIR FRY function and cook in two batches at 360ºF (182ºC) for 6 to 8 minutes, shaking the basket once during cooking time, until the beef is at least 145ºF (63ºC) and the outside is crisp and brown.
4. Serve hot.

Cheesy Apple Roll-Ups

Prep time: 5 minutes | Cook time: 4 to 5 minutes | Makes 8 roll-ups

8 slices whole wheat sandwich bread
4 ounces (113 g) Colby Jack cheese, grated
½ small apple, chopped
2 tablespoons butter, melted

1. Remove the crusts from the bread and flatten the slices with a rolling pin. Don't be gentle. Press hard so that bread will be very thin.
2. Top bread slices with cheese and chopped apple, dividing the ingredients evenly.
3. Roll up each slice tightly and secure each with one or two toothpicks.
4. Brush outside of rolls with melted butter.
5. Place in air fryer basket. Select the AIR FRY function and cook at 390ºF (199ºC) for 4 to 5 minutes, or until outside is crisp and nicely browned.
6. Serve hot.

Cheesy Steak Fries

Prep time: 5 minutes | Cook time: 20 minutes | Serves 5

1 (28-ounce / 794-g) bag frozen steak fries
Cooking spray
Salt and pepper, to taste
½ cup beef gravy
1 cup shredded Mozzarella cheese
2 scallions, green parts only, chopped

1. Place the frozen steak fries in the air fryer oven. Select the AIR FRY function and cook at 400ºF (204ºC) for 10 minutes. Shake the basket and spritz the fries with cooking spray. Sprinkle with salt and pepper. Air fry for an additional 8 minutes.
2. Pour the beef gravy into a medium, microwave-safe bowl. Microwave for 30 seconds, or until the gravy is warm.
3. Sprinkle the fries with the cheese. Air fry for an additional 2 minutes, until the cheese is melted.
4. Transfer the fries to a serving dish. Drizzle the fries with gravy and sprinkle the scallions on top for a green garnish. Serve.

Cheesy Jalapeño Poppers

Prep time: 5 minutes | Cook time: 10 minutes | Serves 4

8 jalapeño peppers
½ cup whipped cream cheese
¼ cup shredded Cheddar cheese

1. Use a paring knife to carefully cut off the jalapeño tops, then scoop out the ribs and seeds. Set aside.
2. In a medium bowl, combine the whipped cream cheese and shredded Cheddar cheese. Place the mixture in a sealable plastic bag, and using a pair of scissors, cut off one corner from the bag. Gently squeeze some cream cheese mixture into each pepper until almost full.
3. Place a piece of parchment paper on the bottom of the air fryer basket and place the poppers on top, distributing evenly. Select the AIR FRY function and cook at 360ºF (182ºC) for 10 minutes.
4. Allow the poppers to cool for 5 to 10 minutes before serving.

Poutine with Waffle Fries

Prep time: 10 minutes | Cook time: 15 to 17 minutes | Serves 4

2 cups frozen waffle cut fries
2 teaspoons olive oil
1 red bell pepper, chopped
2 green onions, sliced
1 cup shredded Swiss cheese
½ cup bottled chicken gravy

1. Toss the waffle fries with the olive oil and place in the air fryer basket. Select the AIR FRY function and cook at 380ºF (193ºC) for 10 to 12 minutes, or until the fries are crisp and light golden brown, shaking the basket halfway through the cooking time.
2. Transfer the fries to a baking pan and top with the pepper, green onions, and cheese. Air fry for 3 minutes, or until the vegetables are crisp and tender.
3. Remove the pan from the air fryer oven and drizzle the gravy over the fries. Air fry for 2 minutes, or until the gravy is hot.
4. Serve immediately.

Cheesy Hash Brown Bruschetta

Prep time: 5 minutes | Cook time: 6 to 8 minutes | Serves 4

4 frozen hash brown patties
1 tablespoon olive oil
1/3 cup chopped cherry tomatoes
3 tablespoons diced fresh Mozzarella
2 tablespoons grated Parmesan cheese
1 tablespoon balsamic vinegar
1 tablespoon minced fresh basil

1. Place the hash brown patties in the air fryer basket in a single layer. Select the AIR FRY function and cook at 400ºF (204ºC) for 6 to 8 minutes, or until the potatoes are crisp, hot, and golden brown.
2. Meanwhile, combine the olive oil, tomatoes, Mozzarella, Parmesan, vinegar, and basil in a small bowl.
3. When the potatoes are done, carefully remove from the basket and arrange on a serving plate. Top with the tomato mixture and serve.

Crispy Cajun Dill Pickle Chips

Prep time: 5 minutes | Cook time: 10 minutes | Makes 16 slices

¼ cup all-purpose flour
½ cup panko bread crumbs
1 large egg, beaten
2 teaspoons Cajun seasoning
2 large dill pickles, sliced into 8 rounds each
Cooking spray

1. Place the all-purpose flour, panko bread crumbs, and egg into 3 separate shallow bowls, then stir the Cajun seasoning into the flour.
2. Dredge each pickle chip in the flour mixture, then the egg, and finally the bread crumbs. Shake off any excess, then place each coated pickle chip on a plate.
3. Spritz the air fryer basket with cooking spray, then place 8 pickle chips in the basket. Select the AIR FRY function and cook at 390°F (199°C) for 5 minutes, or until crispy and golden brown. Repeat this process with the remaining pickle chips.
4. Remove the chips and allow to slightly cool on a wire rack before serving.

Crispy Mozzarella Sticks

Prep time: 5 minutes | Cook time: 6 to 7 minutes | Serves 4 to 8

1 egg
1 tablespoon water
8 eggroll wraps
8 Mozzarella string cheese "sticks"

1. Beat together egg and water in a small bowl.
2. Lay out eggroll wraps and moisten edges with egg wash.
3. Place one piece of string cheese on each wrap near one end.
4. Fold in sides of eggroll wrap over ends of cheese, and then roll up.
5. Brush outside of wrap with egg wash and press gently to seal well.
6. Place in air fryer basket in a single layer. Select the AIR FRY function and cook at 390°F (199°C) for 5 minutes. Air fry for an additional 1 or 2 minutes, if necessary, or until they are golden brown and crispy.
7. Serve immediately.

Cajun Zucchini Chips

Prep time: 5 minutes | Cook time: 15 to 16 minutes | Serves 4

2 large zucchini, cut into ⅛-inch-thick slices
2 teaspoons Cajun seasoning
Cooking spray

1. Spray the air fryer basket lightly with cooking spray.
2. Put the zucchini slices in a medium bowl and spray them generously with cooking spray.
3. Sprinkle the Cajun seasoning over the zucchini and stir to make sure they are evenly coated with oil and seasoning.
4. Place the slices in a single layer in the air fryer basket, making sure not to overcrowd. You will need to cook these in several batches.
5. Select the AIR FRY function and cook at 370°F (188°C) for 8 minutes. Flip the slices over and air fry for an additional 7 to 8 minutes, or until they are as crisp and brown as you prefer.
6. Serve immediately.

Zucchini and Potato Tots

Prep time: 5 minutes | Cook time: 20 minutes | Serves 4

1 large zucchini, grated
1 medium baked potato, skin removed and mashed
¼ cup shredded Cheddar cheese
1 large egg, beaten
½ teaspoon kosher salt
Cooking spray

1. Wrap the grated zucchini in a paper towel and squeeze out any excess liquid, then combine the zucchini, baked potato, shredded Cheddar cheese, egg, and kosher salt in a large bowl.
2. Spray a baking pan with cooking spray, then place individual tablespoons of the zucchini mixture in the pan.
3. Select the AIR FRY function and cook at 390°F (199°C) for 10 minutes. Repeat with the remaining mixture.
4. Remove the tots and allow to cool on a wire rack for 5 minutes before serving.

Spiced Mixed Nuts

Prep time: 5 minutes | Cook time: 6 minutes | Makes 2 cups

½ cup raw cashews
½ cup raw pecan halves
½ cup raw walnut halves
½ cup raw whole almonds
2 tablespoons olive oil
1 tablespoon light brown sugar
1 teaspoon chopped fresh rosemary

leaves
1 teaspoon chopped fresh thyme leaves
1 teaspoon kosher salt
½ teaspoon ground coriander
¼ teaspoon onion powder
¼ teaspoon freshly ground black pepper
⅛ teaspoon garlic powder

1. In a large bowl, combine all the ingredients and toss until the nuts are evenly coated in the herbs, spices, and sugar.
2. Scrape the nuts and seasonings into the air fryer oven. Select the AIR FRY function and cook at 350ºF (177ºC) for 6 minutes, or until golden brown and fragrant, shaking the basket halfway through.
3. Transfer the nuts to a bowl and serve warm.

Artichoke-Spinach Dip

Prep time: 10 minutes | Cook time: 10 minutes | Makes 3 cups

1 (14-ounce / 397-g) can artichoke hearts packed in water, drained and chopped
1 (10-ounce / 284-g) package frozen spinach, thawed and drained
1 teaspoon minced garlic
2 tablespoons

mayonnaise
¼ cup nonfat plain Greek yogurt
¼ cup shredded part-skim Mozzarella cheese
¼ cup grated Parmesan cheese
¼ teaspoon freshly ground black pepper
Cooking spray

1. Wrap the artichoke hearts and spinach in a paper towel and squeeze out any excess liquid, then transfer the vegetables to a large bowl.

2. Add the minced garlic, mayonnaise, plain Greek yogurt, Mozzarella, Parmesan, and black pepper to the large bowl, stirring well to combine.
3. Spray a baking pan with cooking spray, then transfer the dip mixture to the pan. Select the AIR FRY function and cook at 360ºF (182ºC) for 10 minutes.
4. Remove the dip from the air fryer oven and allow to cool in the pan on a wire rack for 10 minutes before serving.

Spinach and Crab Meat Cups

Prep time: 10 minutes | Cook time: 10 minutes | Makes 30 cups

1 (6-ounce / 170-g) can crab meat, drained to yield ⅓ cup meat
¼ cup frozen spinach, thawed, drained, and chopped
1 clove garlic, minced
½ cup grated

Parmesan cheese
3 tablespoons plain yogurt
¼ teaspoon lemon juice
½ teaspoon Worcestershire sauce
30 mini frozen phyllo shells, thawed
Cooking spray

1. Remove any bits of shell that might remain in the crab meat.
2. Mix the crab meat, spinach, garlic, and cheese together.
3. Stir in the yogurt, lemon juice, and Worcestershire sauce and mix well.
4. Spoon a teaspoon of filling into each phyllo shell.
5. Spray the air fryer basket with cooking spray and arrange half the shells in the basket.
6. Select the AIR FRY function and cook at 390ºF (199ºC) for 5 minutes. Repeat with the remaining shells.
7. Serve immediately.

Rosemary Baked Cashews

Prep time: 5 minutes | Cook time: 3 minutes | Makes 2 cups

2 sprigs of fresh rosemary (1 chopped and 1 whole)
1 teaspoon olive oil
1 teaspoon kosher

salt
½ teaspoon honey
2 cups roasted and unsalted whole cashews
Cooking spray

1. Select the BAKE function and preheat MAXX to 300ºF (149ºC).
2. In a medium bowl, whisk together the chopped rosemary, olive oil, kosher salt, and honey. Set aside.
3. Spray the air fryer basket with cooking spray, then place the cashews and the whole rosemary sprig in the basket and bake for 3 minutes.
4. Remove the cashews and rosemary from the air fryer oven, then discard the rosemary and add the cashews to the olive oil mixture, tossing to coat.
5. Allow to cool for 15 minutes before serving.

Breaded Artichoke Hearts

Prep time: 5 minutes | Cook time: 8 minutes | Serves 14

14 whole artichoke hearts, packed in water
1 egg
½ cup all-purpose flour

⅓ cup panko bread crumbs
1 teaspoon Italian seasoning
Cooking spray

1. Squeeze excess water from the artichoke hearts and place them on paper towels to dry.
2. In a small bowl, beat the egg. In another small bowl, place the flour. In a third small bowl, combine the bread crumbs and Italian seasoning, and stir.
3. Spritz the air fryer basket with cooking spray.
4. Dip the artichoke hearts in the flour, then the egg, and then the bread crumb mixture.
5. Place the breaded artichoke hearts in the air fryer basket. Spray them with cooking spray.
6. Select the AIR FRY function and cook at 380ºF (193ºC) for 8 minutes, or until the artichoke hearts have browned and are crisp, flipping once halfway through.
7. Let cool for 5 minutes before serving.

Pigs in a Blanket

Prep time: 5 minutes | Cook time: 14 minutes | Serves 4 to 6

24 cocktail smoked sausages
6 slices deli-sliced Cheddar cheese, each cut into 8

rectangular pieces
1 (8-ounce / 227-g) tube refrigerated crescent roll dough

1. Unroll the crescent roll dough into one large sheet. If your crescent roll dough has perforated seams, pinch or roll all the perforated seams together. Cut the large sheet of dough into 4 rectangles. Then cut each rectangle into 6 pieces by making one slice lengthwise in the middle and 2 slices horizontally. You should have 24 pieces of dough.
2. Make a deep slit lengthwise down the center of the cocktail sausage. Stuff two pieces of cheese into the slit in the sausage. Roll one piece of crescent dough around the stuffed cocktail sausage, leaving the ends of the sausage exposed. Pinch the seam together. Repeat with the remaining sausages.
3. Transfer to the air fryer basket, seam-side down.
4. Select the AIR FRY function and cook in 2 batches at 350ºF (177ºC) for 7 minutes.
5. Serve hot.

Root Veggie Chips with Herb Salt

Prep time: 10 minutes | Cook time: 8 minutes | Serves 2

1 parsnip, washed
1 small beet, washed
1 small turnip, washed
½ small sweet potato, washed
1 teaspoon olive oil
Cooking spray
Herb Salt:
¼ teaspoon kosher salt
2 teaspoons finely chopped fresh parsley

1. Peel and thinly slice the parsnip, beet, turnip, and sweet potato, then place the vegetables in a large bowl, add the olive oil, and toss.
2. Spray the air fryer basket with cooking spray, then place the vegetables in the basket. Select the AIR FRY function and cook at 360ºF (182ºC) for 8 minutes, gently shaking the basket halfway through.
3. While the chips cook, make the herb salt in a small bowl by combining the kosher salt and parsley.
4. Remove the chips and place on a serving plate, then sprinkle the herb salt on top and allow to cool for 2 to 3 minutes before serving.

Mozzarella Arancini

Prep time: 5 minutes | Cook time: 8 to 11 minutes | Makes 16 arancini

2 cups cooked rice, cooled
2 eggs, beaten
1½ cups panko bread crumbs, divided
½ cup grated
Parmesan cheese
2 tablespoons minced fresh basil
16 ¾-inch cubes Mozzarella cheese
2 tablespoons olive oil

1. In a medium bowl, combine the rice, eggs, ½ cup of the bread crumbs, Parmesan cheese, and basil. Form this mixture into 16 1½-inch balls.
2. Poke a hole in each of the balls with your finger and insert a Mozzarella cube. Form the rice mixture firmly around the cheese.

3. On a shallow plate, combine the remaining 1 cup of the bread crumbs with the olive oil and mix well. Roll the rice balls in the bread crumbs to coat. Transfer to the air fryer basket.
4. Select the AIR FRY function and cook at 400ºF (204ºC) for 8 to 11 minutes, or until golden brown. You may need to work in batches.
5. Serve hot.

Cayenne Sesame Nut Mix

Prep time: 10 minutes | Cook time: 2 minutes | Makes 4 cups

1 tablespoon buttery spread, melted
2 teaspoons honey
¼ teaspoon cayenne pepper
2 teaspoons sesame seeds
¼ teaspoon kosher salt
¼ teaspoon freshly ground black pepper
1 cup cashews
1 cup almonds
1 cup mini pretzels
1 cup rice squares cereal
Cooking spray

1. Select the BAKE function and preheat MAXX to 360ºF (182ºC).
2. In a large bowl, combine the buttery spread, honey, cayenne pepper, sesame seeds, kosher salt, and black pepper, then add the cashews, almonds, pretzels, and rice squares, tossing to coat.
3. Spray a baking pan with cooking spray, then pour the mixture into the pan and bake for 2 minutes.
4. Remove the sesame mix from the air fryer oven and allow to cool in the pan on a wire rack for 5 minutes before serving.

Air Fried Pot Stickers

Prep time: 10 minutes | Cook time: 18 to 20 minutes | Makes 30 pot stickers

½ cup finely chopped cabbage
¼ cup finely chopped red bell pepper
2 green onions, finely chopped
1 egg, beaten

2 tablespoons cocktail sauce
2 teaspoons low-sodium soy sauce
30 wonton wrappers
1 tablespoon water, for brushing the wrappers

1. In a small bowl, combine the cabbage, pepper, green onions, egg, cocktail sauce, and soy sauce, and mix well.
2. Put about 1 teaspoon of the mixture in the center of each wonton wrapper. Fold the wrapper in half, covering the filling; dampen the edges with water, and seal. You can crimp the edges of the wrapper with your fingers so they look like the pot stickers you get in restaurants. Brush them with water.
3. Place the pot stickers in the air fryer basket. Select the AIR FRY function and cook at 360°F (182°C) for 9 to 10 minutes, or until the pot stickers are hot and the bottoms are lightly browned.
4. Serve hot.

Bruschetta with Basil Pesto

Prep time: 10 minutes | Cook time: 5 to 11 minutes | Serves 4

8 slices French bread, ½ inch thick
2 tablespoons softened butter
1 cup shredded Mozzarella cheese

½ cup basil pesto
1 cup chopped grape tomatoes
2 green onions, thinly sliced

1. Select the BAKE function and preheat MAXX to 350°F (177°C).
2. Spread the bread with the butter and place butter-side up in the air fryer basket. Bake for 3 to 5 minutes, or until the bread is light golden brown.
3. Remove the bread from the basket and top each piece with some of the cheese. Return to the basket in 2 batches and bake for 1 to 3 minutes, or until the cheese melts.

4. Meanwhile, combine the pesto, tomatoes, and green onions in a small bowl.
5. When the cheese has melted, remove the bread from the air fryer oven and place on a serving plate. Top each slice with some of the pesto mixture and serve.

Tortellini with Spicy Dipping Sauce

Prep time: 5 minutes | Cook time: 20 minutes | Serves 4

¾ cup mayonnaise
2 tablespoons mustard
1 egg
½ cup flour
½ teaspoon dried oregano

1½ cups bread crumbs
2 tablespoons olive oil
2 cups frozen cheese tortellini

1. In a small bowl, combine the mayonnaise and mustard and mix well. Set aside.
2. In a shallow bowl, beat the egg. In a separate bowl, combine the flour and oregano. In another bowl, combine the bread crumbs and olive oil, and mix well.
3. Drop the tortellini, a few at a time, into the egg, then into the flour, then into the egg again, and then into the bread crumbs to coat. Put into the air fryer basket, cooking in batches.
4. Select the AIR FRY function and cook at 380°F (193°C) for 10 minutes, shaking halfway through the cooking time, or until the tortellini are crisp and golden brown on the outside. Serve with the mayonnaise mixture.

Chapter 10 Desserts

Bourbon Bread Pudding

Prep time: 10 minutes | Cook time: 20 minutes | Serves 4

3 slices whole grain bread, cubed
1 large egg
1 cup whole milk
2 tablespoons bourbon
½ teaspoons vanilla extract
¼ cup maple syrup, divided
½ teaspoons ground cinnamon
2 teaspoons sparkling sugar

1. Select the BAKE function and preheat MAXX to 270ºF (132ºC).
2. Spray a baking pan with nonstick cooking spray, then place the bread cubes in the pan.
3. In a medium bowl, whisk together the egg, milk, bourbon, vanilla extract, 3 tablespoons of maple syrup, and cinnamon. Pour the egg mixture over the bread and press down with a spatula to coat all the bread, then sprinkle the sparkling sugar on top and bake for 20 minutes.
4. Remove the pudding from the air fryer oven and allow to cool in the pan on a wire rack for 10 minutes. Drizzle the remaining 1 tablespoon of maple syrup on top. Slice and serve warm.

Applesauce and Chocolate Brownies

Prep time: 10 minutes | Cook time: 15 minutes | Serves 8

¼ cup unsweetened cocoa powder
¼ cup all-purpose flour
¼ teaspoon kosher salt
½ teaspoons baking powder
3 tablespoons unsalted butter, melted
½ cup granulated sugar
1 large egg
3 tablespoons unsweetened applesauce
¼ cup miniature semisweet chocolate chips
Coarse sea salt, to taste

1. Select the BAKE function and preheat MAXX to 300ºF (149ºC).
2. In a large bowl, whisk together the cocoa powder, all-purpose flour, kosher salt, and baking powder.
3. In a separate large bowl, combine the butter, granulated sugar, egg, and applesauce, then use a spatula to fold in the cocoa powder mixture and the chocolate chips until well combined.
4. Spray a baking pan with nonstick cooking spray, then pour the mixture into the pan. Place the pan in the air fryer oven and bake for 15 minutes or until a toothpick comes out clean when inserted in the middle.
5. Remove the brownies from the air fryer oven, sprinkle some coarse sea salt on top, and allow to cool in the pan on a wire rack for 20 minutes before cutting and serving.

Lemony Apple Butter

Prep time: 10 minutes | Cook time: 1 hour | Makes 1¼ cups

Cooking spray
2 cups unsweetened applesauce
⅔ cup packed light brown sugar
3 tablespoons fresh lemon juice
½ teaspoon kosher salt
¼ teaspoon ground cinnamon
⅛ teaspoon ground allspice

1. Select the BAKE function and preheat MAXX to 340ºF (171ºC).
2. Spray a metal cake pan with cooking spray. Whisk together all the ingredients in a bowl until smooth, then pour into the greased pan. Set the pan in the air fryer oven and bake until the apple mixture is caramelized, reduced to a thick purée, and fragrant, about 1 hour.
3. Remove the pan from the air fryer oven, stir to combine the caramelized bits at the edge with the rest, then let cool completely to thicken.
4. Serve immediately.

Pineapple Galette

Prep time: 10 minutes | Cook time: 40 minutes | Serves 2

¼ medium-size pineapple, peeled, cored, and cut crosswise into ¼-inch-thick slices
2 tablespoons dark rum
1 teaspoon vanilla extract
½ teaspoon kosher salt
Finely grated zest of

½ lime
1 store-bought sheet puff pastry, cut into an 8-inch round
3 tablespoons granulated sugar
2 tablespoons unsalted butter, cubed and chilled
Coconut ice cream, for serving

1. Select the BAKE function and preheat MAXX to 310ºF (154ºC).
2. In a small bowl, combine the pineapple slices, rum, vanilla, salt, and lime zest and let stand for at least 10 minutes to allow the pineapple to soak in the rum.
3. Meanwhile, press the puff pastry round into the bottom and up the sides of a round metal cake pan and use the tines of a fork to dock the bottom and sides.
4. Arrange the pineapple slices on the bottom of the pastry in more or less a single layer, then sprinkle with the sugar and dot with the butter. Drizzle with the leftover juices from the bowl. Put the pan in the air fryer oven and bake until the pastry is puffed and golden brown and the pineapple is lightly caramelized on top, about 40 minutes.
5. Transfer the pan to a wire rack to cool for 15 minutes. Unmold the galette from the pan and serve warm with coconut ice cream.

Easy Almond Shortbread

Prep time: 5 minutes | Cook time: 12 minutes | Serves 8

½ cup (1 stick) unsalted butter
½ cup sugar
1 teaspoon pure

almond extract
1 cup all-purpose flour

1. Select the BAKE function and preheat MAXX to 375ºF (191ºC).

2. In a bowl of a stand mixer fitted with the paddle attachment, beat the butter and sugar on medium speed until fluffy, 3 to 4 minutes. Add the almond extract and beat until combined, about 30 seconds. Turn the mixer to low. Add the flour a little at a time and beat for about 2 minutes more until well incorporated.
3. Pat the dough into an even layer in a round baking pan. Put the pan in the air fryer basket and bake for 12 minutes.
4. Carefully remove the pan from air fryer basket. While the shortbread is still warm and soft, cut it into 8 wedges.
5. Let cool in the pan on a wire rack for 5 minutes. Remove the wedges from the pan and let cool on the rack before serving.

Chickpea Brownies

Prep time: 10 minutes | Cook time: 20 minutes | Serves 6

Vegetable oil
1 (15-ounce / 425-g) can chickpeas, drained and rinsed
4 large eggs
1/3 cup coconut oil, melted
1/3 cup honey
3 tablespoons unsweetened cocoa

powder
1 tablespoon espresso powder (optional)
1 teaspoon baking powder
1 teaspoon baking soda
½ cup chocolate chips

1. Select the BAKE function and preheat MAXX to 325ºF (163ºC).
2. Generously grease a baking pan with vegetable oil.
3. In a blender or food processor, combine the chickpeas, eggs, coconut oil, honey, cocoa powder, espresso powder (if using), baking powder, and baking soda. Blend or process until smooth. Transfer to the prepared pan and stir in the chocolate chips by hand.
4. Set the pan in the air fryer basket and bake for 20 minutes, or until a toothpick inserted into the center comes out clean.
5. Let cool in the pan on a wire rack for 30 minutes before cutting into squares.
6. Serve immediately.

Simple Apple Turnovers

Prep time: 10 minutes | Cook time: 10 minutes | Serves 4

1 apple, peeled, quartered, and thinly sliced
½ teaspoons pumpkin pie spice
Juice of ½ lemon

1 tablespoon granulated sugar
Pinch of kosher salt
6 sheets phyllo dough

1. Select the BAKE function and preheat MAXX to 330ºF (166ºC).
2. In a medium bowl, combine the apple, pumpkin pie spice, lemon juice, granulated sugar, and kosher salt.
3. Cut the phyllo dough sheets into 4 equal pieces and place individual tablespoons of apple filling in the center of each piece, then fold in both sides and roll from front to back.
4. Spray the air fryer basket with nonstick cooking spray, then place the turnovers in the basket and bake for 10 minutes or until golden brown.
5. Remove the turnovers from the air fryer oven and allow to cool on a wire rack for 10 minutes before serving.

Oatmeal and Carrot Cookie Cups

Prep time: 10 minutes | Cook time: 8 minutes | Makes 16 cups

3 tablespoons unsalted butter, at room temperature
¼ cup packed brown sugar
1 tablespoon honey
1 egg white
½ teaspoon vanilla extract

⅓ cup finely grated carrot
½ cup quick-cooking oatmeal
⅓ cup whole-wheat pastry flour
½ teaspoon baking soda
¼ cup dried cherries

1. Select the BAKE function and preheat MAXX to 350ºF (177ºC)
2. In a medium bowl, beat the butter, brown sugar, and honey until well combined.
3. Add the egg white, vanilla, and carrot. Beat to combine.
4. Stir in the oatmeal, pastry flour, and baking soda.
5. Stir in the dried cherries.

6. Double up 32 mini muffin foil cups to make 16 cups. Fill each with about 4 teaspoons of dough. Bake the cookie cups, 8 at a time, for 8 minutes, or until light golden brown and just set. Serve warm.

Ricotta Lemon Poppy Seed Cake

Prep time: 15 minutes | Cook time: 55 minutes | Serves 4

Unsalted butter, at room temperature
1 cup almond flour
½ cup sugar
3 large eggs
¼ cup heavy cream
¼ cup full-fat ricotta cheese
¼ cup coconut oil, melted

2 tablespoons poppy seeds
1 teaspoon baking powder
1 teaspoon pure lemon extract
Grated zest and juice of 1 lemon, plus more zest for garnish

1. Select the BAKE function and preheat MAXX to 325ºF (163ºC).
2. Generously butter a round baking pan. Line the bottom of the pan with parchment paper cut to fit.
3. In a large bowl, combine the almond flour, sugar, eggs, cream, ricotta, coconut oil, poppy seeds, baking powder, lemon extract, lemon zest, and lemon juice. Beat with a hand mixer on medium speed until well blended and fluffy.
4. Pour the batter into the prepared pan. Cover the pan tightly with aluminum foil. Set the pan in the air fryer basket and bake for 45 minutes. Remove the foil and bake for 10 to 15 minutes more until a knife (do not use a toothpick) inserted into the center of the cake comes out clean.
5. Let the cake cool in the pan on a wire rack for 10 minutes. Remove the cake from pan and let it cool on the rack for 15 minutes before slicing.
6. Top with additional lemon zest, slice and serve.

Chocolate Cake

Prep time: 10 minutes | Cook time: 55 minutes | Serves 4

Unsalted butter, at room temperature
3 large eggs
1 cup almond flour
²/₃ cup sugar
¹/₃ cup heavy cream
¼ cup coconut oil,

melted
¼ cup unsweetened cocoa powder
1 teaspoon baking powder
¼ cup chopped walnuts

1. Select the BAKE function and preheat MAXX to 400ºF (204ºC).
2. Generously butter a round baking pan. Line the bottom of the pan with parchment paper cut to fit.
3. In a large bowl, combine the eggs, almond flour, sugar, cream, coconut oil, cocoa powder, and baking powder. Beat with a hand mixer on medium speed until well blended and fluffy. (This will keep the cake from being too dense, as almond flour cakes can sometimes be.) Fold in the walnuts.
4. Pour the batter into the prepared pan. Cover the pan tightly with aluminum foil. Set the pan in the air fryer basket and bake for 45 minutes. Remove the foil and bake for 10 to 15 minutes more until a knife (do not use a toothpick) inserted into the center of the cake comes out clean.
5. Let the cake cool in the pan on a wire rack for 10 minutes. Remove the cake from the pan and let cool on the rack for 20 minutes before slicing and serving.

Oatmeal Raisin Bars

Prep time: 15 minutes | Cook time: 15 minutes | Serves 8

¹/₃ cup all-purpose flour
¼ teaspoon kosher salt
¼ teaspoon baking powder
¼ teaspoon ground cinnamon
¼ cup light brown sugar, lightly packed

¼ cup granulated sugar
½ cup canola oil
1 large egg
1 teaspoon vanilla extract
1¹/₃ cups quick-cooking oats
¹/₃ cup raisins

1. Select the BAKE function and preheat MAXX to 360ºF (182ºC).
2. In a large bowl, combine the all-purpose flour, kosher salt, baking powder, ground cinnamon, light brown sugar, granulated sugar, canola oil, egg, vanilla extract, quick-cooking oats, and raisins.
3. Spray a baking pan with nonstick cooking spray, then pour the oat mixture into the pan and press down to evenly distribute. Place the pan in the air fryer oven and bake for 15 minutes or until golden brown.
4. Remove from the air fryer oven and allow to cool in the pan on a wire rack for 20 minutes before slicing and serving.

Orange Cake

Prep time: 10 minutes | Cook time: 23 minutes | Serves 8

Nonstick baking spray with flour
1¼ cups all-purpose flour
¹/₃ cup yellow cornmeal
¾ cup white sugar
1 teaspoon baking

soda
¼ cup safflower oil
1¼ cups orange juice, divided
1 teaspoon vanilla
¼ cup powdered sugar

1. Select the BAKE function and preheat MAXX to 350ºF (177ºC).
2. Spray a baking pan with nonstick spray and set aside.
3. In a medium bowl, combine the flour, cornmeal, sugar, baking soda, safflower oil, 1 cup of the orange juice, and vanilla, and mix well.
4. Pour the batter into the baking pan and place in the air fryer oven. Bake for 23 minutes or until a toothpick inserted in the center of the cake comes out clean.
5. Remove the cake from the basket and place on a cooling rack. Using a toothpick, make about 20 holes in the cake.
6. In a small bowl, combine remaining ¼ cup of orange juice and the powdered sugar and stir well. Drizzle this mixture over the hot cake slowly so the cake absorbs it.
7. Cool completely, then cut into wedges to serve.

Pineapple and Chocolate Cake

Prep time: 10 minutes | Cook time: 35 to 40 minutes | Serves 4

2 cups flour
4 ounces (113 g) butter, melted
¼ cup sugar
½ pound (227 g) pineapple, chopped
½ cup pineapple

juice
1 ounce (28 g) dark chocolate, grated
1 large egg
2 tablespoons skimmed milk

1. Select the BAKE function and preheat MAXX to 370ºF (188ºC).
2. Grease a cake tin with a little oil or butter.
3. In a bowl, combine the butter and flour to create a crumbly consistency.
4. Add the sugar, chopped pineapple, juice, and grated dark chocolate and mix well.
5. In a separate bowl, combine the egg and milk. Add this mixture to the flour mixture and stir well until a soft dough forms.
6. Pour the mixture into the cake tin and transfer to the air fryer oven.
7. Bake for 35 to 40 minutes.
8. Serve immediately.

Berry Crumble

Prep time: 10 minutes | Cook time: 15 minutes | Serves 4

For the Filling:
2 cups mixed berries
2 tablespoons sugar
1 tablespoon

cornstarch
1 tablespoon fresh lemon juice

For the Topping:
¼ cup all-purpose flour
¼ cup rolled oats
1 tablespoon sugar
2 tablespoons cold

unsalted butter, cut into small cubes
Whipped cream or ice cream (optional)

1. For the filling: In a round baking pan, gently mix the berries, sugar, cornstarch, and lemon juice until thoroughly combined.
2. For the topping: In a small bowl, combine the flour, oats, and sugar. Stir the butter into the flour mixture until the mixture has the consistency of bread crumbs.

3. Sprinkle the topping over the berries. Put the pan in the air fryer basket.
4. Select the AIR FRY function and cook at 400ºF (204ºC) for 15 minutes.
5. Let cool for 5 minutes on a wire rack.
6. Serve topped with whipped cream or ice cream, if desired.

Simple Pineapple Sticks

Prep time: 5 minutes | Cook time: 10 minutes | Serves 4

½ fresh pineapple, cut into sticks

¼ cup desiccated coconut

1. Coat the pineapple sticks in the desiccated coconut and put each one in the air fryer basket.
2. Select the AIR FRY function and cook at 400ºF (204ºC) for 10 minutes.
3. Serve immediately

Brazilian Pineapple Bake

Prep time: 5 minutes | Cook time: 16 minutes | Serves 4

½ cup brown sugar
2 teaspoons ground cinnamon
1 small pineapple, peeled, cored, and

cut into spears
3 tablespoons unsalted butter, melted

1. Select the BAKE function and preheat MAXX to 400ºF (204ºC).
2. In a small bowl, mix the brown sugar and cinnamon until thoroughly combined.
3. Brush the pineapple spears with the melted butter. Sprinkle the cinnamon-sugar over the spears, pressing lightly to ensure it adheres well.
4. Put the spears in the air fryer basket in a single layer. (Depending on the size of the air fryer oven, you may have to do this in batches.) Bake for 10 minutes for the first batch (6 to 8 minutes for the next batch, as the air fryer oven will be preheated). Halfway through the cooking time, brush the spears with butter.
5. The pineapple spears are done when they are heated through and the sugar is bubbling. Serve hot.

Chocolate Coconut Brownies

Prep time: 15 minutes | Cook time: 15 minutes | Serves 8

½ cup coconut oil
2 ounces (57 g) dark chocolate
1 cup sugar
2½ tablespoons water
4 whisked eggs
¼ teaspoon ground cinnamon
½ teaspoons ground

anise star
¼ teaspoon coconut extract
½ teaspoons vanilla extract
1 tablespoon honey
½ cup flour
½ cup desiccated coconut
Sugar, for dusting

1. Select the BAKE function and preheat MAXX to 355ºF (179ºC).
2. Melt the coconut oil and dark chocolate in the microwave.
3. Combine with the sugar, water, eggs, cinnamon, anise, coconut extract, vanilla, and honey in a large bowl.
4. Stir in the flour and desiccated coconut. Incorporate everything well.
5. Lightly grease a baking dish with butter. Transfer the mixture to the dish.
6. Put the dish in the air fryer oven and bake for 15 minutes.
7. Remove from the air fryer oven and allow to cool slightly.
8. Take care when taking it out of the baking dish. Slice it into squares.
9. Dust with sugar before serving.

Spice Cookies

Prep time: 15 minutes | Cook time: 12 minutes | Serves 4

4 tablespoons (½ stick) unsalted butter, at room temperature
2 tablespoons agave nectar
1 large egg
2 tablespoons water
2½ cups almond flour
½ cup sugar

2 teaspoons ground ginger
1 teaspoon ground cinnamon
½ teaspoon freshly grated nutmeg
1 teaspoon baking soda
¼ teaspoon kosher salt

1. Select the BAKE function and preheat MAXX to 325ºF (163ºC).
2. Line the bottom of the air fryer basket with parchment paper cut to fit.
3. In a large bowl using a hand mixer, beat together the butter, agave, egg, and water on medium speed until fluffy.
4. Add the almond flour, sugar, ginger, cinnamon, nutmeg, baking soda, and salt. Beat on low speed until well combined.
5. Roll the dough into 2-tablespoon balls and arrange them on the parchment paper in the basket. (They don't really spread too much, but try to leave a little room between them.) Bake for 12 minutes, or until the tops of cookies are lightly browned.
6. Transfer to a wire rack and let cool completely.
7. Serve immediately

Honey-Roasted Pears

Prep time: 5 minutes | Cook time: 20 minutes | Serves 4

2 large Bosc pears, halved and deseeded
3 tablespoons honey
1 tablespoon unsalted butter
½ teaspoon ground

cinnamon
¼ cup walnuts, chopped
¼ cup part skim low-fat ricotta cheese, divided

1. Select the ROAST function and preheat MAXX to 350ºF (177ºC).
2. In a baking pan, place the pears, cut side up.
3. In a small microwave-safe bowl, melt the honey, butter, and cinnamon. Brush this mixture over the cut sides of the pears.
4. Pour 3 tablespoons of water around the pears in the pan. Roast the pears for 20 minutes, or until tender when pierced with a fork and slightly crisp on the edges, basting once with the liquid in the pan.
5. Carefully remove the pears from the pan and place on a serving plate. Drizzle each with some liquid from the pan, sprinkle the walnuts on top, and serve with a spoonful of ricotta cheese.

Baked Apples

Prep time: 5 minutes | Cook time: 10 minutes | Serves 4

4 small apples, cored and cut in half	1 teaspoon apple pie spice
2 tablespoons salted butter or coconut oil, melted	Ice cream, heavy cream, or whipped cream, for serving
2 tablespoons sugar	

1. Select the BAKE function and preheat MAXX to 350°F (177°C).
2. Put the apples in a large bowl. Drizzle with the melted butter and sprinkle with the sugar and apple pie spice. Use the hands to toss, ensuring the apples are evenly coated.
3. Put the apples in the air fryer basket and bake for 10 minutes. Pierce the apples with a fork to ensure they are tender.
4. Serve with ice cream, or top with a splash of heavy cream or a spoonful of whipped cream.

Cardamom and Vanilla Custard

Prep time: 5 minutes | Cook time: 25 minutes | Serves 2

1 cup whole milk	bean paste or pure vanilla extract
1 large egg	¼ teaspoon ground cardamom, plus more for sprinkling
2 tablespoons plus 1 teaspoon sugar	
¼ teaspoon vanilla	

1. Select the BAKE function and preheat MAXX to 350°F (177°C).
2. In a medium bowl, beat together the milk, egg, sugar, vanilla, and cardamom.
3. Put two ramekins in the air fryer basket. Divide the mixture between the ramekins. Sprinkle lightly with cardamom. Cover each ramekin tightly with aluminum foil. Bake for 25 minutes, or until a toothpick inserted in the center comes out clean.
4. Let the custards cool on a wire rack for 5 to 10 minutes.
5. Serve warm, or refrigerate until cold and serve chilled.

Cinnamon Almonds

Prep time: 5 minutes | Cook time: 8 minutes | Serves 4

1 cup whole almonds	1 tablespoon sugar
2 tablespoons salted butter, melted	½ teaspoon ground cinnamon

1. Select the BAKE function and preheat MAXX to 300°F (149°C).
2. In a medium bowl, combine the almonds, butter, sugar, and cinnamon. Mix well to ensure all the almonds are coated with the spiced butter.
3. Transfer the almonds to the air fryer basket and shake so they are in a single layer. Bake for 8 minutes, stirring the almonds halfway through the cooking time.
4. Let cool completely before serving.

Easy Chocolate Donuts

Prep time: 5 minutes | Cook time: 8 minutes | Serves 8

1 (8-ounce / 227-g) can jumbo biscuits	Chocolate sauce, for drizzling
Cooking oil	

1. Separate the biscuit dough into 8 biscuits and place them on a flat work surface. Use a small circle cookie cutter or a biscuit cutter to cut a hole in the center of each biscuit. You can also cut the holes using a knife.
2. Spray the air fryer basket with cooking oil.
3. Put 4 donuts in the air fryer oven. Do not stack. Spray with cooking oil.
4. Select the AIR FRY function and cook at 375°F (191°C) for 4 minutes.
5. Open the air fryer oven and flip the donuts. Air fry for an additional 4 minutes.
6. Remove the cooked donuts from the air fryer oven. Repeat with the remaining 4 donuts.
7. Drizzle chocolate sauce over the donuts and enjoy while warm.

Jelly Doughnuts

Prep time: 5 minutes | Cook time: 5 minutes | Serves 8

1 (16.3-ounce / 462-g) package large refrigerator biscuits
Cooking spray

1¼ cups good-quality raspberry jam
Confectioners' sugar, for dusting

1. Separate biscuits into 8 rounds. Spray both sides of rounds lightly with oil.
2. Spray the basket with oil and place 3 to 4 rounds in the basket.
3. Select the AIR FRY function and cook at 350ºF (177ºC) for 5 minutes, or until golden brown. Transfer to a wire rack; let cool. Repeat with the remaining rounds.
4. Fill a pastry bag, fitted with small plain tip, with raspberry jam; use tip to poke a small hole in the side of each doughnut, then fill the centers with the jam. Dust doughnuts with confectioners' sugar.
5. Serve immediately.

Pecan and Cherry Stuffed Apples

Prep time: 10 minutes | Cook time: 20 minutes | Serves 4

4 apples (about 1¼ pounds / 567 g)
¼ cup chopped pecans
1/3 cup dried tart cherries
1 tablespoon melted

butter
3 tablespoons brown sugar
¼ teaspoon allspice
Pinch salt
Ice cream, for serving

1. Cut off top ½ inch from each apple; reserve tops. With a melon baller, core through stem ends without breaking through the bottom. (Do not trim bases.)
2. Combine pecans, cherries, butter, brown sugar, allspice, and a pinch of salt. Stuff mixture into the hollow centers of the apples. Cover with apple tops. Put in the air fryer basket, using tongs.
3. Select the AIR FRY function and cook at 350ºF (177ºC) for 20 to 25 minutes, or just until tender.
4. Serve warm with ice cream.

Apple, Peach, and Cranberry Crisp

Prep time: 10 minutes | Cook time: 12 minutes | Serves 8

1 apple, peeled and chopped
2 peaches, peeled and chopped
1/3 cup dried cranberries

2 tablespoons honey
1/3 cup brown sugar
¼ cup flour
½ cup oatmeal
3 tablespoons softened butter

1. Select the BAKE function and preheat MAXX to 370ºF (188ºC).
2. In a baking pan, combine the apple, peaches, cranberries, and honey, and mix well.
3. In a medium bowl, combine the brown sugar, flour, oatmeal, and butter, and mix until crumbly. Sprinkle this mixture over the fruit in the pan.
4. Bake for 10 to 12 minutes or until the fruit is bubbly and the topping is golden brown. Serve warm.

Banana and Walnut Cake

Prep time: 10 minutes | Cook time: 25 minutes | Serves 6

1 pound (454 g) bananas, mashed
8 ounces (227 g) flour
6 ounces (170 g) sugar
3.5 ounces (99 g)

walnuts, chopped
2.5 ounces (71 g) butter, melted
2 eggs, lightly beaten
¼ teaspoon baking soda

1. Select the BAKE function and preheat MAXX to 355ºF (179ºC).
2. In a bowl, combine the sugar, butter, egg, flour, and baking soda with a whisk. Stir in the bananas and walnuts.
3. Transfer the mixture to a greased baking dish. Put the dish in the air fryer oven and bake for 10 minutes.
4. Reduce the temperature to 330ºF (166ºC) and bake for another 15 minutes. Serve hot.

Graham Cracker Cheesecake

Prep time: 10 minutes | Cook time: 20 minutes | Serves 8

1 cup graham cracker crumbs
3 tablespoons softened butter
1½ (8-ounce / 227-g) packages cream cheese, softened

⅓ cup sugar
2 eggs
1 tablespoon flour
1 teaspoon vanilla
¼ cup chocolate syrup

1. For the crust, combine the graham cracker crumbs and butter in a small bowl and mix well. Press into the bottom of a baking pan and put in the freezer to set.
2. For the filling, combine the cream cheese and sugar in a medium bowl and mix well. Beat in the eggs, one at a time. Add the flour and vanilla.
3. Select the BAKE function and preheat MAXX to 450ºF (232ºC).
4. Remove ⅔ cup of the filling to a small bowl and stir in the chocolate syrup until combined.
5. Pour the vanilla filling into the pan with the crust. Drop the chocolate filling over the vanilla filling by the spoonful. With a clean butter knife, stir the fillings in a zigzag pattern to marbleize them.
6. Bake for 20 minutes or until the cheesecake is just set.
7. Cool on a wire rack for 1 hour, then chill in the refrigerator until the cheesecake is firm.
8. Serve immediately.

Rich Chocolate Cookie

Prep time: 10 minutes | Cook time: 9 minutes | Serves 4

Nonstick baking spray with flour
3 tablespoons softened butter
⅓ cup plus 1 tablespoon brown sugar
1 egg yolk
½ cup flour

2 tablespoons ground white chocolate
¼ teaspoon baking soda
½ teaspoon vanilla
¾ cup chocolate chips

1. Select the BAKE function and preheat MAXX to 350ºF (177ºC).
2. In a medium bowl, beat the butter and brown sugar together until fluffy. Stir in the egg yolk.
3. Add the flour, white chocolate, baking soda, and vanilla, and mix well. Stir in the chocolate chips.
4. Line a baking pan with parchment paper. Spray the parchment paper with nonstick baking spray with flour.
5. Spread the batter into the prepared pan, leaving a ½-inch border on all sides.
6. Bake for about 9 minutes or until the cookie is light brown and just barely set.
7. Remove the pan from the air fryer oven and let cool for 10 minutes. Remove the cookie from the pan, remove the parchment paper, and let cool on a wire rack.
8. Serve immediately.

Lemony Blackberry Crisp

Prep time: 5 minutes | Cook time: 20 minutes | Serves 1

2 tablespoons lemon juice
⅓ cup powdered erythritol
¼ teaspoon

xantham gum
2 cup blackberries
1 cup crunchy granola

1. Select the BAKE function and preheat MAXX to 350ºF (177ºC).
2. In a bowl, combine the lemon juice, erythritol, xantham gum, and blackberries. Transfer to a round baking dish and cover with aluminum foil.
3. Put the dish in the air fryer oven and bake for 12 minutes.
4. Take care when removing the dish from the air fryer oven. Give the blackberries a stir and top with the granola.
5. Return the dish to the air fryer oven and bake for an additional 3 minutes, this time at 320ºF (160ºC). Serve once the granola has turned brown and enjoy.

Chocolate and Peanut Butter Lava Cupcakes

Prep time: 10 minutes | Cook time: 10 to 13 minutes | Serves 8

Nonstick baking spray with flour
1 1/3 cups chocolate cake mix
1 egg
1 egg yolk
1/4 cup safflower oil

1/4 cup hot water
1/3 cup sour cream
3 tablespoons peanut butter
1 tablespoon powdered sugar

1. Select the BAKE function and preheat MAXX to 350ºF (177ºC).
2. Double up 16 foil muffin cups to make 8 cups. Spray each lightly with nonstick spray; set aside.
3. In a medium bowl, combine the cake mix, egg, egg yolk, safflower oil, water, and sour cream, and beat until combined.
4. In a small bowl, combine the peanut butter and powdered sugar and mix well. Form this mixture into 8 balls.
5. Spoon about 1/4 cup of the chocolate batter into each muffin cup and top with a peanut butter ball. Spoon remaining batter on top of the peanut butter balls to cover them.
6. Arrange the cups in the air fryer basket, leaving some space between each. Bake for 10 to 13 minutes or until the tops look dry and set.
7. Let the cupcakes cool for about 10 minutes, then serve warm.

Chocolate S'mores

Prep time: 5 minutes | Cook time: 3 minutes | Serves 12

12 whole cinnamon graham crackers
2 (1.55-ounce / 44-g) chocolate bars,

broken into 12 pieces
12 marshmallows

1. Select the BAKE function and preheat MAXX to 350ºF (177ºC).
2. Halve each graham cracker into 2 squares.
3. Put 6 graham cracker squares in the air fryer oven. Do not stack. Put a piece of chocolate into each. Bake for 2 minutes.
4. Open the air fryer oven and add a marshmallow onto each piece of melted chocolate. Bake for 1 additional minute.
5. Remove the cooked s'mores from the air fryer oven, then repeat with the remaining 6 s'mores.
6. Top with the remaining graham cracker squares and serve.

Black Forest Pies

Prep time: 10 minutes | Cook time: 15 minutes | Serves 6

3 tablespoons milk or dark chocolate chips
2 tablespoons thick, hot fudge sauce
2 tablespoons chopped dried cherries

1 (10-by-15-inch) sheet frozen puff pastry, thawed
1 egg white, beaten
2 tablespoons sugar
1/2 teaspoon cinnamon

1. Select the BAKE function and preheat MAXX to 350ºF (177ºC).
2. In a small bowl, combine the chocolate chips, fudge sauce, and dried cherries.
3. Roll out the puff pastry on a floured surface. Cut into 6 squares with a sharp knife.
4. Divide the chocolate chip mixture into the center of each puff pastry square. Fold the squares in half to make triangles. Firmly press the edges with the tines of a fork to seal.
5. Brush the triangles on all sides sparingly with the beaten egg white. Sprinkle the tops with sugar and cinnamon.
6. Put in the air fryer basket and bake for 15 minutes or until the triangles are golden brown. The filling will be hot, so cool for at least 20 minutes before serving.

Fried Golden Bananas

Prep time: 5 minutes | Cook time: 7 minutes | Serves 6

1 large egg
¼ cup cornstarch
¼ cup plain bread crumbs
3 bananas, halved crosswise
Cooking oil
Chocolate sauce, for drizzling

1. In a small bowl, beat the egg. In another bowl, place the cornstarch. Put the bread crumbs in a third bowl.
2. Dip the bananas in the cornstarch, then the egg, and then the bread crumbs.
3. Spray the air fryer basket with cooking oil.
4. Put the bananas in the basket and spray them with cooking oil.
5. Select the AIR FRY function and cook at 350ºF (177ºC) for 5 minutes.
6. Open the air fryer oven and flip the bananas. Air fry for an additional 2 minutes.
7. Transfer the bananas to plates. Drizzle the chocolate sauce over the bananas, and serve.

Chocolate Croissants

Prep time: 5 minutes | Cook time: 24 minutes | Serves 8

1 sheet frozen puff pastry, thawed
⅓ cup chocolate-hazelnut spread
1 large egg, beaten

1. On a lightly floured surface, roll puff pastry into a 14-inch square. Cut pastry into quarters to form 4 squares. Cut each square diagonally to form 8 triangles.
2. Spread 2 teaspoons chocolate-hazelnut spread on each triangle; from wider end, roll up pastry. Brush egg on top of each roll. Place in the air fryer basket.
3. Select the AIR FRY function and cook at 375ºF (191ºC) for 8 minutes, or until pastry is golden brown. You may need to work in batches.
4. Cool on a wire rack; serve while warm or at room temperature.

Curry Peaches, Pears, and Plums

Prep time: 5 minutes | Cook time: 5 minutes | Serves 6 to 8

2 peaches
2 firm pears
2 plums
2 tablespoons
melted butter
1 tablespoon honey
2 to 3 teaspoons curry powder

1. Select the BAKE function and preheat MAXX to 325ºF (163ºC).
2. Cut the peaches in half, remove the pits, and cut each half in half again. Cut the pears in half, core them, and remove the stem. Cut each half in half again. Do the same with the plums.
3. Spread a large sheet of heavy-duty foil on the work surface. Arrange the fruit on the foil and drizzle with the butter and honey. Sprinkle with the curry powder.
4. Wrap the fruit in the foil, making sure to leave some air space in the packet.
5. Put the foil package in the basket and bake for 5 to 8 minutes, shaking the basket once during the cooking time, until the fruit is soft.
6. Serve immediately.

Pumpkin Pudding

Prep time: 10 minutes | Cook time: 15 minutes | Serves 4

3 cups pumpkin purée
3 tablespoons honey
1 tablespoon ginger
1 tablespoon cinnamon
1 teaspoon clove
1 teaspoon nutmeg
1 cup full-fat cream
2 eggs
1 cup sugar

1. Select the BAKE function and preheat MAXX to 390ºF (199ºC).
2. In a bowl, stir all the ingredients together to combine.
3. Scrape the mixture into the a greased dish and transfer to the air fryer oven. Bake for 15 minutes. Serve warm.

Cinnamon and Pecan Pie

Prep time: 10 minutes | Cook time: 25 minutes | Serves 4

1 pie dough
½ teaspoons cinnamon
¾ teaspoon vanilla extract
2 eggs
¾ cup maple syrup
⅛ teaspoon nutmeg
3 tablespoons melted butter, divided
2 tablespoons sugar
½ cup chopped pecans

1. In a small bowl, coat the pecans in 1 tablespoon of melted butter.
2. Transfer the pecans to the air fryer oven. Select the AIR FRY function and cook at 370ºF (188ºC) for 10 minutes.
3. Put the pie dough in a greased pie pan and add the pecans on top.
4. In a bowl, mix the rest of the ingredients. Pour this over the pecans.
5. Put the pan in the air fryer oven. Switch from AIR FRY to BAKE and bake for 25 minutes.
6. Serve immediately.

Chocolate Molten Cake

Prep time: 5 minutes | Cook time: 10 minutes | Serves 4

3.5 ounces (99 g) butter, melted
3½ tablespoons sugar
3.5 ounces (99 g)
chocolate, melted
1½ tablespoons flour
2 eggs

1. Select the BAKE function and preheat MAXX to 375ºF (191ºC).
2. Grease four ramekins with a little butter.
3. Rigorously combine the eggs, butter, and sugar before stirring in the melted chocolate.
4. Slowly fold in the flour.
5. Spoon an equal amount of the mixture into each ramekin.
6. Put them in the air fryer oven and bake for 10 minutes
7. Put the ramekins upside-down on plates and let the cakes fall out. Serve hot.

Pear and Apple Crisp

Prep time: 10 minutes | Cook time: 20 minutes | Serves 6

½ pound (227 g) apples, cored and chopped
½ pound (227 g) pears, cored and chopped
1 cup flour
1 cup sugar
1 tablespoon butter
1 teaspoon ground
cinnamon
¼ teaspoon ground cloves
1 teaspoon vanilla extract
¼ cup chopped walnuts
Whipped cream, for serving

1. Select the BAKE function and preheat MAXX to 340ºF (171ºC).
2. Lightly grease a baking dish and place the apples and pears inside.
3. Combine the rest of the ingredients, minus the walnuts and the whipped cream, until a coarse, crumbly texture is achieved.
4. Pour the mixture over the fruits and spread it evenly. Top with the chopped walnuts.
5. Bake for 20 minutes or until the top turns golden brown.
6. Serve at room temperature with whipped cream.

Chapter 11 Holiday Specials

Bourbon Monkey Bread

Prep time: 15 minutes | Cook time: 25 minutes | Serves 6 to 8

1 (16.3-ounce / 462-g) can store-bought refrigerated biscuit dough
¼ cup packed light brown sugar
1 teaspoon ground cinnamon
½ teaspoon freshly grated nutmeg
½ teaspoon ground ginger
½ teaspoon kosher salt
¼ teaspoon ground allspice
⅛ teaspoon ground cloves
4 tablespoons (½ stick) unsalted butter, melted
½ cup powdered sugar
2 teaspoons bourbon
2 tablespoons chopped candied cherries
2 tablespoons chopped pecans

1. Select the BAKE function and preheat MAXX to 310ºF (154ºC).
2. Open the can and separate the biscuits, then cut each into quarters. Toss the biscuit quarters in a large bowl with the brown sugar, cinnamon, nutmeg, ginger, salt, allspice, and cloves until evenly coated. Transfer the dough pieces and any sugar left in the bowl to a round cake pan, metal cake pan, or foil pan and drizzle evenly with the melted butter. Put the pan in the air fryer oven and bake until the monkey bread is golden brown and cooked through in the middle, about 25 minutes. Transfer the pan to a wire rack and let cool completely. Unmold from the pan.
3. In a small bowl, whisk the powdered sugar and the bourbon into a smooth glaze. Drizzle the glaze over the cooled monkey bread and, while the glaze is still wet, sprinkle with the cherries and pecans to serve.

Whole Chicken Roast

Prep time: 10 minutes | Cook time: 1 hour | Serves 6

1 teaspoon salt
1 teaspoon Italian seasoning
½ teaspoon freshly ground black pepper
½ teaspoon paprika
½ teaspoon garlic powder
½ teaspoon onion powder
2 tablespoons olive oil, plus more as needed
1 (4-pound / 1.8-kg) fryer chicken

1. Grease the air fryer basket lightly with olive oil.
2. In a small bowl, mix the salt, Italian seasoning, pepper, paprika, garlic powder, and onion powder.
3. Remove any giblets from the chicken. Pat the chicken dry thoroughly with paper towels, including the cavity.
4. Brush the chicken all over with the olive oil and rub it with the seasoning mixture.
5. Truss the chicken or tie the legs with butcher's twine. This will make it easier to flip the chicken during cooking.
6. Put the chicken in the air fryer basket, breast-side down. Select the AIR FRY function and cook at 360ºF (182ºC) for 30 minutes. Flip the chicken over and baste it with any drippings collected in the bottom drawer of the air fryer oven. Lightly brush the chicken with olive oil.
7. Air fry for 20 minutes. Flip the chicken over one last time and air fry until a thermometer inserted into the thickest part of the thigh reaches at least 165ºF (74ºC) and it's crispy and golden, 10 more minutes. Continue to cook, checking every 5 minutes until the chicken reaches the correct internal temperature.
8. Let the chicken rest for 10 minutes before carving and serving.

Hearty Honey Yeast Rolls

Prep time: 10 minutes | Cook time: 20 minutes | Makes 8 rolls

¼ cup whole milk, heated to 115°F (46°C) in the microwave
½ teaspoon active dry yeast
1 tablespoon honey
²⁄₃ cup all-purpose flour, plus more for dusting

½ teaspoon kosher salt
2 tablespoons unsalted butter, at room temperature, plus more for greasing
Flaky sea salt, to taste

1. In a large bowl, whisk together the milk, yeast, and honey and let stand until foamy, about 10 minutes.
2. Stir in the flour and salt until just combined. Stir in the butter until absorbed. Scrape the dough onto a lightly floured work surface and knead until smooth, about 6 minutes. Transfer the dough to a lightly greased bowl, cover loosely with a sheet of plastic wrap or a kitchen towel, and let sit until nearly doubled in size, about 1 hour.
3. Uncover the dough, lightly press it down to expel the bubbles, then portion it into 8 equal pieces. Prep the work surface by wiping it clean with a damp paper towel (if there is flour on the work surface, it will prevent the dough from sticking lightly to the surface, which helps it form a ball). Roll each piece into a ball by cupping the palm of the hand around the dough against the work surface and moving the heel of the hand in a circular motion while using the thumb to contain the dough and tighten it into a perfectly round ball. Once all the balls are formed, nestle them side by side in the air fryer basket.
4. Cover the rolls loosely with a kitchen towel or a sheet of plastic wrap and let sit until lightly risen and puffed, 20 to 30 minutes.
5. Uncover the rolls and gently brush with more butter, being careful not to press the rolls too hard. Place the rolls in the air fryer basket.
6. Select the AIR FRY function and cook at 270°F (132°C) for 12 minutes, or until the rolls are light golden brown and fluffy.
7. Remove the rolls from the air fryer oven and brush liberally with more butter, if you like, and sprinkle each roll with a pinch of sea salt. Serve warm.

Mushroom and Green Bean Casserole

Prep time: 10 minutes | Cook time: 15 minutes | Serves 4

4 tablespoons unsalted butter
¼ cup diced yellow onion
½ cup chopped white mushrooms
½ cup heavy whipping cream
1 ounce (28 g) full-

fat cream cheese
½ cup chicken broth
¼ teaspoon xanthan gum
1 pound (454 g) fresh green beans, edges trimmed
½ ounce (14 g) pork rinds, finely ground

1. In a medium skillet over medium heat, melt the butter. Sauté the onion and mushrooms until they become soft and fragrant, about 3 to 5 minutes.
2. Add the heavy whipping cream, cream cheese, and broth to the pan. Whisk until smooth. Bring to a boil and then reduce to a simmer. Sprinkle the xanthan gum into the pan and remove from heat.
3. Select the BAKE function and preheat MAXX to 320°F (160°C).
4. Chop the green beans into 2-inch pieces and place into a baking dish. Pour the sauce mixture over them and stir until coated. Top the dish with ground pork rinds. Put into the air fryer basket and bake for 15 minutes.
5. Top will be golden and green beans fork-tender when fully cooked. Serve warm.

Eggnog Bread

Prep time: 10 minutes | Cook time: 18 minutes | Serves 6 to 8

1 cup flour, plus more for dusting
¼ cup sugar
1 teaspoon baking powder
¼ teaspoon salt
¼ teaspoon nutmeg
½ cup eggnog
1 egg yolk

1 tablespoon plus 1 teaspoon butter, melted
¼ cup pecans
¼ cup chopped candied fruit (cherries, pineapple, or mixed fruits)
Cooking spray

1. Select the BAKE function and preheat MAXX to 360ºF (182ºC).
2. In a medium bowl, stir together the flour, sugar, baking powder, salt, and nutmeg.
3. Add eggnog, egg yolk, and butter. Mix well but do not beat.
4. Stir in nuts and fruit.
5. Spray a baking pan with cooking spray and dust with flour.
6. Spread batter into prepared pan and bake for 18 minutes or until top is dark golden brown and bread starts to pull away from sides of pan.
7. Serve immediately.

Hasselback Potatoes

Prep time: 5 minutes | Cook time: 50 minutes | Serves 4

4 russet potatoes, peeled
Salt and freshly ground black pepper,

to taste
¼ cup grated Parmesan cheese
Cooking spray

1. Spray the air fryer basket lightly with cooking spray.
2. Make thin parallel cuts into each potato, ⅛-inch to ¼-inch apart, stopping at about ½ of the way through. The potato needs to stay intact along the bottom.
3. Spray the potatoes with cooking spray and use the hands or a silicone brush to completely coat the potatoes lightly in oil.
4. Put the potatoes, sliced side up, in the air fryer basket in a single layer. Leave a little room between each potato. Sprinkle the potatoes lightly with salt and black pepper.
5. Select the AIR FRY function and cook at 400ºF (204ºC) for 20 minutes. Reposition the potatoes and spritz lightly with cooking spray again. Air fry until the potatoes are fork-tender and crispy and browned, another 20 to 30 minutes.
6. Sprinkle the potatoes with Parmesan cheese and serve.

Air Fried Spicy Olives

Prep time: 10 minutes | Cook time: 5 minutes | Serves 4

12 ounces (340 g) pitted black extra-large olives
¼ cup all-purpose flour
1 cup panko bread crumbs
2 teaspoons dried thyme

1 teaspoon red pepper flakes
1 teaspoon smoked paprika
1 egg beaten with 1 tablespoon water
Vegetable oil for spraying

1. Drain the olives and place them on a paper towel–lined plate to dry.
2. Put the flour on a plate. Combine the panko, thyme, red pepper flakes, and paprika on a separate plate. Dip an olive in the flour, shaking off any excess, then coat with egg mixture. Dredge the olive in the panko mixture, pressing to make the crumbs adhere, and place the breaded olive on a platter. Repeat with the remaining olives.
3. Spray the olives with oil and place them in a single layer in the air fryer basket. Work in batches if necessary so as not to overcrowd the basket. Select the AIR FRY function and cook at 400ºF (204ºC) for 5 minutes until the breading is browned and crispy. Serve warm

Lush Snack Mix

Prep time: 10 minutes | Cook time: 10 minutes | Serves 10

½ cup honey
3 tablespoons butter, melted
1 teaspoon salt
2 cups sesame sticks
2 cup pumpkin seeds

2 cups granola
1 cup cashews
2 cups crispy corn puff cereal
2 cup mini pretzel crisps

1. In a bowl, combine the honey, butter, and salt.
2. In another bowl, mix the sesame sticks, pumpkin seeds, granola, cashews, corn puff cereal, and pretzel crisps.
3. Combine the contents of the two bowls.
4. Put the mixture in the air fryer basket. Select the AIR FRY function and cook at 370ºF (188ºC) for 10 to 12 minutes, shaking the basket frequently. Do this in two batches.
5. Put the snack mix on a cookie sheet and allow it to cool fully.
6. Serve immediately.

Holiday Spicy Beef Roast

Prep time: 10 minutes | Cook time: 45 minutes | Serves 8

2 pounds (907 g) roast beef, at room temperature
2 tablespoons extra-virgin olive oil
1 teaspoon sea salt flakes
1 teaspoon black pepper, preferably freshly

ground
1 teaspoon smoked paprika
A few dashes of liquid smoke
2 jalapeño peppers, thinly sliced

1. Select the ROAST function and preheat MAXX to 330ºF (166ºC).
2. Pat the roast dry using kitchen towels. Rub with extra-virgin olive oil and all seasonings along with liquid smoke.
3. Roast for 30 minutes in the preheated air fryer oven. Turn the roast over and roast for additional 15 minutes.
4. Check for doneness using a meat thermometer and serve sprinkled with sliced jalapeños. Bon appétit!

Chapter 12 Fast and Easy Everyday Favorites

Simple and Easy Croutons

Prep time: 5 minutes | Cook time: 8 minutes | Serves 4

2 slices friendly bread
1 tablespoon olive
oil
Hot soup, for serving

1. Cut the slices of bread into medium-size chunks.
2. Brush the air fryer basket with the oil and place the chunks inside.
3. Select the AIR FRY function and cook at 390ºF (199ºC) for 8 minutes.
4. Serve with hot soup.

Spinach and Carrot Balls

Prep time: 10 minutes | Cook time: 10 minutes | Serves 4

2 slices toasted bread
1 carrot, peeled and grated
1 package fresh spinach, blanched and chopped
½ onion, chopped
1 egg, beaten
½ teaspoon garlic
powder
1 teaspoon minced garlic
1 teaspoon salt
½ teaspoon black pepper
1 tablespoon nutritional yeast
1 tablespoon flour

1. In a food processor, pulse the toasted bread to form bread crumbs. Transfer into a shallow dish or bowl.
2. In a bowl, mix together all the other ingredients.
3. Use your hands to shape the mixture into small-sized balls. Roll the balls in the bread crumbs, ensuring to cover them well.
4. Put in the air fryer basket. Select the AIR FRY function and cook at 390ºF (199ºC) for 10 minutes.
5. Serve immediately.

Simple Pea Delight

Prep time: 5 minutes | Cook time: 15 minutes | Serves 2 to 4

1 cup flour
1 teaspoon baking powder
3 eggs
1 cup coconut milk
1 cup cream cheese
3 tablespoons pea
protein
½ cup chicken or turkey strips
Pinch of sea salt
1 cup Mozzarella cheese

1. Select the BAKE function and preheat MAXX to 390ºF (199ºC).
2. In a large bowl, mix all ingredients together using a large wooden spoon.
3. Spoon equal amounts of the mixture into muffin cups and bake for 15 minutes.
4. Serve immediately.

Scalloped Veggie Mix

Prep time: 10 minutes | Cook time: 15 minutes | Serves 4

1 Yukon Gold potato, thinly sliced
1 small sweet potato, peeled and thinly sliced
1 medium carrot, thinly sliced
¼ cup minced onion
3 garlic cloves, minced
¾ cup 2 percent milk
2 tablespoons cornstarch
½ teaspoon dried thyme

1. Select the BAKE function and preheat MAXX to 380ºF (193ºC).
2. In a baking pan, layer the potato, sweet potato, carrot, onion, and garlic.
3. In a small bowl, whisk the milk, cornstarch, and thyme until blended. Pour the milk mixture evenly over the vegetables in the pan.
4. Bake for 15 minutes. Check the casserole—it should be golden brown on top, and the vegetables should be tender.
5. Serve immediately.

Cheesy Sausage Balls

Prep time: 5 minutes | Cook time: 15 minutes | Serves 6

12 ounces (340 g) Jimmy Dean's Sausage
6 ounces (170 g) shredded Cheddar cheese
10 Cheddar cubes

1. Mix the shredded cheese and sausage.
2. Divide the mixture into 12 equal parts to be stuffed.
3. Add a cube of cheese to the center of the sausage and roll into balls.
4. Select the AIR FRY function and cook at 375ºF (191ºC) for 15 minutes, or until crisp.
5. Serve immediately.

Sweet Corn and Carrot Fritters

Prep time: 10 minutes | Cook time: 8 to 11 minutes | Serves 4

1 medium-sized carrot, grated
1 yellow onion, finely chopped
4 ounces (113 g) canned sweet corn kernels, drained
1 teaspoon sea salt flakes
1 tablespoon chopped fresh cilantro
1 medium-sized egg, whisked
2 tablespoons plain milk
1 cup grated Parmesan cheese
¼ cup flour
1/3 teaspoon baking powder
1/3 teaspoon sugar
Cooking spray

1. Select the BAKE function and preheat MAXX to 350ºF (177ºC).
2. Place the grated carrot in a colander and press down to squeeze out any excess moisture. Dry it with a paper towel.
3. Combine the carrots with the remaining ingredients.
4. Mold 1 tablespoon of the mixture into a ball and press it down with your hand or a spoon to flatten it. Repeat until the rest of the mixture is used up.
5. Spritz the balls with cooking spray.
6. Arrange in the air fryer basket, taking care not to overlap any balls. Bake for 8 to 11 minutes, or until they're firm.
7. Serve warm.

Air Fried Broccoli

Prep time: 5 minutes | Cook time: 6 minutes | Serves 1

4 egg yolks
¼ cup butter, melted
2 cups coconut flower
Salt and pepper, to taste
2 cups broccoli florets

1. In a bowl, whisk the egg yolks and melted butter together. Throw in the coconut flour, salt and pepper, then stir again to combine well.
2. Dip each broccoli floret into the mixture and place in the air fryer basket. Select the AIR FRY function and cook at 400ºF (204ºC) for 6 minutes.
3. Work in batches if necessary. Take care when removing them from the air fryer oven and serve immediately.

Cheesy Potato Patties

Prep time: 5 minutes | Cook time: 10 minutes | Serves 8

2 pounds (907 g) white potatoes
½ cup finely chopped scallions
½ teaspoon freshly ground black pepper, or more to taste
1 tablespoon fine
sea salt
½ teaspoon hot paprika
2 cups shredded Colby cheese
¼ cup canola oil
1 cup crushed crackers

1. Select the BAKE function and preheat MAXX to 360ºF (182ºC).
2. Boil the potatoes until soft. Dry them off and peel them before mashing thoroughly, leaving no lumps.
3. Combine the mashed potatoes with scallions, pepper, salt, paprika, and cheese.
4. Mold the mixture into balls with your hands and press with your palm to flatten them into patties.
5. In a shallow dish, combine the canola oil and crushed crackers. Coat the patties in the crumb mixture.
6. Bake the patties for about 10 minutes, in multiple batches if necessary.
7. Serve hot.

Bacon-Wrapped Beef Hot Dog

Prep time: 5 minutes | Cook time: 10 minutes | Serves 4

4 slices sugar-free bacon
4 beef hot dogs

1. Select the BAKE function and preheat MAXX to 370ºF (188ºC).
2. Take a slice of bacon and wrap it around the hot dog, securing it with a toothpick. Repeat with the other pieces of bacon and hot dogs, placing each wrapped dog in the air fryer basket.
3. Bake for 10 minutes, turning halfway through.
4. Once hot and crispy, the hot dogs are ready to serve.

Beef Bratwursts

Prep time: 5 minutes | Cook time: 15 minutes | Serves 4

4 (3-ounce / 85-g) beef bratwursts

1. Place the beef bratwursts in the air fryer basket.
2. Select the AIR FRY function and cook at 375ºF (191ºC) for 15 minutes, turning once halfway through.
3. Serve hot.

Carrot and Celery Croquettes

Prep time: 10 minutes | Cook time: 6 minutes | Serves 4

2 medium-sized carrots, trimmed and grated
2 medium-sized celery stalks, trimmed and grated
½ cup finely chopped leek
1 tablespoon garlic paste
¼ teaspoon freshly cracked black pepper
1 teaspoon fine sea salt
1 tablespoon finely chopped fresh dill
1 egg, lightly whisked
¼ cup flour
¼ teaspoon baking powder
½ cup bread crumbs
Cooking spray
Chive mayo, for serving

1. Drain any excess liquid from the carrots and celery by placing them on a paper towel.
2. Stir together the vegetables with all of the other ingredients, save for the bread crumbs and chive mayo.
3. Use your hands to mold 1 tablespoon of the vegetable mixture into a ball and repeat until all of the mixture has been used up. Press down on each ball with your hand or a palette knife. Cover completely with bread crumbs. Spritz the croquettes with cooking spray.
4. Arrange the croquettes in a single layer in the air fryer basket. Select the AIR FRY function and cook at 360ºF (182ºC) for 6 minutes.
5. Serve warm with the chive mayo on the side.

Purple Potato Chips with Rosemary

Prep time: 10 minutes | Cook time: 9 to 14 minutes | Serves 6

1 cup Greek yogurt
2 chipotle chiles, minced
2 tablespoons adobo sauce
1 teaspoon paprika
1 tablespoon lemon juice
10 purple fingerling potatoes
1 teaspoon olive oil
2 teaspoons minced fresh rosemary leaves
⅛ teaspoon cayenne pepper
¼ teaspoon coarse sea salt

1. In a medium bowl, combine the yogurt, minced chiles, adobo sauce, paprika, and lemon juice. Mix well and refrigerate.
2. Wash the potatoes and dry them with paper towels. Slice the potatoes lengthwise, as thinly as possible. You can use a mandoline, a vegetable peeler, or a very sharp knife.
3. Combine the potato slices in a medium bowl and drizzle with the olive oil; toss to coat. Transfer the potato slices to the air fryer basket.
4. Select the AIR FRY function and cook at 400ºF (204ºC) for 9 to 14 minutes. Use tongs to gently rearrange the chips halfway during cooking time.
5. Sprinkle the chips with the rosemary, cayenne pepper, and sea salt. Serve with the chipotle sauce for dipping.

Bistro Potato Wedges

Prep time: 10 minutes | Cook time: 13 minutes | Serves 4

1 pound (454 g) fingerling potatoes, cut into wedges
1 teaspoon extra-virgin olive oil
½ teaspoon garlic powder
Salt and pepper, to taste
½ cup raw cashews, soaked in water overnight
½ teaspoon ground turmeric
½ teaspoon paprika
1 tablespoon nutritional yeast
1 teaspoon fresh lemon juice
2 tablespoons to ¼ cup water

1. In a bowl, toss together the potato wedges, olive oil, garlic powder, and salt and pepper, making sure to coat the potatoes well.
2. Transfer the potatoes to the air fryer basket. Select the AIR FRY function and cook at 400ºF (204ºC) for 10 minutes.
3. In the meantime, prepare the cheese sauce. Pulse the cashews, turmeric, paprika, nutritional yeast, lemon juice, and water together in a food processor. Add more water to achieve your desired consistency.
4. When the potatoes are finished cooking, transfer to a bowl and add the cheese sauce on top. Air fry for an additional 3 minutes.
5. Serve hot.

Baked Chorizo Scotch Eggs

Prep time: 5 minutes | Cook time: 15 to 20 minutes | Makes 4 eggs

1 pound (454 g) Mexican chorizo or other seasoned sausage meat
4 soft-boiled eggs plus 1 raw egg
1 tablespoon water
½ cup all-purpose flour
1 cup panko bread crumbs
Cooking spray

1. Divide the chorizo into 4 equal portions. Flatten each portion into a disc. Place a soft-boiled egg in the center of each disc. Wrap the chorizo around the egg, encasing it completely. Place the encased eggs on a plate and chill for at least 30 minutes.

2. Select the BAKE function and preheat MAXX to 360ºF (182ºC).
3. Beat the raw egg with 1 tablespoon of water. Place the flour on a small plate and the panko on a second plate. Working with 1 egg at a time, roll the encased egg in the flour, then dip it in the egg mixture. Dredge the egg in the panko and place on a plate. Repeat with the remaining eggs.
4. Spray the eggs with oil and place in the air fryer basket. Bake for 10 minutes. Turn and bake for an additional 5 to 10 minutes, or until browned and crisp on all sides.
5. Serve immediately.

Pomegranate Avocado Fries

Prep time: 5 minutes | Cook time: 7 to 8 minutes | Serves 4

1 cup panko bread crumbs
1 teaspoon kosher salt, plus more for sprinkling
1 teaspoon garlic powder
½ teaspoon cayenne pepper
2 ripe but firm avocados
1 egg, beaten with 1 tablespoon water
Cooking spray
Pomegranate molasses, for serving

1. Select the BAKE function and preheat MAXX to 375ºF (191ºC).
2. Whisk together the panko, salt, and spices on a plate. Cut each avocado in half and remove the pit. Cut each avocado half into 4 slices and scoop the slices out with a large spoon, taking care to keep the slices intact.
3. Dip each avocado slice in the egg wash and then dredge it in the panko. Place the breaded avocado slices on a plate.
4. Working in 2 batches, arrange half of the avocado slices in a single layer in the air fryer basket. Spray lightly with oil. Bake the slices for 7 to 8 minutes, turning once halfway through. Remove the cooked slices to a platter and repeat with the remaining avocado slices.
5. Sprinkle the warm avocado slices with salt and drizzle with pomegranate molasses. Serve immediately.

Buttery Sweet Potatoes

Prep time: 5 minutes | Cook time: 10 minutes | Serves 4

2 tablespoons butter, melted
1 tablespoon light brown sugar

2 sweet potatoes, peeled and cut into ½-inch cubes
Cooking spray

1. Line the air fryer basket with parchment paper.
2. In a medium bowl, stir together the melted butter and brown sugar until blended. Toss the sweet potatoes in the butter mixture until coated.
3. Place the sweet potatoes on the parchment and spritz with oil.
4. Select the AIR FRY function and cook at 400ºF (204ºC) for 5 minutes. Shake the basket, spritz the sweet potatoes with oil, and air fry for 5 minutes more until they're soft enough to cut with a fork.
5. Serve immediately.

Rosemary and Orange Roasted Chickpeas

Prep time: 5 minutes | Cook time: 10 to 12 minutes | Makes 4 cups

4 cups cooked chickpeas
2 tablespoons vegetable oil
1 teaspoon kosher salt

1 teaspoon cumin
1 teaspoon paprika
Zest of 1 orange
1 tablespoon chopped fresh rosemary

1. Make sure the chickpeas are completely dry prior to roasting. In a medium bowl, toss the chickpeas with oil, salt, cumin, and paprika.
2. Working in batches, spread the chickpeas in a single layer in the air fryer basket.
3. Select the AIR FRY function and cook at 400ºF (204ºC) for 10 to 12 minutes, or until crisp, shaking once halfway through.
4. Return the warm chickpeas to the bowl and toss with the orange zest and rosemary. Allow to cool completely.
5. Serve.

Easy Roasted Asparagus

Prep time: 5 minutes | Cook time: 6 minutes | Serves 4

1 pound (454 g) asparagus, trimmed and halved crosswise
1 teaspoon extra-

virgin olive oil
Salt and pepper, to taste
Lemon wedges, for serving

1. Select the ROAST function and preheat MAXX to 400ºF (204ºC).
2. Toss the asparagus with the oil, ⅛ teaspoon salt, and ⅛ teaspoon pepper in bowl. Transfer to air fryer basket.
3. Place the basket in air fryer oven and roast for 6 to 8 minutes, or until tender and bright green, tossing halfway through cooking.
4. Season with salt and pepper and serve with lemon wedges.

Crunchy Fried Okra

Prep time: 5 minutes | Cook time: 8 to 10 minutes | Serves 4

1 cup self-rising yellow cornmeal
1 teaspoon Italian-style seasoning
1 teaspoon paprika
1 teaspoon salt

½ teaspoon freshly ground black pepper
2 large eggs, beaten
2 cups okra slices
Cooking spray

1. Line the air fryer basket with parchment paper.
2. In a shallow bowl, whisk the cornmeal, Italian-style seasoning, paprika, salt, and pepper until blended. Place the beaten eggs in a second shallow bowl.
3. Add the okra to the beaten egg and stir to coat. Add the egg and okra mixture to the cornmeal mixture and stir until coated.
4. Place the okra on the parchment and spritz it with oil.
5. Select the AIR FRY function and cook at 400ºF (204ºC) for 4 minutes. Shake the basket, spritz the okra with oil, and air fry for 4 to 6 minutes more until lightly browned and crispy.
6. Serve immediately.

Easy Devils on Horseback

Prep time: 5 minutes | Cook time: 7 minutes | Serves 12

24 petite pitted prunes (4½ ounces / 128 g)
¼ cup crumbled

blue cheese, divided
8 slices center-cut bacon, cut crosswise into thirds

1. Halve the prunes lengthwise, but don't cut them all the way through. Place ½ teaspoon of cheese in the center of each prune. Wrap a piece of bacon around each prune and secure the bacon with a toothpick.
2. Working in batches, arrange a single layer of the prunes in the air fryer basket.
3. Select the AIR FRY function and cook at 400ºF (204ºC) for 7 minutes, flipping halfway, until the bacon is cooked through and crisp.
4. Let cool slightly and serve warm.

Bacon and Green Beans

Prep time: 15 minutes | Cook time: 8 to 10 minutes | Serves 4

2 (14.5-ounce / 411-g) cans cut green beans, drained
4 bacon slices, air-fried and diced
¼ cup minced onion
1 tablespoon distilled white

vinegar
1 teaspoon freshly squeezed lemon juice
½ teaspoon salt
½ teaspoon freshly ground black pepper
Cooking spray

1. Spritz a baking pan with oil. In the prepared pan, stir together the green beans, bacon, onion, vinegar, lemon juice, salt, and pepper until blended.
2. Place the pan on the air fryer basket.
3. Select the AIR FRY function and cook at 370ºF (188ºC) for 4 minutes. Stir the green beans and air fry for 4 to 6 minutes more until soft.
4. Serve immediately.

Bacon-Wrapped Jalapeño Poppers

Prep time: 5 minutes | Cook time: 12 minutes | Serves 6

6 large jalapeños
4 ounces (113 g) ¹/₃-less-fat cream cheese
¼ cup shredded reduced-fat sharp

Cheddar cheese
2 scallions, green tops only, sliced
6 slices center-cut bacon, halved

1. Select the BAKE function and preheat MAXX to 325ºF (163ºC).
2. Wearing rubber gloves, halve the jalapeños lengthwise to make 12 pieces. Scoop out the seeds and membranes and discard.
3. In a medium bowl, combine the cream cheese, Cheddar, and scallions. Using a small spoon or spatula, fill the jalapeños with the cream cheese filling. Wrap a bacon strip around each pepper and secure with a toothpick.
4. Working in batches, place the stuffed peppers in a single layer in the air fryer basket. Bake for about 12 minutes, until the peppers are tender, the bacon is browned and crisp, and the cheese is melted.
5. Serve warm.

Air-Fried Chicken Wings

Prep time: 5 minutes | Cook time: 19 minutes | Serves 6

2 pounds (907 g) chicken wings, tips

removed
⅛ teaspoon salt

1. Season the wings with salt.
2. Working in 2 batches, place half the chicken wings in the basket. Select the AIR FRY function and cook at 400ºF (204ºC) for 15 minutes, or until the skin is browned and cooked through, turning the wings with tongs halfway through cooking.
3. Combine both batches in the air fryer oven and air fry for 4 minutes more. Transfer to a large bowl and serve immediately.

Baked Cheese Sandwich

Prep time: 5 minutes | Cook time: 8 minutes | Serves 2

2 tablespoons mayonnaise
4 thick slices sourdough bread

4 thick slices Brie cheese
8 slices hot capicola

1. Select the BAKE function and preheat MAXX to 350ºF (177ºC).
2. Spread the mayonnaise on one side of each slice of bread. Place 2 slices of bread in the air fryer basket, mayonnaise-side down.
3. Place the slices of Brie and capicola on the bread and cover with the remaining two slices of bread, mayonnaise-side up.
4. Bake for 8 minutes, or until the cheese has melted.
5. Serve immediately.

Indian-Style Sweet Potato Fries

Prep time: 5 minutes | Cook time: 8 minutes | Makes 20 fries

Seasoning Mixture:
¾ teaspoon ground coriander
½ teaspoon garam masala
½ teaspoon garlic

powder
½ teaspoon ground cumin
¼ teaspoon ground cayenne pepper

Fries:
2 large sweet potatoes, peeled
2 teaspoons olive oil

1. In a small bowl, combine the coriander, garam masala, garlic powder, cumin, and cayenne pepper.
2. Slice the sweet potatoes into ¼-inch-thick fries.
3. In a large bowl, toss the sliced sweet potatoes with the olive oil and the seasoning mixture.
4. Transfer the seasoned sweet potatoes to the air fryer basket. Select the AIR FRY function and cook at 400ºF (204ºC) for 8 minutes, or until crispy.
5. Serve warm.

Herb-Roasted Veggies

Prep time: 10 minutes | Cook time: 14 to 18 minutes | Serves 4

1 red bell pepper, sliced
1 (8-ounce / 227-g) package sliced mushrooms
1 cup green beans, cut into 2-inch pieces
¹⁄₃ cup diced red

onion
3 garlic cloves, sliced
1 teaspoon olive oil
½ teaspoon dried basil
½ teaspoon dried tarragon

1. Select the ROAST function and preheat MAXX to 350ºF (177ºC).
2. In a medium bowl, mix the red bell pepper, mushrooms, green beans, red onion, and garlic. Drizzle with the olive oil. Toss to coat.
3. Add the herbs and toss again.
4. Place the vegetables in the air fryer basket. Roast for 14 to 18 minutes, or until tender. Serve immediately.

Peppery Brown Rice Fritters

Prep time: 10 minutes | Cook time: 8 to 10 minutes | Serves 4

1 (10-ounce / 284-g) bag frozen cooked brown rice, thawed
1 egg
3 tablespoons brown rice flour
¹⁄₃ cup finely grated

carrots
¹⁄₃ cup minced red bell pepper
2 tablespoons minced fresh basil
3 tablespoons grated Parmesan cheese
2 teaspoons olive oil

1. In a small bowl, combine the thawed rice, egg, and flour and mix to blend.
2. Stir in the carrots, bell pepper, basil, and Parmesan cheese.
3. Form the mixture into 8 fritters and drizzle with the olive oil.
4. Put the fritters carefully into the air fryer basket.
5. Select the AIR FRY function and cook at 380ºF (193ºC) for 8 to 10 minutes, or until the fritters are golden brown and cooked through.
6. Serve immediately.

Classic Mexican Street Corn

Prep time: 5 minutes | Cook time: 7 minutes | Serves 4

4 medium ears corn, husked
Cooking spray
2 tablespoons mayonnaise
1 tablespoon fresh lime juice
½ teaspoon ancho chile powder
¼ teaspoon kosher salt
2 ounces (57 g) crumbled Cotija or feta cheese
2 tablespoons chopped fresh cilantro

1. Spritz the corn with cooking spray. Working in batches, arrange the ears of corn in the air fryer basket in a single layer.
2. Select the AIR FRY function and cook at 375°F (191°C) for 7 minutes, flipping halfway, until the kernels are tender when pierced with a paring knife. When cool enough to handle, cut the corn kernels off the cob.
3. In a large bowl, mix together mayonnaise, lime juice, ancho powder, and salt. Add the corn kernels and mix to combine. Transfer to a serving dish and top with the Cotija and cilantro.
4. Serve immediately.

Baked Halloumi with Greek Salsa

Prep time: 15 minutes | Cook time: 6 minutes | Serves 4

Salsa:
1 small shallot, finely diced
3 garlic cloves, minced
2 tablespoons fresh lemon juice
2 tablespoons extra-virgin olive oil
1 teaspoon freshly cracked black pepper
Pinch of kosher salt
½ cup finely diced English cucumber
1 plum tomato, deseeded and finely diced
2 teaspoons chopped fresh parsley
1 teaspoon snipped fresh dill
1 teaspoon snipped fresh oregano

Cheese:
8 ounces (227 g) Halloumi cheese, sliced into ½-inch-thick pieces
1 tablespoon extra-virgin olive oil

1. Select the BAKE function and preheat MAXX to 375°F (191°C).
2. For the salsa: Combine the shallot, garlic, lemon juice, olive oil, pepper, and salt in a medium bowl. Add the cucumber, tomato, parsley, dill, and oregano. Toss gently to combine; set aside.
3. For the cheese: Place the cheese slices in a medium bowl. Drizzle with the olive oil. Toss gently to coat. Arrange the cheese in a single layer in the air fryer basket. Bake for 6 minutes.
4. Divide the cheese among four serving plates. Top with the salsa and serve immediately.

Air Fried Green Tomatoes

Prep time: 5 minutes | Cook time: 6 to 8 minutes | Serves 4

4 medium green tomatoes
⅓ cup all purpose flour
2 egg whites
¼ cup almond milk
1 cup ground
almonds
½ cup panko bread crumbs
2 teaspoons olive oil
1 teaspoon paprika
1 clove garlic, minced

1. Rinse the tomatoes and pat dry. Cut the tomatoes into ½-inch slices, discarding the thinner ends.
2. Put the flour on a plate. In a shallow bowl, beat the egg whites with the almond milk until frothy. And in another plate, combine the almonds, bread crumbs, olive oil, paprika, and garlic and mix well.
3. Dip the tomato slices into the flour, then into the egg white mixture, then into the almond mixture to coat.
4. Place four of the coated tomato slices in the air fryer basket.
5. Select the AIR FRY function and cook at 400°F (204°C) for 6 to 8 minutes, or until the tomato coating is crisp and golden brown. Repeat with remaining tomato slices and serve immediately.

Cheesy Baked Grits

Prep time: 10 minutes | Cook time: 12 minutes | Serves 6

¾ cup hot water
2 (1-ounce / 28-g) packages instant grits
1 large egg, beaten
1 tablespoon butter, melted
2 cloves garlic,
minced
½ to 1 teaspoon red pepper flakes
1 cup shredded Cheddar cheese or jalapeño Jack cheese

1. In a baking pan, combine the water, grits, egg, butter, garlic, and red pepper flakes. Stir until well combined. Stir in the shredded cheese.
2. Place the pan in the air fryer basket. Select the AIR FRY function and cook at 400°F (204°C) for 12 minutes, or until the grits have cooked through and a knife inserted near the center comes out clean.
3. Let stand for 5 minutes before serving.

Simple Sweet Potato Soufflé

Prep time: 10 minutes | Cook time: 30 minutes | Serves 4

1 sweet potato, baked and mashed
2 tablespoons unsalted butter, divided
1 large egg, separated
¼ cup whole milk
½ teaspoon kosher salt

1. Select the BAKE function and preheat MAXX to 330°F (166°C).
2. In a medium bowl, combine the sweet potato, 1 tablespoon of melted butter, egg yolk, milk, and salt. Set aside.
3. In a separate medium bowl, whisk the egg white until stiff peaks form.
4. Using a spatula, gently fold the egg white into the sweet potato mixture.
5. Coat the inside of four 3-inch ramekins with the remaining 1 tablespoon of butter, then fill each ramekin halfway full. Place 2 ramekins in the air fryer basket and bake for 15 minutes. Repeat this process with the remaining ramekins.
6. Remove the ramekins from the air fryer oven and allow to cool on a wire rack for 10 minutes before serving

Corn Fritters

Prep time: 15 minutes | Cook time: 8 minutes | Serves 6

1 cup self-rising flour
1 tablespoon sugar
1 teaspoon salt
1 large egg, lightly
beaten
¼ cup buttermilk
¾ cup corn kernels
¼ cup minced onion
Cooking spray

1. Select the BAKE function and preheat MAXX to 350°F (177°C). Line the air fryer basket with parchment paper.
2. In a medium bowl, whisk the flour, sugar, and salt until blended. Stir in the egg and buttermilk. Add the corn and minced onion. Mix well. Shape the corn fritter batter into 12 balls.
3. Place the fritters on the parchment and spritz with oil. Bake for 4 minutes. Flip the fritters, spritz them with oil, and bake for 4 minutes more until firm and lightly browned.
4. Serve immediately.

Indian Masala Omelet

Prep time: 10 minutes | Cook time: 12 minutes | Serves 2

4 large eggs
½ cup diced onion
½ cup diced tomato
¼ cup chopped fresh cilantro
1 jalapeño, deseeded and finely chopped
½ teaspoon ground turmeric
½ teaspoon kosher salt
½ teaspoon cayenne pepper
Olive oil, for greasing the pan

1. Select the BAKE function and preheat MAXX to 250°F (121°C). Generously grease a 3-cup Bundt pan.
2. In a large bowl, beat the eggs. Stir in the onion, tomato, cilantro, jalapeño, turmeric, salt, and cayenne.
3. Pour the egg mixture into the prepared pan. Place the pan in the air fryer basket. Bake for 12 minutes, or until the eggs are cooked through. Carefully unmold and cut the omelet into four pieces.
4. Serve immediately.

Cheesy Chile Toast

Prep time: 5 minutes | Cook time: 5 minutes | Serves 1

2 tablespoons grated Parmesan cheese
2 tablespoons grated Mozzarella cheese
2 teaspoons salted butter, at room temperature

10 to 15 thin slices serrano chile or jalapeño
2 slices sourdough bread
½ teaspoon black pepper

1. Select the BAKE function and preheat MAXX to 325ºF (163ºC).
2. In a small bowl, stir together the Parmesan, Mozzarella, butter, and chiles.
3. Spread half the mixture onto one side of each slice of bread. Sprinkle with the pepper. Place the slices, cheese-side up, in the air fryer basket. Bake for 5 minutes, or until the cheese has melted and started to brown slightly.
4. Serve immediately.

Beet Salad with Lemon Vinaigrette

Prep time: 10 minutes | Cook time: 12 to 15 minutes | Serves 4

6 medium red and golden beets, peeled and sliced
1 teaspoon olive oil
¼ teaspoon kosher

salt
½ cup crumbled feta cheese
8 cups mixed greens
Cooking spray

Vinaigrette:
2 teaspoons olive oil
2 tablespoons

chopped fresh chives
Juice of 1 lemon

1. In a large bowl, toss the beets, olive oil, and kosher salt.
2. Spray the air fryer basket with cooking spray, then place the beets in the basket. Select the AIR FRY function and cook at 360ºF (182ºC) for 12 to 15 minutes, or until tender.
3. While the beets cook, make the vinaigrette in a large bowl by whisking together the olive oil, lemon juice, and chives.
4. Remove the beets from the air fryer oven, toss in the vinaigrette, and allow to cool for 5 minutes. Add the feta and serve on top of the mixed greens.

Traditional Queso Fundido

Prep time: 10 minutes | Cook time: 25 minutes | Serves 4

4 ounces (113 g) fresh Mexican chorizo, casings removed
1 medium onion, chopped
3 cloves garlic, minced
1 cup chopped tomato
2 jalapeños,

deseeded and diced
2 teaspoons ground cumin
2 cups shredded Oaxaca or Mozzarella cheese
½ cup half-and-half
Celery sticks or tortilla chips, for serving

1. In a baking pan, combine the chorizo, onion, garlic, tomato, jalapeños, and cumin. Stir to combine.
2. Place the pan in the air fryer basket. Select the AIR FRY function and cook at 400ºF (204ºC) for 15 minutes, or until the sausage is cooked, stirring halfway through the cooking time to break up the sausage.
3. Add the cheese and half-and-half; stir to combine. Air fry for 10 minutes, or until the cheese has melted.
4. Serve with celery sticks or tortilla chips.

Cheesy Jalapeño Poppers

Prep time: 5 minutes | Cook time: 25 minutes | Serves 6

2 slices bacon, halved
¾ cup whole milk ricotta cheese
½ cup shredded sharp Cheddar cheese
1 green onion, finely

chopped
¼ teaspoon salt
6 large jalapeños, halved lengthwise and deseeded
½ cup finely crushed potato chips

1. Lay bacon in single layer in basket. Select the AIR FRY function and cook at 400ºF (204ºC) for 5 minutes, or until crisp. Remove bacon and place on paper towels to drain. When cool, finely chop.
2. Stir together ricotta, Cheddar, green onion, bacon, and salt. Spoon into jalapeños; top with potato chips.
3. Place half the jalapeños in the basket and air fry for 8 minutes, or until tender. Repeat with the remaining jalapeños.
4. Serve immediately.

Chapter 13 Sauces, Dips, and Dressings

Avocado Dressing

Prep time: 5 minutes | Cook time: 0 minutes | Makes 12 tablespoons

1 large avocado, pitted and peeled
½ cup water
2 tablespoons tahini
2 tablespoons freshly squeezed lemon juice
1 teaspoon dried

basil
1 teaspoon white wine vinegar
1 garlic clove
¼ teaspoon pink Himalayan salt
¼ teaspoon freshly ground black pepper

1. Combine all the ingredients in a food processor and blend until smooth.

Cauliflower Alfredo Sauce

Prep time: 2 minutes | Cook time: 0 minutes | Makes 4 cups

2 tablespoons olive oil
6 garlic cloves, minced
3 cups unsweetened almond milk
1 (1-pound / 454-g) head cauliflower, cut

into florets
1 teaspoon salt
¼ teaspoon freshly ground black pepper
Juice of 1 lemon
4 tablespoons nutritional yeast

1. In a medium saucepan, heat the olive oil over medium-high heat. Add the garlic and sauté for 1 minute or until fragrant. Add the almond milk, stir, and bring to a boil.
2. Gently add the cauliflower. Stir in the salt and pepper and return to a boil. Continue cooking over medium-high heat for 5 minutes or until the cauliflower is soft. Stir frequently and reduce heat if needed to prevent the liquid from boiling over.
3. Carefully transfer the cauliflower and cooking liquid to a food processor, using a slotted spoon to scoop out the larger pieces of cauliflower before pouring in the liquid. Add the lemon and nutritional yeast and blend for 1 to 2 minutes until smooth.
4. Serve immediately.

Red Buffalo Sauce

Prep time: 5 minutes | Cook time: 20 minutes | Makes 2 cups

¼ cup olive oil
4 garlic cloves, roughly chopped
1 (5-ounce / 142-g) small red onion, roughly chopped
6 red chiles, roughly chopped (about 2

ounces / 56 g in total)
1 cup water
½ cup apple cider vinegar
½ teaspoon salt
½ teaspoon freshly ground black pepper

1. In a large nonstick sauté pan, heat ¼ cup olive oil over medium-high heat. Once it's hot, add the garlic, onion, and chiles. Cook for 5 minutes, stirring occasionally, until onions are golden brown.
2. Add the water and bring to a boil. Cook for about 10 minutes or until the water has nearly evaporated.
3. Transfer the cooked onion and chile mixture to a food processor or blender and blend briefly to combine. Add the apple cider vinegar, salt, and pepper. Blend again for 30 seconds.
4. Using a mesh sieve, strain the sauce into a bowl. Use a spoon or spatula to scrape and press all the liquid from the pulp.

Cashew Ranch Dressing

Prep time: 15 minutes | Cook time: 0 minutes | Serves 12

1 cup cashews, soaked in warm water for at least 1 hour
½ cup water
2 tablespoons freshly squeezed lemon juice

1 tablespoon vinegar
1 teaspoon garlic powder
1 teaspoon onion powder
2 teaspoons dried dill

1. In a food processor, combine the cashews, water, lemon juice, vinegar, garlic powder, and onion powder. Blend until creamy and smooth. Add the dill and pulse a few times until combined.

Dijon and Balsamic Vinaigrette

Prep time: 5 minutes | Cook time: 0 minutes | Makes 12 tablespoons

6 tablespoons water
4 tablespoons Dijon mustard
4 tablespoons balsamic vinegar
1 teaspoon maple syrup
½ teaspoon pink Himalayan salt
¼ teaspoon freshly ground black pepper

1. In a bowl, whisk together all the ingredients.

Hemp Dressing

Prep time: 5 minutes | Cook time: 0 minutes | Makes 12 tablespoons

½ cup white wine vinegar
¼ cup tahini
¼ cup water
1 tablespoon hemp seeds
½ tablespoon freshly squeezed lemon juice
1 teaspoon garlic powder
1 teaspoon dried oregano
1 teaspoon dried basil
1 teaspoon red pepper flakes
½ teaspoon onion powder
½ teaspoon pink Himalayan salt
½ teaspoon freshly ground black pepper

1. In a bowl, combine all the ingredients and whisk until mixed well.

Cashew Pesto

Prep time: 10 minutes | Cook time: 0 minutes | Makes 1 cup

¼ cup raw cashews
Juice of 1 lemon
2 garlic cloves
⅓ red onion (about 2 ounces / 56 g in total)
1 tablespoon olive oil
4 cups basil leaves, packed
1 cup wheatgrass
¼ cup water
¼ teaspoon salt

1. Put the cashews in a heatproof bowl and add boiling water to cover. Soak for 5 minutes and then drain.
2. Put all ingredients in a blender and blend for 2 to 3 minutes or until fully combined.

Mushroom Apple Gravy

Prep time: 5 minutes | Cook time: 10 minutes | Serves 4

2 cups vegetable broth
½ cup finely chopped mushrooms
2 tablespoons whole wheat flour
1 tablespoon unsweetened applesauce
1 teaspoon onion powder
½ teaspoon dried thyme
¼ teaspoon dried rosemary
⅛ teaspoon pink Himalayan salt
Freshly ground black pepper, to taste

1. In a nonstick saucepan over medium-high heat, combine all the ingredients and mix well. Bring to a boil, stirring frequently, reduce the heat to low, and simmer, stirring constantly, until it thickens.

Cashew Vodka Sauce

Prep time: 15 minutes | Cook time: 5 minutes | Makes 3 cups

¾ cup raw cashews
¼ cup boiling water
1 tablespoon olive oil
4 garlic cloves, minced
1½ cups unsweetened almond milk
1 tablespoon arrowroot powder
1 teaspoon salt
1 tablespoon nutritional yeast
1¼ cups marinara sauce

1. Put the cashews in a heatproof bowl and add boiling water to cover. Let soak for 10 minutes. Drain the cashews and place them in a blender. Add ¼ cup boiling water and blend for 1 to 2 minutes or until creamy. Set aside.
2. In a small saucepan, heat the olive oil over medium heat. Add the garlic and sauté for 2 minutes until golden. Whisk in the almond milk, arrowroot powder, and salt. Bring to a simmer. Continue to simmer, whisking frequently, for about 5 minutes or until the sauce thickens.
3. Carefully transfer the hot almond milk mixture to the blender with the cashews. Blend for 30 seconds to combine, then add the nutritional yeast and marinara sauce. Blend for 1 minute or until creamy.

Cashew Mayo

Prep time: 5 minutes | Cook time: 0 minutes | Makes 18 tablespoons

1 cup cashews, soaked in hot water for at least 1 hour
¼ cup plus 3 tablespoons milk
1 tablespoon apple cider vinegar
1 tablespoon freshly squeezed lemon juice
1 tablespoon Dijon mustard
1 tablespoon aquafaba
⅛ teaspoon pink Himalayan salt

1. In a food processor, combine all the ingredients and blend until creamy and smooth.

Pico de Gallo

Prep time: 5 minutes | Cook time: 0 minutes | Serves 2

3 large tomatoes, chopped
½ small red onion, diced
⅛ cup chopped fresh cilantro
3 garlic cloves, chopped
2 tablespoons chopped pickled jalapeño pepper
1 tablespoon lime juice
¼ teaspoon pink Himalayan salt (optional)

1. In a medium bowl, combine all the ingredients and mix with a wooden spoon.

Balsamic Dressing

Prep time: 5 minutes | Cook time: 0 minutes | Makes 1 cup

2 tablespoons Dijon mustard
¼ cup balsamic vinegar
¾ cup olive oil

1. Put all ingredients in a jar with a tight-fitting lid. Put on the lid and shake vigorously until thoroughly combined. Refrigerate until ready to use and shake well before serving.

Hummus

Prep time: 5 minutes | Cook time: 0 minutes | Serves 2

1 (19-ounce / 539-g) can chickpeas, drained and rinsed
¼ cup tahini
3 tablespoons cold water
2 tablespoons freshly squeezed lemon juice
1 garlic clove
½ teaspoon turmeric powder
⅛ teaspoon black pepper
Pinch pink Himalayan salt, to taste

1. Combine all the ingredients in a food processor and blend until smooth.

Lemony Tahini

Prep time: 5 minutes | Cook time: 0 minutes | Serves 4

¾ cup water
½ cup tahini
3 garlic cloves, minced
Juice of 3 lemons
½ teaspoon pink Himalayan salt

1. In a bowl, whisk together all the ingredients until mixed well.

Ginger Sweet Sauce

Prep time: 5 minutes | Cook time: 5 minutes | Makes ²/₃ cup

3 tablespoons ketchup
2 tablespoons water
2 tablespoons maple syrup
1 tablespoon rice vinegar
2 teaspoons peeled
minced fresh ginger root
2 teaspoons soy sauce (or tamari, which is a gluten-free option)
1 teaspoon cornstarch

1. In a small saucepan over medium heat, combine all the ingredients and stir continuously for 5 minutes, or until slightly thickened. Enjoy warm or cold.

Chapter 14 Casseroles, Frittatas, and Quiches

Cheesy Bacon Quiche

Prep time: 15 minutes | Cook time: 20 minutes | Serves 4

1 tablespoon olive oil
1 shortcrust pastry
3 tablespoons Greek yogurt
½ cup grated Cheddar cheese
3 ounces (85 g) chopped bacon
4 eggs, beaten
¼ teaspoon garlic powder
Pinch of black pepper
¼ teaspoon onion powder
¼ teaspoon sea salt
Flour, for sprinkling

1. Select the BAKE function and preheat MAXX to 330ºF (166ºC).
2. Take 8 ramekins and grease with olive oil. Coat with a sprinkling of flour, tapping to remove any excess.
3. Cut the shortcrust pastry in 8 and place each piece at the bottom of each ramekin.
4. Put all the other ingredients in a bowl and combine well. Spoon equal amounts of the filling into each piece of pastry.
5. Bake the ramekins in the air fryer oven for 20 minutes.
6. Serve warm.

Easy Mac and Cheese

Prep time: 10 minutes | Cook time: 10 minutes | Serves 2

1 cup cooked macaroni
1 cup grated Cheddar cheese
½ cup warm milk
Salt and ground black pepper, to taste
1 tablespoon grated Parmesan cheese

1. Select the BAKE function and preheat MAXX to 350ºF (177ºC).
2. In a baking dish, mix all the ingredients, except for Parmesan.
3. Put the dish inside the air fryer oven and bake for 10 minutes.
4. Add the Parmesan cheese on top and serve.

Mini Quiche Cups

Prep time: 15 minutes | Cook time: 16 minutes | Makes 10 quiche cups

4 ounces (113 g) ground pork sausage
3 eggs
¾ cup milk
Cooking spray
4 ounces (113 g) sharp Cheddar cheese, grated

Special Equipment:
20 foil muffin cups

1. Spritz the air fryer basket with cooking spray.
2. Divide sausage into 3 portions and shape each into a thin patty.
3. Put patties in air fryer basket. Select the AIR FRY function and cook at 390ºF (199ºC) for 6 minutes.
4. While sausage is cooking, prepare the egg mixture. Combine the eggs and milk in a large bowl and whisk until well blended. Set aside.
5. When sausage has cooked fully, remove patties from the basket, drain well, and use a fork to crumble the meat into small pieces.
6. Double the foil cups into 10 sets. Remove paper liners from the top muffin cups and spray the foil cups lightly with cooking spray.
7. Divide crumbled sausage among the 10 muffin cup sets.
8. Top each with grated cheese, divided evenly among the cups.
9. Put 5 cups in air fryer basket.
10. Pour egg mixture into each cup, filling until each cup is at least ²/₃ full.
11. Switch from AIR FRY to BAKE. Bake for 8 minutes and test for doneness. A knife inserted into the center shouldn't have any raw egg on it when removed.
12. Repeat with the remaining quiches.
Serve warm.

Shrimp Quiche

Prep time: 15 minutes | Cook time: 20 minutes | Serves 2

2 teaspoons vegetable oil
4 large eggs
½ cup half-and-half
4 ounces (113 g) raw shrimp, chopped
1 cup shredded Parmesan or Swiss cheese
¼ cup chopped

scallions
1 teaspoon sweet smoked paprika
1 teaspoon herbes de Provence
1 teaspoon black pepper
½ to 1 teaspoon kosher salt

1. Select the BAKE function and preheat MAXX to 300ºF (149ºC). Generously grease a round baking pan with 4-inch sides with vegetable oil.
2. In a large bowl, beat together the eggs and half-and-half. Add the shrimp, ¾ cup of the cheese, the scallions, paprika, herbes de Provence, pepper, and salt. Stir with a fork to thoroughly combine. Pour the egg mixture into the prepared pan.
3. Put the pan in the air fryer basket and bake for 20 minutes. After 17 minutes, sprinkle the remaining ¼ cup cheese on top and bake for the remaining 3 minutes, or until the cheese has melted, the eggs are set, and a toothpick inserted into the center comes out clean.
4. Serve the quiche warm.

Creamy Tomato Casserole

Prep time: 5 minutes | Cook time: 30 minutes | Serves 4

5 eggs
2 tablespoons heavy cream
3 tablespoons chunky tomato

sauce
2 tablespoons grated Parmesan cheese, plus more for topping

1. Select the BAKE function and preheat MAXX to 350ºF (177ºC).
2. Combine the eggs and cream in a bowl.
3. Mix in the tomato sauce and add the cheese.
4. Spread into a glass baking dish and bake in the preheated air fryer oven for 30 minutes.
5. Top with extra cheese and serve.

Chicken and Mushroom Casserole

Prep time: 15 minutes | Cook time: 20 minutes | Serves 4

4 chicken breasts
1 tablespoon curry powder
1 cup coconut milk
Salt, to taste
1 broccoli, cut into

florets
1 cup mushrooms
½ cup shredded Parmesan cheese
Cooking spray

1. Select the BAKE function and preheat MAXX to 350ºF (177ºC). Spritz a casserole dish with cooking spray.
2. Cube the chicken breasts and combine with curry powder and coconut milk in a bowl. Season with salt.
3. Add the broccoli and mushroom and mix well.
4. Pour the mixture into the casserole dish. Top with the cheese.
5. Transfer to the air fryer oven and bake for about 20 minutes.
6. Serve warm.

Spinach Casserole

Prep time: 10 minutes | Cook time: 20 minutes | Serves 4

1 (13.5-ounce / 383-g) can spinach, drained and squeezed
1 cup cottage cheese
2 large eggs, beaten
¼ cup crumbled feta cheese
2 tablespoons all-purpose flour

2 tablespoons butter, melted
1 clove garlic, minced, or more to taste
1 ½ teaspoons onion powder
⅛ teaspoon ground nutmeg
Cooking spray

1. Grease an 8-inch pie pan with cooking spray and set aside.
2. Combine spinach, cottage cheese, eggs, feta cheese, flour, butter, garlic, onion powder, and nutmeg in a bowl. Stir until all ingredients are well incorporated. Pour into the prepared pie pan.
3. Select the AIR FRY function and cook at 375ºF (191ºC) for 18 to 20 minutes, or until the center is set.
4. Serve warm.

Shrimp Green Casserole

Prep time: 15 minutes | Cook time: 22 minutes | Serves 4

1 pound (454 g) shrimp, cleaned and deveined
2 cups cauliflower, cut into florets
2 green bell pepper, sliced
1 shallot, sliced
2 tablespoons sesame oil
1 cup tomato paste
Cooking spray

1. Select the BAKE function and preheat MAXX to 360ºF (182ºC). Spritz a baking pan with cooking spray.
2. Arrange the shrimp and vegetables in the baking pan. Then, drizzle the sesame oil over the vegetables. Pour the tomato paste over the vegetables.
3. Bake for 10 minutes in the preheated air fryer oven. Stir with a large spoon and bake for a further 12 minutes.
4. Serve warm.

Western Prosciutto Casserole

Prep time: 5 minutes | Cook time: 10 minutes | Serves 2

1 cup day-old whole grain bread, cubed
3 large eggs, beaten
2 tablespoons water
⅛ teaspoon kosher salt
1 ounce (28 g) prosciutto, roughly chopped
1 ounce (28 g) Pepper Jack cheese, roughly chopped
1 tablespoon chopped fresh chives
Nonstick cooking spray

1. Select the BAKE function and preheat MAXX to 360ºF (182ºC).
2. Spray a baking pan with nonstick cooking spray, then place the bread cubes in the pan. Transfer the baking pan to the air fryer oven.
3. In a medium bowl, stir together the beaten eggs and water, then stir in the kosher salt, prosciutto, cheese, and chives.
4. Pour the egg mixture over the bread cubes and bake for 10 minutes, or until the eggs are set and the top is golden brown.
5. Serve warm.
6.

Ritzy Vegetable Frittata

Prep time: 15 minutes | Cook time: 21 minutes | Serves 2

4 eggs
¼ cup milk
Sea salt and ground black pepper, to taste
1 zucchini, sliced
½ bunch asparagus, sliced
½ cup mushrooms, sliced
½ cup spinach, shredded
½ cup red onion, sliced
½ tablespoon olive oil
5 tablespoons feta cheese, crumbled
4 tablespoons Cheddar cheese, grated
¼ bunch chives, minced

1. In a bowl, mix the eggs, milk, salt and pepper.
2. Over a medium heat, sauté the vegetables for 6 minutes with the olive oil in a nonstick pan.
3. Put some parchment paper in the base of a baking tin. Pour in the vegetables, followed by the egg mixture. Top with the feta and grated Cheddar.
4. Select the BAKE function and preheat MAXX to 320ºF (160ºC).
5. Transfer the baking tin to the air fryer oven and bake for 15 minutes. Remove the frittata from the air fryer oven and leave to cool for 5 minutes.
6. Top with the minced chives and serve.

Appendix 1 Measurement Conversion Chart

US STANDARD	METRIC (APPROXIMATE)
1/8 teaspoon	0.5 mL
1/4 teaspoon	1 mL
1/2 teaspoon	2 mL
3/4 teaspoon	4 mL
1 teaspoon	5 mL
1 tablespoon	15 mL
1/4 cup	59 mL
1/2 cup	118 mL
3/4 cup	177 mL
1 cup	235 mL
2 cups	475 mL
3 cups	700 mL
4 cups	1 L

US STANDARD	US STANDARD (OUNCES)	METRIC (APPROXIMATE)
2 tablespoons	1 fl.oz.	30 mL
1/4 cup	2 fl.oz.	60 mL
1/2 cup	4 fl.oz.	120 mL
1 cup	8 fl.oz.	240 mL
1 1/2 cup	12 fl.oz.	355 mL
2 cups or 1 pint	16 fl.oz.	475 mL
4 cups or 1 quart	32 fl.oz.	1 L
1 gallon	128 fl.oz.	4 L

TEMPERATURES EQUIVALENTS

FAHRENHEIT(F)	CELSIUS(C) (APPROXIMATE)
225 °F	107 °C
250 °F	120 °C
275 °F	135 °C
300 °F	150 °C
325 °F	160 °C
350 °F	180 °C
375 °F	190 °C
400 °F	205 °C
425 °F	220 °C
450 °F	235 °C
475 °F	245 °C
500 °F	260 °C

WEIGHT EQUIVALENTS

US STANDARD	METRIC (APPROXIMATE)
1 ounce	28 g
2 ounces	57 g
5 ounces	142 g
10 ounces	284 g
15 ounces	425 g
16 ounces (1 pound)	455 g
1.5 pounds	680 g
2 pounds	907 g

Appendix 2: Air Fryer Cooking Chart

Beef

Item	Temp (°F)	Time (mins)	Item	Temp (°F)	Time (mins)
Beef Eye Round Roast (4 lbs.)	400 °F	45 to 55	Meatballs (1-inch)	370 °F	7
Burger Patty (4 oz.)	370 °F	16 to 20	Meatballs (3-inch)	380 °F	10
Filet Mignon (8 oz.)	400 °F	18	Ribeye, bone-in (1-inch, 8 oz)	400 °F	10 to 15
Flank Steak (1.5 lbs.)	400 °F	12	Sirloin steaks (1-inch, 12 oz)	400 °F	9 to 14
Flank Steak (2 lbs.)	400 °F	20 to 28			

Chicken

Item	Temp (°F)	Time (mins)	Item	Temp (°F)	Time (mins)
Breasts, bone in (1 ¼ lb.)	370 °F	25	Legs, bone-in (1 ¾ lb.)	380 °F	30
Breasts, boneless (4 oz)	380 °F	12	Thighs, boneless (1 ½ lb.)	380 °F	18 to 20
Drumsticks (2 ½ lb.)	370 °F	20	Wings (2 lb.)	400 °F	12
Game Hen (halved 2 lb.)	390 °F	20	Whole Chicken	360 °F	75
Thighs, bone-in (2 lb.)	380 °F	22	Tenders	360 °F	8 to 10

Pork & Lamb

Item	Temp (°F)	Time (mins)	Item	Temp (°F)	Time (mins)
Bacon (regular)	400 °F	5 to 7	Pork Tenderloin	370 °F	15
Bacon (thick cut)	400 °F	6 to 10	Sausages	380 °F	15
Pork Loin (2 lb.)	360 °F	55	Lamb Loin Chops (1-inch thick)	400 °F	8 to 12
Pork Chops, bone in (1-inch, 6.5 oz)	400 °F	12	Rack of Lamb (1.5 – 2 lb.)	380 °F	22

Fish & Seafood

Item	Temp (°F)	Time (mins)	Item	Temp (°F)	Time (mins)
Calamari (8 oz)	400 °F	4	Tuna Steak	400 °F	7 to 10
Fish Fillet (1-inch, 8 oz)	400 °F	10	Scallops	400 °F	5 to 7
Salmon, fillet (6 oz)	380 °F	12	Shrimp	400 °F	5
Swordfish steak	400 °F	10			

Vegetables

INGREDIENT	AMOUNT	PREPARATION	OIL	TEMP	COOK TIME
Asparagus	2 bunches	Cut in half, trim stems	2 Tbsp	420°F	12-15 mins
Beets	1½ lbs	Peel, cut in ½-inch cubes	1Tbsp	390°F	28-30 mins
Bell peppers (for roasting)	4 peppers	Cut in quarters, remove seeds	1Tbsp	400°F	15-20 mins
Broccoli	1 large head	Cut in 1-2-inch florets	1Tbsp	400°F	15-20 mins
Brussels sprouts	1lb	Cut in half, remove stems	1Tbsp	425°F	15-20 mins
Carrots	1lb	Peel, cut in ¼-inch rounds	1 Tbsp	425°F	10-15 mins
Cauliflower	1 head	Cut in 1-2-inch florets	2 Tbsp	400°F	20-22 mins
Corn on the cob	7 ears	Whole ears, remove husks	1 Tbps	400°F	14-17 mins
Green beans	1 bag (12 oz)	Trim	1 Tbps	420°F	18-20 mins
Kale (for chips)	4 oz	Tear into pieces, remove stems	None	325°F	5-8 mins
Mushrooms	16 oz	Rinse, slice thinly	1 Tbps	390°F	25-30 mins
Potatoes, russet	1½ lbs	Cut in 1-inch wedges	1 Tbps	390°F	25-30 mins
Potatoes, russet	1lb	Hand-cut fries, soak 30 mins in cold water, then pat dry	½ -3 Tbps	400°F	25-28 mins
Potatoes, sweet	1lb	Hand-cut fries, soak 30 mins in cold water, then pat dry	1 Tbps	400°F	25-28 mins
Zucchini	1lb	Cut in eighths lengthwise, then cut in half	1 Tbps	400°F	15-20 mins

Appendix 3: Recipe Index

S

Salmon Burgers   55
Salmon Patties   54
Saltine Wax Beans   35
Scalloped Veggie Mix   163
Seasoned Breaded Shrimp   62
Sesame Glazed Salmon   65
Sesame Taj Tofu   37
Shishito Peppers with Herb Dressing   130
Shrimp Dejonghe Skewers   51
Shrimp Green Casserole   180
Shrimp Quiche   179
Simple and Easy Croutons   163
Simple Apple Turnovers   147
Simple Buffalo Cauliflower   36
Simple Chicken Shawarma   77
Simple Cinnamon Toasts   15
Simple Pea Delight   163
Simple Pesto Gnocchi   38
Simple Pineapple Sticks   149
Simple Salmon Patty Bites   66
Simple Scotch Eggs   13
Simple Sweet Potato Soufflé   171
Smoked Beef   113
Smoky Chicken Sandwich   127
Sole and Asparagus Bundles   47
Soufflé   23
Sourdough Croutons   13
Spaghetti Squash Lasagna   115
Spanish Garlic Shrimp   63
Spice Cookies   150
Spiced Mixed Nuts   140
Spiced Sweet Potato Fries   131
Spiced Turkey Tenderloin   90
Spicy Cauliflower Roast   31
Spicy Chicken Bites   134
Spicy Chicken Wings   132
Spicy Kale Chips   136
Spicy Orange Shrimp   58
Spinach and Beef Braciole   102
Spinach and Carrot Balls   163
Spinach and Crab Meat Cups   140
Spinach Casserole   179
Spinach Omelet   18
Spinach with Scrambled Eggs   20
Sriracha Golden Cauliflower   39
Sriracha Honey Pork Tenderloin   96
Sumptuous Pizza Tortilla Rolls   117
Sun-dried Tomato Crusted Chops   102
Super Bacon with Meat   101
Super Easy Bacon Cups   10
Super Veg Rolls   26
Super Vegetable Burger   30

Swedish Beef Meatballs   119
Sweet and Sour Tofu 20   36
Sweet and Spicy Turkey Meatballs   89
Sweet Bacon Tater Tots   135
Sweet Corn and Carrot Fritters   164
Sweet Potato Fries   37
Sweet Potatoes with Tofu   28
Sweet Potatoes with Zucchini   29
Sweet-and-Sour Drumsticks   86
Swordfish Skewers with Caponata   48

T

Tandoori-Spiced Salmon and Potatoes   45
Tempero Baiano Brazilian Chicken   86
Teriyaki Pork and Mushroom Rolls   119
Tex-Mex Chicken Breasts   73
Tex-Mex Turkey Burgers   92
Thai Cornish Game Hens   80
Thai Curry Meatballs   77
Thai Shrimp Skewers with Peanut Dipping Sauce 54
Tofu Bites   34
Tomato and Mozzarella Bruschetta   18
Tortellini with Spicy Dipping Sauce   143
Tortilla Shrimp Tacos   56
Traditional Queso Fundido   172
Traditional Tuna Melt   64
Trout Amandine with Lemon Butter Sauce 46
Tuna and Lettuce Wraps   123
Tuna Muffin Sandwich   126
Tuna Patty Sliders   65
Tuna-Stuffed Quinoa Patties   52
Turkey and Cranberry Quesadillas   80
Turkey Hoisin Burgers   91
Turkey Stuffed Bell Peppers   88
Turkey, Hummus, and Cheese Wraps   90
Turkish Chicken Kebabs   84

V

Vegetable and Fish Tacos   57
Veggie Pita Sandwich   126
Veggie Salmon Nachos   137
Veggie Salsa Wraps   124
Veggie Shrimp Toast   137
Vietnamese Pork Chops   118

W

Western Prosciutto Casserole   180
Whole Chicken Roast   158
Whole Rotisserie Chicken   98

Y-Z

Yellow Curry Chicken Thighs with Peanuts 84
Zucchini and Potato Tots   139
Zucchini Balls   34

Manufactured by Amazon.ca
Bolton, ON

18668175R00109